Decoding
RUSSIA-CHINA
Axis

Decoding RUSSIA-CHINA Axis

Neil Nayak

HOW
ACADEMICS
an imprint of Highlyy Publishing LLP

ISBN: 978-93-6009-960-2
First Published : 2024

Published by : HOW ACADEM/CS
an imprint of Highlyy Publishing LLP

Correspondence Address :
4/30 A II Floor, Double Storey Buildings
Vijay Nagar, Delhi-110009
Editorial: +91 9811026449
Sales : +91 9999953412
Email: info@howacademics.com
Website: www.howacademics.com

Contents

List of Figures

List of Tables

Preface

In the complex tapestry of international relations, the evolving partnership between Russia and China stands out as a pivotal force that has garnered attention and speculation from scholars, policymakers, and observers around the globe. This book, "Decoding Russia-China Axis," delves into the intricacies of this relationship, seeking to unravel the nuances that define the strategic alliance between these two influential nations.

The chapters that follow offer a comprehensive exploration of China and Russia's entwined destinies, addressing key facets of their collaboration and examining the motives and implications that underpin this formidable alliance. From the historical roots to the contemporary dynamics, we embark on a journey that scrutinizes the multifaceted dimensions of Sino-Russian relations.

The introductory chapter, "China and Russia in a Nutshell: An Introduction," sets the stage by providing a broad overview, allowing readers to grasp the historical context and the foundational elements of this geopolitical alliance. As we progress, we navigate through the intricate landscape of China-Russia relations, probing into the intricacies that define this geopolitical partnership. We also explore the nature of their collaboration in multilateral organizations, questioning whether it is a tactical alignment or a strategic alliance with lasting implications.

The exploration continues to Central and Eastern Europe, where we assess the substance of Sino-Russian relations in the region. The following chapter delves into the theoretical frameworks of international relations, probing the prospects and challenges of a military alliance between Russia and China. The pivotal question of whether these two nations can form an alliance to balance the United States is examined with a critical eye.

This book is a scholarly endeavor aimed at unraveling the layers of the Russia-China axis, providing readers with a nuanced understanding of the motives, challenges, and potential trajectories of this significant geopolitical partnership. By decoding the intricacies of Sino-Russian relations, we aim to contribute to the ongoing discourse surrounding global politics and alliances in the 21st century.

Chapter 1
China and Russia in a Nutshell: An Introduction

The strategic relationship between China and Russia already has a lot of geopolitical weight, and if it works well, it could change the balance of power around the world.

The fast rise of China compared to Russia, which is clearly weaker than it used to be and may even be falling, is making it hard for both Beijing and Moscow to change. In fact, history shows that changing big powers has always been hard, in terms of politics, the economy, culture, and safety. Moscow and Beijing say that their relationship has never been stronger and that it is the most important strategic relationship for both countries. However, it is getting harder and harder to adapt to the changing balance of power.

This chapter gives a thorough look at this strategically important (but sometimes troublesome) relationship between China and Russia.

The writers all agree that the relationship sounds and looks a lot better on paper than it really is when it comes to actual results. This chapter tries to explain the link between China and Russia from the point of view of political power. What kinds of problems does the current shift in the balance of power around the world cause for the relationship between China and Russia?

In his part called "Sino-Russian relations: an analytical overview," Peter Ferdinand talks about the history of the relationship, what China hopes to get out of it, and the problems it causes in eight points. Russia's economic policy and Russia-China economic ties by Jouko Rautava changes the subject to Russian economic policies and the economic relationship between China and Russia. Rautava's careful and thorough study of the economic relationship shows that it is unbalanced. There aren't many chances for greater economic integration, mostly because there isn't enough political will and vision.

Pavel Salin's part, "How Russians See China," is an interesting look at how Russians' ideas about China's rise are changing over time. In this paper, he looks at how the anti-China and pro-China sides of the Russian elite, experts, and the media talk about and interact with the rise of China. In his chapter called "Russo-Chinese relations at a crossroads: an American view," Stephen Blank looks at how the connection between China and Russia is talked about (or not talked about) in the US political system. After that, the author makes some suggestions for how the US might handle the relationship between China and Russia in the larger setting of the region. In the last chapter, Arkady Moshes talks about how hard it is to try to balance this relationship that is becoming more unbalanced, as both countries are unhappy with each other over a number of bilateral, regional, and global problems.

Assessing the Structural Transformation of Rising and Declining Powers

One important question in the current study of international relations is what part and nature of state power there is. Globalisation is creating new ways for economies and societies to connect across borders and making existing ones more complicated and interdependent. As globalisation continues to grow, many things happen that are commonly thought to be caused by a mix of economic, financial, technological, social, cultural, and political forces. As Thomas Friedman put it, the "flattening of the world" is being caused by the growing globalisation of the economy that began in the 1980s.

States and multilateral organisations have sped up this process by loosening restrictions on world trade. Now, thanks to new technologies and changes in the way organisations work, resources, people, money, and knowledge are moving quickly across continents and national lines. The process that was meant to boost trade is now dealing with a new political reality: resources and wealth are being moved around the world from the developed West to the big emerging economies and energy providers. The difference between the rates of economic and industrial growth, along with the fast buildup of foreign exchange reserves, give rising powers a new kind of economic independence that gives them great political leverage, both in theory and in practise. Because of this, the whole process is changing and making it harder for states to keep their normal balance of power.

It's hard to figure out how the competition for resources, wealth, and political power is affected by globalisation and the complex web of relationships between them. This is because traditional world-system analysis, conventional structural and political realism, and different globalisation theories can only give partial accounts of the process. It doesn't matter what angle you look at it from, the process hasn't made it less important or less important for rising or existing powers to protect their own national interests or get access to raw materials, markets, and economic benefits outside of their own borders, even though the relationships between them are getting more complicated. One good example of this is the heated discussion over what China is doing in Africa. As these activities are carried out by new economic powers or their main economic institutions, which in the case of Russia and China are mostly state-owned or controlled businesses, they will either make things more competitive or cause a response in the current system. Because of this, the rise of new great powers poses both threats and opportunities for the current international order, even though global and regional interdependencies are growing. These basic realist ideas are still true in this way: This line of thinking says that as the rising powers get stronger and more powerful, they will want more impact. This will make them more eager to show their power and protect their own national interests in international situations. In the end, economic strength is what gives a country its political and armed power. Paul Kennedy's book The Rise and Fall of the Great Powers, which has become popular again since it came out in 1989, shows how countries' ability to keep and use their economic and productive power has been directly linked to their ability to maintain and use their global hegemony.

There are a number of important questions that shape the general process of states adjusting to today's more complicated international order. First, how unhappy are the new powers with the way things are done and the international order? Second, does the rise of a new great power threaten the way things are done in the world now? The third question is what changes rising forces want to see? In most discussions about China and Russia, people say they are unhappy with the way the world is run by the US. This is the main thing that brings these two powerful countries together. As we look for the answer to the second question, we quickly realise that China's rise is not only changing the international order and the order of the great powers, but it is also making Russia less powerful politically and economically in relation to China, both in the region and around the world. Moscow and Beijing could agree on one answer to the third question, though: they both want the world to be more fair and have more than one power. Even though they want the current order to be more fair from their point of view, Russia and China have not been destructive in their actions in international multilateral institutions, such as Russia's actions in the G8 or China's happiness with getting more voting rights in the IMF.

However, while many people have spoken out against the current Bretton Woods system, both China and Russia have reaped the benefits of the globalising economy. But the rewards have come from different places. The rising costs of oil, gas, and raw materials in the first ten years of the 21st century helped Russia's economy and foreign exchange reserves. But Russia's experience isn't even close to China's. China may be both the biggest winner and the most important force behind the new age of globalisation. To put it simply, China's huge success is due in large part to its economic policies and the fact that it is deeply and intricately connected to the rest of the world's economic, industrial, technology, and financial systems. That is, the complicated way China is linked and dependent on other countries The main thing that is changing the balance of power in the world right now is the global economic system.

The Recalibration Strategies of Beijing

Beijing is well aware that China's rapid growth is making its neighbours nervous. Beijing has settled all of its land-border disputes with its neighbours except for India. This is to create a peaceful environment for its own growth and to reassure its friends that it wants to live in peace. But China has had a lot less luck settling its disagreements over maritime territory. In fact, eight of the nine countries that are close to China and border its territorial waters have a dispute with the country over marine land.

Early in the 21st century, China worked hard to come up with new ideas for its foreign policy that would stay true to its traditional core principles of non-intervention and non-conditional behaviour. At the same time, China used its fast growth to promote the idea that it wanted to keep things peaceful. "The peaceful rise of China" was the first idea put forward in 2003. The idea became well known that same year when Zheng Bijian, who was Vice Principal of the Central Party School at the time, spoke at the Boao Forum for Asia. In his speech, Zheng said that the rise of new powers has often led to big changes in the way the world's governments work, sometimes through war. He said again that the PRC was working towards a peaceful foreign policy and would not go down this road of dominance. The Leader of China, Wen Jiaobao, used the same idea in a speech in 2004, which means it has the government stamp of approval. Regardless, the word "rise" proved to be too controversial, and it was criticised by both countries nearby and people around the world. So, Beijing quickly changed the phrase to "peaceful development of China" in 2004, which was a more neutral term.

In 2006, the current leadership came up with the idea of "a harmonious society" as a more general growth principle. This idea also includes the idea of making the world a more harmonious place to live. Chinese leaders promise that their country will strongly oppose any actions that meddle in the internal affairs of other countries that are not in line with a United Nations decision. The leaders of China say that they will instead work to make the world a more fair and equal place. However, Beijing has stepped up its efforts to promote the idea of "win-win solutions" for nations that are ready to work with China. These new rules are meant to reassure China's neighbours and the rest of the world that its rise should not be seen as a danger but as a chance. Besides these government rules, Beijing has been actively spreading a one-sided interpretation of China's non-expansionist and non-aggressive strategic culture. This is another attempt to persuade the world that China has never been one to fight expansionist wars.

Even though Beijing is doing everything it can to convince its neighbours that China's rise is peaceful, people in the region are worried about the country's economic growth and growing political power. One important new thing that has happened in the last few years is that the official party-backed media have used the terms "core interest" and "national interest" more often. It used to be that the phrase "national interest" was often used to criticise the US's dominant policies. But as China's investments and interests grow outside of China, the idea of the country's national interest is getting more positive attention in both popular and official circles. The 12th Five-Year Plan and the 2010 National Defence White Paper, which came out in the spring of 2011, are important papers in this situation.

These two important papers give us a look at how the new leaders who will take office in 2012 will understand the direction of global development and how China should set priorities for its own development plans. These papers say that states and players will become more dependent on each other and that there will be a big change in the balance of power around the world. In the future, China should pay more attention to its own national interests in this changing world. These papers also make it clear that China needs to get better at managing risks in order to further its own national goals. In this context of becoming more aware of and responsive to China's national interests, the fast growth and reform of the Chinese military, especially the deep-sea navy, air carriers, and submarines, suggest that China is becoming more politically aware and building the tools to protect its national interests beyond its own borders.

China's national security policy now includes maritime security as an important part of it. As Beijing's interests in other countries continue to grow, it is clear that its security boundary has already grown much further than its sea-territory boundary. Still, the fact that China's goals and efforts to build up its own capabilities are not always clear makes its neighbours nervous. China talks about its own national interests and flexes its muscles to show its power beyond its own territorial seas. Its neighbours wonder why it does these things. If this unclear progress keeps up, it will definitely make China's neighbours even more worried, no matter how much the country spends on resources to reassure others of its peaceful aims.

Also, China is quickly becoming one of the most important places for foreign businesses to get money. As a result, China's neighbours are growing worried that China will use its money to gain more economic and political power in the countries it borrows from. The realist school of thought says that this is the straight road that a great power should take. It is very hard to give a precise number for China's investments and loan provisions in foreign business. But a study by the Financial Times shows that between 2009 and 2010, China's two biggest loan providers, the China Development Bank and the Exim Bank, gave at least $100 billion to developing countries. This is more than what the World Bank's major lending arms have given out.

Chinese leaders have been telling their neighbours and the rest of the world that they don't need to worry about the political effects of their investments. China is trying to calm the fears of worried countries by sending mixed messages. It says that China's foreign policy is and always will be built on non-interference and that China only wants to make business deals where everyone wins. At the same time, it strongly condemns Western interventionism. Beijing's joke is that China does not put political conditions on the money or loans it gives out. However, surprisingly few studies have been done to see if these arguments are true and to see if a rising power like China can really act as selflessly as it says it can. This idea that there are "no strings attached to Chinese finance" is only partly true, according to a study by the Bank of Finland. The study comes up with four possible types of conditions that are either set by the government or happen as a result of the large amount of business and financial activities that Chinese state-run banks and companies do in developing countries. The study gives some weak proof that China does not always follow its own rules for foreign policy. Naturally, China's neighbours are keeping a close eye on the situation to see if China plans to use its economic and financial power in a more organised way in the future to gain political, economic, or security advantages in other countries.

Bilateral Relationship

The political relationship between China and Russia since the early 1990s can be seen as a success if we only look at the top-level politics and don't take into account how the two countries eventually settled their political differences, resolved land border issues, reduced the risk of armed conflict, and eventually formed a strategic partnership in 1996. At that time, the warming up was based on a number of strong strategic goals that both sides shared. First, there was enough trust between the two countries for Moscow and Beijing to deal with the tricky border and security problems. Second, both countries admitted that they were modernising in different ways and knew that working together more on the economy would be good for both of them. Third, and this may be the most important point, both countries' strategic and security situations were changing. It was clear to Moscow that the former Eastern bloc and the freshly independent states of the old Soviet Union were criticising the EU and NATO. Also, Russia had to look to the East for a more stable dance partner after Boris Yeltsin's short-lived relationship with the West and NATO fell through. At the same time, China had to deal with the US becoming more present in the Pacific. Also, Beijing looked at how the high-tech weapons and war technology used by the US in the first Iraq war affected the situation and realised that it needed to quickly improve its military power. After Tiananmen Square, the West put an arms ban in place, so Russia was the only place that could be used to buy military high-tech. Fourth, in the early years after the Cold War, both Beijing and Moscow were very worried about the US's position and power as the world's most powerful country. They were also strongly against the Western countries' plan for a one-power world order.

The connection between China and Russia is now like a Potemkin village turned around, after about fifteen years of the strategic partnership being in place. In this flipped village, it's not minsters like Grigory Potyomkin who are famous for building fake villages to impress Catherine the Great, who was travelling. Instead, it's the Emperors of both countries who are always putting on a show of a strategic partnership to trick the villagers. This skewed understanding of the metaphor works to some extent if we look at what the countries have actually done over the last ten years compared to the repeated claims from the top that the relationship is strategic. In fact, some scholars have said that the relationship fell into strategic stagnation as early as ten years after the papers for the strategic partnership were signed.

China's fast growth and successful modernization have made the country a part of the global economy. As a result, China depends less on Russia than Russia depends on China in many important areas of their relationship, including politics, energy, raw materials, and even military technology. If things keep going the way they are, China will have the upper hand in all strategic problems and the relationship between China and Russia will become imbalanced.

In addition, it is clear that the countries don't have many strategic goals in common. The main thing that both Moscow and Beijing want is for things to stay peaceful and stable between them. Still, if you take the words "strategic" and "partnership" literally, the strategic partnership should be based on a broad and shared set of values that give the relationship depth, meaning, and purpose, as well as a way to predict how each party will likely respond to changes in the situation. On the other hand, most people who have looked at the relationship say that there isn't much trust between the two people and that it is more helpful than romantic. It seems that both Moscow and Beijing share a strong set of values that are often talked about: rejecting the US's dominant policies, calling for a more fair and multipolar world order, and sticking to noninterventionist principles in foreign policy. But when you look more closely at these supposed shared values, you see that the truth isn't black and white, but comes in many shades of grey.

Both Beijing and Moscow have made it clear that they don't agree with the US's policies and role as the world's leader. On the other hand, Moscow and Beijing have different strategies with Washington at the same time. From Beijing's point of view, things like Moscow's back and forth between criticising and avoiding Washington, NATO, the changing stance on missile defence, and the US's opening of an air bridge to Afghanistan through Russian airspace are all worrying signs that make the relationship between China and Russia less stable. Moscow is even more worried about how much China and the US depend on each other, since China's only real strategic relationship is with the US. Moscow must have been very annoyed to see how some US government officials, well-known experts, and the global media called for the two biggest economies in the world, China and the US, to join forces to solve the world's economic problems. For China, the idea of a G2 was quickly shot down, but the whole conversation served as a stark warning to Moscow that China alone would be the other pole in the desired future multipolar world, not Russia or the Sino-Russian axel. In the end, China would probably be able to live without Russia but not without the US.

Russia's non-interventionist foreign policy principle was called into question by Chinese experts during interviews. It was said that Beijing is keeping a close eye on how Russia's foreign policy constantly goes against this principle by using different forms of force to get involved in the internal affairs of its neighbours. They talked a lot about the "pipeline diplomacy" that was used against Ukraine and Belarus and the 2008 war in Georgia. One Chinese scholar said this was an example of the behaviours of a former giant that no longer has the power to control the newly independent countries that it used to control when it was the Soviet Union. But the same scholar said that some people in China think there is something wrong with Russian foreign policy because they don't have many good ties with the countries that border them.

But China is also feeling more and more pressure to break away from the non-interventionist and non-conditional foreign policy concept. So far, there is proof that China is currently building up both the political will and the military power to better protect its own national interests when they are at risk outside of China. As was already said, it looks like China has already used its financial power to set terms for some countries that want to get loans.

The Complexities of Russia's Transformation

By looking at the current state of the relationship and the two countries' historical development paths, we can only come to the conclusion that the relationship is moving towards a state where Beijing will have more power and control over Moscow than at any other time in history. This trend can already be seen in the important areas of politics, security, energy, the economy, and business between the two countries. In most of these areas, Russia depends on China more than China depends on Russia. In a balanced way, what options does Moscow have for adjusting its relationship with China, which is becoming more unequal, since both countries are aware that the changing balances of power are making it harder for people to trust each other, even though their leaders say the opposite? Regarding Russia, it looks like only a few possible methods for adjustment could be used in practise. Here is a quick look at the tactics of balancing, containment, multilateral binding, jumping on the bandwagon, and engagement.

Russia will not be able to balance or reduce its political and economic dependence on China as long as it can not deal with its own internal problems. It is also not possible for Russia to form political partnerships with other status quo powers, like the EU, NATO, or the US, against China through external balancing or containment. This can't happen because the US, the EU, and China are all much more economically dependent on and connected to each other than they are with Russia. Also, the economies of the EU and the US are fighting to be recognised by Beijing. This makes it very hard, if not impossible, for the EU to stand united against China. China has also been very good at using the "divide et impera" strategy with the European countries. This means that China is putting economic and diplomatic pressure on countries that are interfering with Chinese internal affairs, while giving benefits to countries that are following Chinese rules. This "divide and conquer" strategy has been used before. The most recent example is the sanctions against Norway and Norwegian companies in China after Liu Xiaobo, a Chinese dissident, won the Nobel Peace Prize in October 2010. So, it's clear that neither the US nor the EU would put their relationship with China at risk to help Russia reach its goals.

Russia also can't use a multilateral approach that binds China because it would be politically impossible. A multilateral binding strategy is a way for a rising power to become part of the world's current institutions and ways of doing things. This plan will not work for Moscow because both Russia and China are strong opponents of the ways that Bretton Woods institutions currently work. Additionally, the Shanghai Cooperation Organisation and the new arrangement of BRIC countries are not united enough and do not have the institutional structure and arrangements that Russia could use for any attempt to bind them. Any efforts by Russia to balance, contain, or bind China would clearly be very bad for the relationship and would almost certainly lead to a response from China.

Russia's only choices are to join the group and work with China as it grows. In this case, "bandwagoning" means going along with the better side, which is China in this case. But Russia has had a hard time jumping on the bandwagon because it means admitting that it has become China's "little brother." This is a politically and psychologically hard thing for a country that was a superpower just twenty years ago, as Salin's chapter in this report brilliantly shows. A lot of people jumping on the train could also have political effects at home, as people might start to doubt the effectiveness of Moscow's reform efforts.

Using an engagement approach with a rising China also comes with its own set of problems. A plan for engagement uses a fair mix of concessions and real threats to make sure that the growing power is using its strength in ways that support peaceful change. To put it another way, the best way to guide and please the growing power is to use both rewards and punishments. On the other hand, Russia doesn't have many sticks to use, and it has been very hesitant to give China the carrots it wants. These are the only sticks Russia has right now: oil and some raw materials. For one thing, China now gets energy and raw materials from a lot of different places, so it is not as reliant on Russian supplies as it used to be. If Russia used this "pipeline diplomacy" against China, on the other hand, it would destroy any trust that China still has in Russia.

Also, Russia has become less willing over the last ten years to give China the things it wants, like the newest, most advanced military weapons and an environment that is good for investing. China is scared that Russia will use reverse engineering to copy its weapons technology. In fact, Russia found out in 2006 that the Chinese were making the Shenyang J-II, a version of the Sukhoi SU-27SK plane that was made in China under a licence deal that was signed in 1995. For its part, China has made a lot of progress in making its own defence gear and no longer needs Russian technology. In this chapter, Blank shows how the Chinese and Russian armies are now under a different kind of stress and distrust.

Russia has also had a hard time with the other carrot, which was to open up the Russian market and make the country's institutions more welcoming to foreign direct investors. Entrepreneurs and state-owned banks in China aren't waiting for Russia to open its markets; they're looking elsewhere for new ones that haven't been explored yet. An expert on China said in an interview, "The Russian markets are very closed and corrupt, and local officials treat Chinese businesspeople badly." "Africa is also corrupt, but there is no bias against Chinese people. That's why Chinese companies generally like African markets more," he said. Of course, the same scholar agreed that the seriously bad business ethics of some Chinese people doing business in Russia hurt the image of all Chinese companies in Russia. In this chapter, Ferdinand points out that China's exports to Africa are now higher than those to the area that used to be the Soviet Union.

It is possible to learn about the goals of a rising power and gain experience through the engagement strategy, but it usually takes a long time and requires a lot of resources. If the engagement plan were put into action, Russia would continue to lose its economic, political, and military great power attributes compared to China. This is because China and Russia are developing at different rates. At the same time, it will be harder to adapt to the new power structure.

China's political and economic actions show that Beijing is and will continue to be more connected to the world markets. The Chinese economy is already the second biggest in the world. If it can grow its own markets, it will have even more economic power. Investors and companies from China going global will likely have a bigger effect on the world economy and system in the coming years than Japan's globalisation did in the 1970s and 1980s. To put it simply, China's enormous wealth and ravenous hunger are far greater than Japan's were in the 1980s. In the 1980s, when Russia was still part of the Soviet Union, it missed out on the economic boost that came from Japanese investments in East Asia, North America, and Europe. If Russia doesn't open its markets to foreign and Chinese investments, it will be in the same situation. In terms of politics and diplomacy, China will probably stick to its current plan of treating Russia equally so as not to hurt the former superpower's pride and reputation, even though it is growing worried about the future of the country.

Overview

The history of the world shows that the rise of new powers has always caused problems and tension within the current power structure. There are universal reasons for how hard it is to change, and they are an important part of the process of changing power between rising powers and powers that are already in place. In the case of the relationship between China and Russia, these universal problems of adjustment are made even more difficult by Moscow's own struggles to get used to the fact that it lost its place at the top of the international order of prestige and influence when the socialist world order it created and led fell apart. Moscow is also seen as China's "little brother" more and more these days. Besides that, the two countries' unique histories, complicated political and psychological makeups, and growing economic differences are also affecting the ways they try to make things work.

The countries' medium- and long-term goals for growth, both of themselves and of each other, are at least as important. These goals shape their strategies and policies towards each other. From Moscow's point of view, it looks like Russia always falls at the first hurdle, no matter how fast it tries to run. The Kremlin can only see how the country is losing power and status to China, which is moving quickly in some areas. At the same time, Beijing is picking up speed quickly as it easily clears each obstacle. As a result, China is building up an advantage in all the important areas it needs to become a real superpower. At the same time, people in charge in Beijing's Zhongnanhai administrative district are growing more worried about Russia's shaky efforts to modernise. Russia is a vital partner of China's. So, it's clear that the rising power shift creates different political and public views, as well as different ways, expectations, resources, and connections for Beijing and Moscow to act.

On a practical level, Beijing's fast rising position and Moscow's relatively falling position create very different opportunities and problems. Zhongnanhai's leaders are thinking about how to balance and adjust the city's growth on a global level without upsetting people in places like Africa, South America, or the European Union. Officials are looking at growth possibilities on a global scale. Thoughts and views in Moscow are, on the other hand, much more close up. As the question of "How to adjust to the rise of China?" becomes more important, the Kremlin's view is limited to the regional and local level. Its main concerns are how to move forward with its Euro-Asian strategy, how to regain control over newly independent states, and whether to turn to Europe or Asia.

But the gap between China and Russia will keep growing as long as Moscow keeps fumbling with its reforms, swaying back and forth between the West and the East, being unsure how to open up its markets and economy, and not being able to make it a good place for foreign investors, including Chinese ones. If this pattern of failing to see the big picture and political indecision continues, Moscow will have even fewer choices for how to deal with the problems that come with China's rise and its own relative fall.

Sino-Russian Relations: An Analytical Overview

China and Russia are getting along better than they have in 50 years. In the past few years, both governments have put in a lot of work to make them better. At the same time, though, their future is still clouded by doubt and even mistrust between them.

Accomplishments

During the Sino-Soviet dispute in the late 1960s and early 1970s, the leaders of the USSR thought about using nuclear weapons against China to stop the fighting on the border. When President Nixon made overtures to Mao, Mao looked to the US for help in keeping the Soviet Union in check. Over the next ten years, things got better, but there was still constant conflict. There was always a chance that new border fights over disputed land would turn into a bigger war. In Siberia and the Far East, the Soviet army built up a huge army that was always a threat to Beijing. China was very worried about Soviet expansion in Asia, and their involvement in Afghanistan made those worries worse. They were always on high watch. At least until the middle of the 1980s, Beijing's official line was that there would be war, possibly a nuclear one, and that the Soviet Union was the most likely enemy.

Since then, things have slowly gotten better. Gorbachev was the first leader to try to make peace. He suggested that both sides pull their troops back from the line, and this quickly turned into a peaceful reconciliation. The fall of the Soviet Union slowed down this process, but China and Russia signed a deal in 1992 to have friendly ties. In 2001, they made this even stronger with a Treaty for Good Neighbourliness, Friendship, and Cooperation.

As tensions dropped, it became easier to settle border disputes with Russia and Central Asian countries. By 2011, all parties had signed agreements that permanently erased the borders, which was a process in which everyone gave and took. So, as long as everyone agrees that the deals will last, there shouldn't be any reason to start fighting again, and people shouldn't have any doubts about their neighbours' long-term territorial goals.

As a result of this loosening, trade between Russia and China has grown. Since they live close to each other, this hasn't progressed as much as either side had thought. Still, China's exports to the FSU as a whole are less than those to the Middle East, and they are very small compared to those to Europe and the US. But China's exports to Africa are now higher than those to the FSU. For China, this means that the FSU as a whole is not as important a market.

These ties are based on the fact that governments agree on what kind of foreign relations and governance are best. Table 1.1 shows a study of how people vote in the UN General Assembly, which shows one example of this. There is a list of all the votes that China has cast compared to all the other regular members of the Security Council.

Table 1.1. Voting records of the permanent members of the UN Security Council in general assembly compared with the People's Republic of China, 1974-2008 (as a percentage of total number of votes cast)

	→	divergence	→
	Identical (yes/no/abstain)	1 yes/no + 1 abstain	1 yes + 1 no
France	36.26	34.84	17.32
Russia	65.99	17.64	6.53
UK	33.42	32.57	22.70
USA	13.21	23.20	50.80

Total number of votes = 3384 (figures do not add up to 100 because of the absence of at least one of the states from individual votes)

Data from: Erik Voeten and Adis Merdzanovic, "United Nations General Assembly Voting Data"

It's important to remember that the UN General Assembly passes most of its resolutions without a vote, and when they do, they pass with a vote of a big majority. As a result, states usually vote "yes," and when they have doubts, they can abstain rather than taking a stand that could cause problems with other countries. And the times when one state votes "yes" and the other states votes "no" are the most interesting. It shows real differences in foreign policy. This table shows that China's vote was very different from those of the other regular members. When it came to voting, the UK and France were about as close to China as each other, with France being a little more similar. Things are very different when it comes to the US. About half of the votes cast in these two states were against the problems at hand. In fact, the difference was even bigger when George W. Bush was president. Only 9.44% of the time did the US and China vote the same way between 2000 and 2008. On the other hand, they voted against each other 64.92 % of the time. But Russia (and the old USSR) and China had the most similar voting habits, even when there was a dispute between China and the USSR. This trend grew stronger under Gorbachev.

In 1997, China and Russia signed a joint statement called "A Multipolar World and the Establishment of a New International Order." This made their shared views on world events even clearer. It looked forward to a world with more than two major powers, to which more and more developing countries would also participate. It said the following:

> *Diversity in the political, cultural and economic development of all countries is becoming the norm... A growing number of countries are beginning to recognise the need for mutual respect, equality and mutual advantage - but*

not for hegemony and power politics - and for dialogue and cooperation - but not for confrontation and conflict.

This is what they said: "mutual respect for sovereignty and territorial integrity, mutual non-aggression, non-interference in each other's internal affairs, equality and mutual advantage, peaceful coexistence and other universally recognised principles of international law." The Declaration reaffirmed the importance of the United Nations and the intention of both states to work towards its strengthening. Larson and Shevchenko both say that both states don't believe in liberal action to protect people's rights.

In 2005, Presidents Putin and Hu signed a new version of this statement that added support for multiethnic states and a call to avoid policies that would divide them. These ideas have also been reaffirmed at more recent BRIC meetings.

China's Objectives with Russia

China's foreign policy has two main goals that come before its ties with Russia. The first goal is to keep the international situation in the area stable so that China can continue to grow its economy. This is a very long-term goal: for China to be a "moderately prosperous" country by 2049, which is the 100th anniversary of the founding of the People's Republic of China. The second is to keep an eye on its "peaceful rise" (heping jueqi) or "peaceful development" (heping fazhan) around the world so that it doesn't start a fight with major powers that could stop its rise. That means that China's leaders are very focused on their "strategic partnerships" with other important countries and its relationship with the US, which is the world's most powerful country.

Along with this, there are two other things to think about. The first is that China always says no to defence alliances. Due to the painful nature of the Sino-Soviet dispute and the threat it posed to the PRC, China's leaders do not want to depend on any other country for its security again, and they also do not want to get too involved with any other power. This was summed up by Mao's doctrine of "selfreliance." China's new strategic concept of 1998 reopened the door to fuller integration in world affairs based on "mutual trust, mutual benefit, equality, and cooperation," but the desire to keep as much independence as possible has not gone away. In fact, China's economic gains since then have made it more likely to happen.

Chinese critics have become very excited about the idea of "soft power" in recent years. They see it as a less dangerous way to lead in world affairs. At the 17th Party Congress, President Hu Jintao stressed how important it was to improve culture as a way to boost the country's "soft power."

The second thing to think about is the advice Deng Xiaoping gave to China's leaders in 1989 about how to best handle its relationships with the rest of the world after the killings in Tiananmen Square and the subsequent isolation by other countries. This was summed up as "observe coldly, protect our positions, deal calmly, hide our skills and bide our time, stay out of the way, never take the lead, and make a contribution." The economic progress of China and the rising respect that other countries show for its leaders have actually pushed the country's leaders to become more assertive and raise the country's profile. Still, Deng's legacy still has a big impact on how the present leadership thinks.

So, China looks to Russia for a stable environment in the area, for business partnerships, and for help with its foreign policy. The Shanghai Cooperation Organisation is the most obvious example of the second type. It was created when President Yeltsin offered a "strategic partnership" with China on the spur of the moment in 1996, because he thought that the West, especially the US, was not treating Russia with the respect and equality it deserved. This made Chinese leaders feel good because they were also worried about how dangerous Afghanistan and maybe even the rest of Central Asia were to Xinjiang's safety. At a meeting in Shanghai, they started a process of working together in the area. Most of the Central Asian states that were there were worried that either of their "big brothers" to the north or south could threaten their newfound independence. This became an official diplomatic route in 1998, and the first meeting of the Shanghai Cooperation Organisation (SCO) took place in 2001. A regional anti-terrorism station (RATS) and a Business Council have been set up by the SCO since then. It has held regular joint military drills, usually aimed at a supposed terrorist danger, and it has worked together to fight drug trafficking.

It has taken the SCO a while to become known on the world stage. A number of things have led to this. First, it has been hard for the members to get over long-standing doubts or grudges they have against each other. Second, this has been a very important learning experience for China. It is the first time that China has been in charge of a multinational group, and because it doesn't like alliances of any kind, it didn't want to make SCO ties that were too tight. Third, the members have different ideas about what the organization's main goals should be. China wanted it to focus on economic cooperation so that it could get its goods into more markets. Russia, on the other hand, wanted it to focus more on military cooperation because it was afraid that China would get more business opportunities. Fourth, Central Asia has been the natural focus of its policies. It is ready to help find a regional solution to Afghanistan's problems, but as long as NATO has been involved, it has not been asked to play a major part. It also didn't want to directly question NATO because it was afraid it would have to deal with the Taliban on its own. It has, however, tried to stop NATO and especially the US from settling down in the area for good. As NATO's operations in Afghanistan come to an end, the SCO is starting to build links with the Afghan government, which wants to become an observer. It is also looking for ways to work together with India, Pakistan, and Iran, which are all neighbours in the area. India, Pakistan, Iran, and Mongolia are all Observers in the SCO. Belarus and Sri Lanka are also Dialogue Partners, which means that the organisation could do more in the future, like in South Asia. India and Iran have both said they want to join, but the process has been put on hold until the international dispute over Iran's nuclear project is over. At the SCO's 10th anniversary meeting in June 2011, the rules for adding new members should be agreed upon. It has also made a deal with the UN to share information as a regional body.

The group is not really a union, though, because its members have not promised to help each other if they are attacked. Also, there isn't a single structure for commanding military activities. Russia may have tried to make it seem like a threat to NATO through rhetoric, but it is not. Another thing is that economic multilateralism, which could lead to a shared market, is not moving forward yet. All economic agreement between states is still done on a two-way street. Despite this, it gives all members confidence in their ability to deal with guerrilla and terrorist threats in the area. Also, the Central Asian states like it because it lets them play Russia off against China instead of having to deal with both of them separately and unfairly.

The second thing China wants from Russia is to work together on business. Table 1.2 shows how their trade relationship has changed over time. Unfortunately, the proof is not good.

Table 1.2. China-Russia trade, selected years (in US $ billions)

China	**1992**	**1995**	**2000**	**2005**	**2010**
Exports from: Russia	2.34	1.67	2.23	13.21	29.59
World	85.62	148.97	249.22	762.65	1580.40
As % of total	2.73	1.12	0.89	1.73	1.87
Imports from: Russia	3.51	3.80	5.80	15.89	25.81
World	81.87	132.16	225.18	660.22	1393.92
As % of total	4.28	2.88	2.58	2.41	1.85
Russia					
Exports from: China	2.74	3.38	5.23	13.05	23.46
World	39.93	77.60	103.00	239.30	403.76

As % of total	6.86	4.36	5.08	5.45	5.81
Imports: from China	1.67	0.86	0.95	7.24	32.55
World	34.98	46.40	33.85	97.41	232.66
As % of total	4.77	1.85	2.81	7.43	14.00

Source: IMF Direction of Trade Statistics database

In almost every way, this table shows that Sino-Russian trade as a share of all trade is smaller now than it was in 1992, which was a bad year for Russian exports in general. Even though they are neighbours and could save money on transportation and other costs because of this, the only area where trade has grown proportionally is when Russia buys things from China. Russia and China sent a total of $53 billion worth of goods and services to each other in 2010. This is a lot less than the $80 billion or even $100 billion goals that the two presidents set earlier in the year. Russia started sending oil to China through a tunnel at the end of 2010. Before that, oil was sent by rail. Russia will likely be able to send three or four times as much oil and gas to China over the next ten years because of this. In June 2011, an important new deal will be signed at the SCO. Also, getting energy from Russia and Central Asia makes China less reliant on getting it by sea from the Middle East and Africa, through dangerous chokepoints like the Straits of Hormuz and Malacca. But these numbers don't show the bigger problem, which is that Russia can't send China a lot of the manufactured things that Chinese people want to buy. The relationship is also not fair on both sides. Russia cares more about China than China cares about Russia. It trades with more countries than any other country except the EU. Russia, on the other hand, is China's seventh biggest trade partner.

But Russia is a key source for two types of things that China needs. The first one is energy and basic goods in general. Since the fall of the Soviet Union, both of these needs have grown by a huge amount. China has been a net importer of oil since 1993, but its need for energy has grown incredibly fast since then. Over half of China's oil needs are met by imports right now. The government thinks that by 2020, that number will have risen to 60%. The timing of China's demand rise was very bad because most major oil producers in the Middle East were already locked into long-term deals with Western companies. This meant that China couldn't get most of its oil from those countries. Because of this, China is working hard to make long-term deals with small suppliers in Latin America and Africa. The former Soviet Union, on the other hand, has the best chance of providing major relief because it is close by and has new oil fields that are not tied to existing customers. Concerns similar to those above also affect China's need for natural gas. Once again, the FSU could be a big supplier, but China has a better chance of getting supplies from other parts of the world.

It's not just about energy, though. As China has become more industrialised, it has increased its need for other minerals and raw materials. Still based on what the Chinese government says, they will have to import a lot of 19 of the 45 key materials they need over the next twenty years. For example, they will need to import 70% of their copper and 40% of their iron ore. Russia is a clear possible source. China is also going through a time of a lot of people moving to cities. By 2030 or even 2025, an extra 300–350 million people, or 60% of the population, will live in cities, up from 40% now. Again, this will bring in huge amounts of products from Russia, like wood. There is also the issue of food security, which is starting to worry the Chinese government. China has always had a tough time balancing its food needs with its population. It has 23% of the world's people but only 7% of the world's farmland. The most crops were grown in China in 1998, and the population will keep growing for another 20 years. To make sure there is food for a long time, Chinese companies have started to buy or rent farmland in Africa. It's possible that Russia could also become a big source of food for China.

Defence technology was the second thing China needed to buy from Russia. Once more, this was a lucky accident for everyone. The allies' win in the first Gulf War in 1991 came as a huge surprise to the Chinese government. It showed how much more advanced Western military technology was than Chinese technology. As it is now, the West has banned the sale of weapons to China after the killings in Tiananmen Square, so China could not buy weapons there. Russia was the only other option. At the same time, Russia's defence sales dropped sharply after 1991, with China becoming its most important customer. Even though it took a while for sales contracts to be signed, China began buying things from Russia, like planes, ships, and later air defence and anti-ship weapons. In the late 1990s and early 2000s, China bought tools from Russia worth between US$1 and US$2 billion a year. In 2006, that number reached a high point. The Chinese military is now much better able to attack because of all of this. But since then, China's overall military equipment imports have dropped sharply, from $3.8 billion in 2006 to $559 million in 2010. A big reason for the drop is that China is making its own similar equipment under licence, which Russia fears is also because China is copying. But near the end of 2010, new deals were made. These deals were mostly for sending Russian engines to China to power planes that China had already bought or built under licence.

On top of that, there is an economic problem for China. This is about how trade with Russia and Central Asian countries can help China's northern provinces grow. These include Heilongjiang, Jilin, Liaoning, and Inner Mongolia, Gansu, Qinghai, and Xinjiang in the central and western ranges. All of these regions have been left behind in the country's growth over the past few years, which has mostly helped the southern coastal region. The reasons for this are different. Heavy industries that are out of date are mainly to blame for the problems in the northeast, especially in Liaoning. These industries have become less competitive as a result of "systemic reform," or the sale of state-owned businesses that began in the late 1990s. Increasing trade with Russia's Far East was something China thought would help bring in investments that would help improve industry. In the late 1990s, China started the well-known "Go West" programme for the central and western provinces. The goal was to bring investment to the western part of the country so that it could catch up to the more developed east over time. Again, having good ties with Russia and the CIS could help with that. In reality, though, these links have not lived up to China's dreams. This is mostly because Russian officials on the other side of the border are not very interested. Additionally, China's continued rapid growth has helped ease the problems in the north by creating extra resources that can be put to use in these areas.

Lastly, there are chances for countries to work together on foreign policy in international groups like the UN Security Council. This was most clear in the case of Iraq, but it has also happened in Iran, Afghanistan, and Libya. In addition, China has said that it wants Russia to join the WTO and the East Asian Summit. But how long this cooperation lasts will rest at least in part on what other states do and how they run their governments. Russia and China could work together if the United States had a more aggressive foreign policy, like it did when George W. Bush was in office. But a "smart" US foreign policy, like the one Joseph Nye supports, would make things more flexible.

Issues

Some of the problems that China experiences in its relations with Russia.

a. The most fundamental reservation of the Chinese leadership concerns the depth of Russian commitment to the strategic partnership, that is the extent to which China can rely upon Russia over the long term. The restoration of the double-headed eagle as the symbol of the Russian state ironically symbolises the problem: the fact that whenever it seems to be looking one way, it can very quickly look in the opposite direction. This nurtures misgivings. A Chinese professor well disposed towards Russia, Zhou Li, has commented on the general unpredictability of Russian foreign policy over the decades. He remarks that Russian culture lacks a sense of the "golden mean", and its foreign policy is instead prey to sudden changes of course. To give an example, the Chinese leadership were profoundly shocked by the collapse of the Soviet Union, but they were also seriously shocked by the way that President Yeltsin (a former communist) then contemplated membership of NATO as well as the EU. Given the previous warming of relations under Gorbachev and the isolation of China at that time so soon after the Tiananmen massacres, the prospect of NATO stretching to Vladivostok was profoundly disturbing. The fact that only four years later President Yeltsin could propose a strategic partnership with China was at one level much more reassuring. So too was the personal chemistry between Presidents Yeltsin and Jiang Zemin. However, the Chinese worried that this might have simply been done as a way of pressuring the West into being more accommodating and that, if this succeeded, relations with China would be sacrificed again. Even though the Russian leadership maintained its commitment through the change of president and indeed found in President Putin someone who was later more combative in his treatment of the West, they also remembered that Putin had initially attempted to win increased cooperation with the US and had raised "hypothetically" the possibility of Russian membership of NATO. Now in President Medvedev they have a leader who has encouraged greater economic liberalisation and who seems more inclined to look westwards again. Even though he told a meeting of Russian ambassadors in 2010 that Asia was now the second foreign policy priority after Europe, that would still make relations with China dependent upon the success of Russia's diplomacy towards Europe. Admittedly the financial difficulties of first the US and later the EU have enhanced the economic attraction of Asia, especially China, which should strengthen Russia's commitment. Nevertheless, even though the new Russia has now demonstrated a sustained commitment to its relations with China, there remains the worry that smart Western diplomacy could lead Russia to look predominantly westwards again. Of course, part of the problem is China's own antipathy towards alliances. Since China is unwilling to make a formal commitment to Russia beyond a "strategic partnership", it is not surprising that other states would want to keep their options open as well. So the problem partly of China's own making. China would like monogamy from Russia, but polygamy for itself. This is not realistic.

b. The next concern follows from this: how comfortable is Russia with a rising China? As a former superpower, how ready is Russia to cede its position to China? This is not just a matter of diplomacy. It also affects military relations. Whilst Russia has supplied China with many more advanced weapons than the Chinese could at that time produce themselves, the Chinese military are only too aware of the fact that Russia has not allowed the transfer of many of the most advanced forms of equipment. Some Russians do not disguise the fact that the main reason for this is the fear that they might at some point be directed back at them. Worse, Russian officials have stated publicly that they would have no problem in transferring more advanced equipment to India - one of China's biggest Asian rivals. Russian commentators have even suggested that Russia would be happy to develop stealth air and naval technology with India, but not with China. All of this keeps Chinese officials disgruntled. Of course, the Russians are not only concerned about power rankings in general. Many in Moscow, and even more in the Far East, are concerned about the long-term viability of Russian rule over Siberia. Even though the Russian and Chinese governments have signed agreements recognising the current frontiers in perpetuity, many Russians do not have faith in their permanence. They fear that at some point in the future, when China is much stronger and Russia weaker, the Chinese government will revive their earlier claims to territory over which they had some authority before 1689 and the Treaty of Nerchinsk. As is reiterated in Russia - and noted by China - even the demographic imbalance between the populations to the north and the south of the frontier is destabilizing, not to mention the possibility of renewed military conflict. It is this fear that keeps Russia from supplying China with the most advanced weapons. But at the same time, given all the reassurances that China has offered, it is not clear what more they could do. If they offer to invest in Siberia, they are suspected of preparing for a takeover. So Chinese officials are entitled to feel a certain exasperation.

c. Linked to this is the Chinese government's specific concern about the Russian government's treatment of Chinese citizens living in Russia. Russian internal security forces are noted for their harsh treatment of ethnic minorities and foreigners living in Russia. In the case of the Chinese there, the problem is compounded by the wide discrepancies in estimates of the numbers of Chinese living in Russia. This can range from a few hundred thousand to several millions. Officials in different agencies, local as well as national, assert wildly varying figures. It contributes to popular paranoia about a Chinese "fifth column" that is allegedly just waiting for the opportunity to take control of large swathes of the country. Serious attempts to come up with an authoritative, more moderate figure have failed to dispel popular prejudice, in part because corrupt Russian officials are known to take bribes, so ordinary Russians are sceptical about official figures. Chinese officials are entitled to feel exasperated by this problem. Despite the fact that Chinese migration to Russia is now regulated by visas, unlike in the early 1990s, there seems no way to take the heat out of the issue. For China the worry is that this prejudice against Chinese living in Russia might lead to violence against them, in which case China would feel that it would have to take steps to protect them, which would damage relations with the Russian government.

d. In terms of business and economics, China's main concern is over energy supplies. One of China's biggest expectations of Russia was that it would seriously help to close their own energy gap. Yet agreements with Russia have taken much longer to achieve than the Chinese expected, and even afterwards have not always been implemented on time. For example, when the possibility of an oil pipeline to China was initially mooted, the Chinese made it clear that they would be willing to take all the oil that Russia could offer. An agreement was signed with the Yukos oil company in 2002 for completion in 2005 costing Russia US $1.7 billion and supplying 20-30 million tonnes of oil per year. China would have only been responsible for the cost of the pipeline inside China - much less than that of Russia. Yet almost immediately the deal became embroiled in the break-up of Yukos after the arrest of its boss Khodorkovsky the following year, and in 2003 Japan also suddenly offered Russia a much larger sum for a pipeline to the Pacific. In the end the Russian government decided to build the longer pipeline to supply China in part, but also Japan and South Korea. It changed the route, citing environmental reasons for one, so as to avoid the risk of spillage from the original route in an earthquake zone around Lake Baikal, but which the previous nearly 10 years of feasibility studies had apparently failed to identify. It was only at the end of 2010 that the pipeline to China was opened. Whilst this was earlier than the longer pipeline to the Pacific which has still not been completed, it was also years later than originally agreed. It only supplies 15 million tonnes per year instead of 20-30 million, while China's demand has escalated in the interim, and it eventually cost $25 billion, of which China paid $15 billion in loans. China suspected that Russian companies procrastinated in the hope that China would have to pay more for the oil as world prices increased. China has also resented being charged European prices by Russia for the supply of energy, especially gas. Given China's growing energy needs, the experience of attracting Russian supplies - and the disputes over Russia's oil and gas shipments to Europe - have not encouraged confidence in Russia as a totally reliable long-term supplier. In turn, China has responded by signing agreements with Central Asian suppliers, especially Kazakhstan and Turkmenistan. The Central Asians have appreciated the possibility of negotiating directly with China and thus reducing their own dependence on Russian cooperation for exporting their energy products. But these states cannot satisfy all of China's needs.

e. Also in terms of economics, China has been disappointed by the relatively leisurely growth in trade. To some extent this is not a crucial problem for either side, given that they both enjoy significant foreign trade surpluses. Nevertheless it shows that Russia has little to offer China by way of advanced technology, apart from the areas of defence, space equipment and nuclear power. Opportunities for joint projects between Chinese and Russian companies are likely to remain limited. There is a mismatch of economic interests between them. On the other hand, the Russian government seems unenthusiastic about increasing imports of Chinese consumer goods, even if it helps China pay for high-priced energy imports. Russia is allegedly more concerned with using its energy exports to enhance its strategic position in Pacific Asia.

f. One problem that both sets of leaders recognised in the middle of the last decade is the relatively thin nature of political and personal ties between them. Even if personal relations are again very good at the very top, there are no longer many middle-level officials who have any direct experience of working with counterparts in the other country. Despite the long years of the Sino-Soviet dispute, there were still many Chinese leaders in the 1990s such as Li Peng and Jiang Zemin who had trained as engineers in the USSR in the 1950s and who could still relate to Russians on a personal level. Their retirement left a big gap, however, and ignorance among their successors exacerbated distrust. Presidents Putin and Hu initiated programmes of mutual familiarisation, most notably with the "Year of Russia in China" in 2006 and the "Year of China in Russia" in 2007. This was intended to spread cultural as well as business awareness, in addition to familiarising middle-level officials at the national and provincial levels with opportunities for mutual cooperation. It has had some effect. However, the numbers of students from both countries going to study in each other's country, for example, are still dwarfed by those going to study in the West, whether in the US or Europe. And provincial officials in the Russian Far East have tended to be less supportive of close ties with China - and more ready to mistreat Chinese citizens - than those in Moscow, so there is no doubt about the need for a change in their mindset if the relationship is to grow.

g. China is anxious about Russia's bouts of robust assertiveness against the West. Both have reasons to feel defensive vis-a-vis the West, but this comes out in different ways, reflecting the differing trajectories of their international power. Russia is or has recently been a declining power and it wants to remind others of its past glory so that it can deter them from taking advantage. It relies upon a harder concept of power. Russia's leaders are nostalgic for hegemony over the "near abroad", namely the war with

Georgia, and they are certainly confronted by serious security challenges, both internally and externally. But sometimes the outbursts of Russian leaders, such as Putin's blistering attack on US international behaviour at the 2007 Munich meeting, seem too provocative. Moreover Russian attempts to reassert hegemony over the "near abroad" sometimes seem to contradict the principles of non-interference in the internal affairs of other states to which both Russia and China have formally committed themselves. It was striking that China - and the rest of the Shanghai Cooperation Organisation as well - refused to endorse Russia's recognition of Abkhazia as a separate state after the conflict with Georgia. China by contrast may have been a great power before the 19th century but not in recent memory. Now it is a rising power and its political leaders are anxious to avoid any provocation that might give other powers, above all the US, a pretext for action to prevent China from developing its full potential (though there are senior Chinese military figures who would be more inclined to stand up to the US). According to Galenovich, Chinese officials and experts seemed to want Russia to take the lead in challenging the US, for example over Iraq. Their chief red line concerns Taiwan, and the SCO has already expressed support for a one-China policy.

h. Finally, from a constructivist view of international relations, the basic problem is that there is only a limited sense of shared values between Russia and China - namely the modest success of the Year of Russia in China and the Year of China in Russia. It is true that the mantra of the current Russian leadership is that it is a Eurasian state and so must share common values with both Europe and Asia. But in practice the Russian leadership presents itself as partly Asian when it is talking to the West, as a way of brushing off excessive Western demands for liberalisation and democratisation. When Russian officials, especially those in the Far East, are talking to counterparts in China or Asia, they easily lapse into thinking of themselves as the last outposts of Western civilisation facing the Tartar hordes.

Conclusion

Even with all of these problems, there are still ways to work together if people have similar interests. China doesn't want any kind of formal alliance, so their relationship will rest on how well soft power works. However, security issues in Afghanistan will also make it possible for them to work together. Having good relations with Iran and Pakistan will bring problems that may be solved in a way that makes those relationships stronger. Their foreign policies can be put together because they have similar views on many problems facing the world, even if they don't always agree on how to carry them out. But as long as the West, especially the US, doesn't get too powerful, soft power is what makes Russia and China work together. China can deal with that better than Russia. China has more natural soft power than Russia on the world stage. China is seen as a growing power with a strong economy. Are they able to change and adapt? In the end, the question is whether China's "soft power" and Russia's "hard power" can be used together to make long-term, dynamic partnership possible.

Russia China Economic Relations and Facts

There are more and more developing countries in the world economy, which has made them more important politically as well. The formation of the G20 group of countries and its growing role as a place for talk may be the most obvious sign of this. Along with this, the big emerging economies have worked to improve their cooperation with each other through the BRICS group's unofficial partnership. China is, of course, the most important player in this new group.

The world economy's growth has been very good for Russia because it has led to more demand for its energy and raw materials and higher sale prices. In the meantime, it has tried to make up for lost economic and political power by getting more involved in new international groups like BRICS and the Shanghai Cooperation Organisation, especially by getting closer to China. Even though Russia and China may have better relations than ever and trade between them has grown quickly, their dealings seem to be a bit shallow and lack vision, and the chances for deeper economic integration are not very good.

This chapter talks about the economic ties between Russia and China and the things that make it hard for them to become more economically integrated. The analysis is mostly from Russia's point of view because, as is stated later in the chapter, progress in integration and opening up would matter more to Russia than to China.

First, we look at the size and growth of the Russian and Chinese economies. These are important factors that affect how the two countries see each other and how likely they are to work together. The next thing we do is look at how trade between the countries has grown, focusing on changes in market share and the way trade is structured. The countries of the Commonwealth of Independent States (CIS) are added to the market share study because they add something interesting to the mix of Russia and China. Energy problems are looked at separately because they are so important to Russia and China's economic relationships. After that, we talk about how Russia and China's industrial strategies might make it harder for their economies to work together. In the last part, the important findings and thoughts on the future are summed up.

The geography and economic potential of Russia and China, as well as how this potential is used, have a big impact on their economic ties. The last ten years have seen interesting changes in how economically powerful Russia and China are compared to each other. These changes are important for understanding how their relationship has changed over time.

The Russian economy has grown strongly since the start of the last decade, even though it was hit hard by the global financial crisis in 2009. Russia's net GDP almost doubled between 2005 and 2010, reaching $1,500 billion. This was made possible by fast economic growth and a stronger rouble. It is now the 11th biggest economy in the world. But, as with any other country, Russia's economic success is not even close to China's. In 2010, China's total GDP was almost $5,900 billion. It passed Japan to become the world's second-largest economy, after the US.

Figure 1.1. Size of the market; nominal GDP in some countries, USD billion

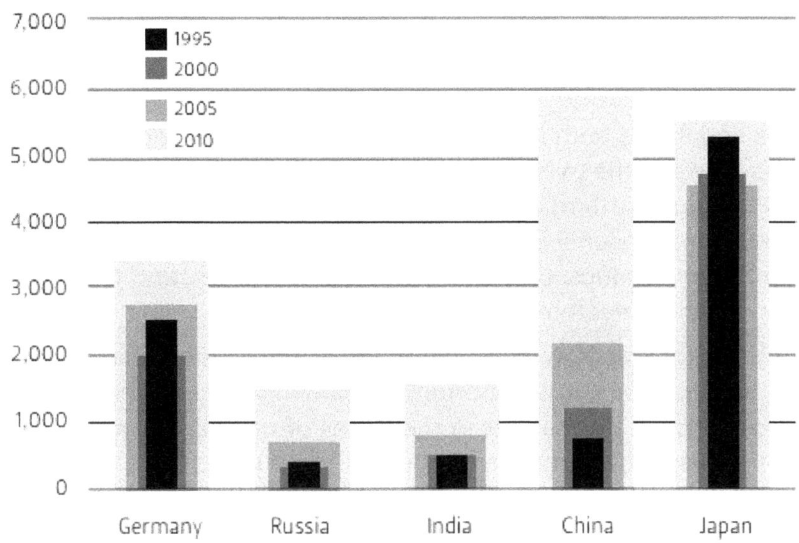

Source: IMF WEO April 2011

The purchasing power parity adjusted GDP (PPP) is a better measure of the "true" size of the economy and how much it uses resources. Nominal GDP shows the size and growth of the market and is used by companies as a key factor when they make strategic business and investment decisions. By this measure, Russia's share of world output has stayed around 3% for the past fifteen years, while China's share has grown from less than 6% to almost 14% during the same time period.

Figure 1.2. Living standards; GDP per capita, USD (PPP)

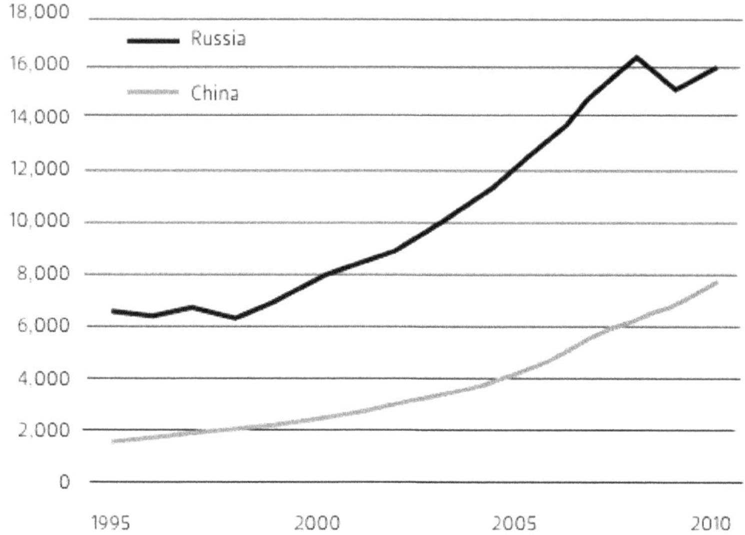

Source: IMF WEO April 2011

China and Russia both have higher growth rates, so the difference in living standards between the two has also shrunk in relative terms. China's per capita GDP (PPP) was only a third of Russia's in the second half of the 1990s. Now, ten years later, China's income is about half that of Russia. The difference in income between the two groups, on the other hand, has grown, and the Chinese will always be much poorer than the Russians.

When we look at how the economies of Russia and China have grown over the last ten years, it is important to remember that Russia's growth has been largely driven by changes in the prices of oil and raw materials. China, on the other hand, has grown even though input prices have gone up, which shows how successful its growth strategy has been. Russia's business situation is bad because it depends too much on export prices that go up and down. Also, energy prices might stay high in the future, but they probably won't rise as quickly as they have in the past ten years. This means that price changes in Russia will have less of an effect on economic growth.

Before we talk about ties between the two countries, it's important to note that China has a big impact on the Russian economy through the world market, which is related to changes in commodity prices. Through a global general equilibrium model, the World Bank found that one of the main ways that the growth of China and India will help Russia is by making its terms of trade better because of higher energy prices. The report says that this way of passing on benefits is very different from how many developing countries gain, which is mostly through more trade with these new giants.

Evolutions in Sino-Russian Trade

Before the Second World War, trade between the two countries was limited by their location, poor transportation links, and the fact that their economies and governments were very difficult. During the 1920s and 1930s, China made up only 3–5% of the Soviet Union's trade with other countries. Back then, when it came to economic problems, the Soviets probably paid more attention to revolutionary activities in China and how they were funded than to normal trade issues.

When the People's Republic of China was founded in 1949, it quickly built an economy similar to the Soviet Union with a lot of help from the Soviet Union. This led to a lot of trade and business between the two countries. The conflict between East and West and the goal of communist countries to become economically independent both showed how important these relationships were. China made up 15-20% of the Soviet Union's foreign trade in the 1950s. China's trade with other countries went up quickly and reached more than half of all trade. It was still only about 40% at the beginning of the 1960s.

But long-standing mistrust between the two countries, competition within the communist block, and a lack of trust between the leaders of Russia and China led to more disagreements between the two nations. By the mid-1960s, there was no longer any formal contact between the two countries, and trade had stopped. In the middle of the decade, China only made up a few percentage points of the Soviet Union's trade with other countries. After the border war in 1969, there wasn't much trade between Russia and China. Even though things got better, especially after President Gorbachev took office in 1985, trade stayed low. China did less than 2% of the Soviet Union's trade with other countries in its last few years. In the mid-1960s, the Soviet Union's share of China's foreign trade dropped below 10%. About 25 years later, just before the Soviet Union broke up, the share was about 3%.

After the fall of the Soviet Union in the 1990s, Russia and China's political ties continued to get better. However, Russia's unstable government and bad economic performance made it harder for the two countries to do business together. On top of that, China's economy hadn't quite reached a point where it would allow for closer cooperation when it came to Russia sending goods to China. Finally, the Asian crisis at the end of the decade made it even harder for them to work together. It slowed China's economic growth and sped up Russia's fall into a full-scale financial crisis in 1998 by causing oil prices to drop.

After the year 2000, trade between Russia and China finally picked up again, even though it had been very slow before. China's fast growth started to be seen in the world economy more and more, as its need for energy and raw materials drove up prices. At the same time, Russia sent more oil and raw materials to China. Because of this, Russia's exports went from being worth $5 billion at the start of the 2000s to $20 billion in 2010. The amount of goods that China sold to Russia, on the other hand, only went up to just over 6%. With a 5% share, China was Russia's fifth biggest export market in 2010.

Russia's imports are where the effects of more trade with China are most noticeable. After the crisis in 1998, Russia's economy started to recover quickly at the start of the 2000s. Rising wages were helped by the rouble's strength and higher prices for energy and raw materials around the world. Also, imports went up very quickly, especially those from China. So, from the beginning of the decade to 2010, the share of Chinese goods in Russian imports rose at an amazing rate, rising from 3% to 17%. China is now by far Russia's most important trade partner when it comes to imports. China's growing market share means that third countries have lost market share in Russia. It also means that Russian companies will have to deal with a lot more competition.

Even though commodity prices went up at the end of last decade, Russia's trade gap with China became bigger because of strong growth in imports. The trade between Russia and China pretty much evened out in 2009. That's when the global financial crisis hit Russia's goods hard. Russia had a trade imbalance with China of about $19 billion in 2010, but Russia had a surplus in all of its other trade, worth about $170 billion.

Figure 1.3. Russia's trade with China, 1995–2010, USD billion

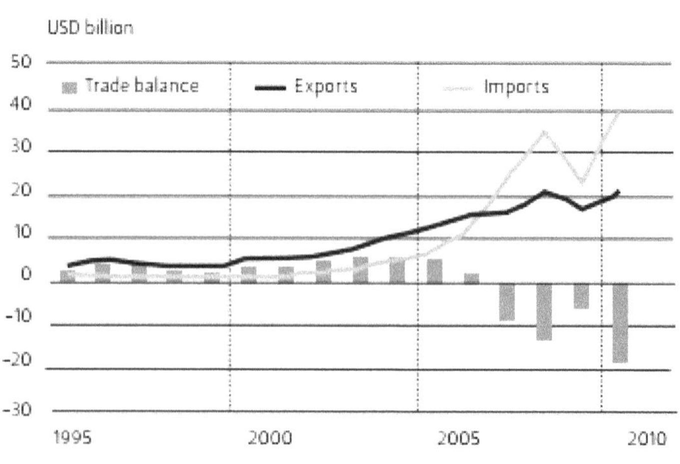

Source: UN Comtrade

Even though trade between Russia and China has grown quickly, Russia has not become very important to China in terms of market share. Post-Soviet Russia's share of China's imports and exports stays steady at around 2%. In the 1950s, China was the weak partner that the Soviet Union helped, but now it is the most important country in the world. This must change how the Russians see not only the economic relationship between Russia and China but also Russia's place in the modern world as a whole.

Figure 1.4. China's share in Russia's foreign trade, %

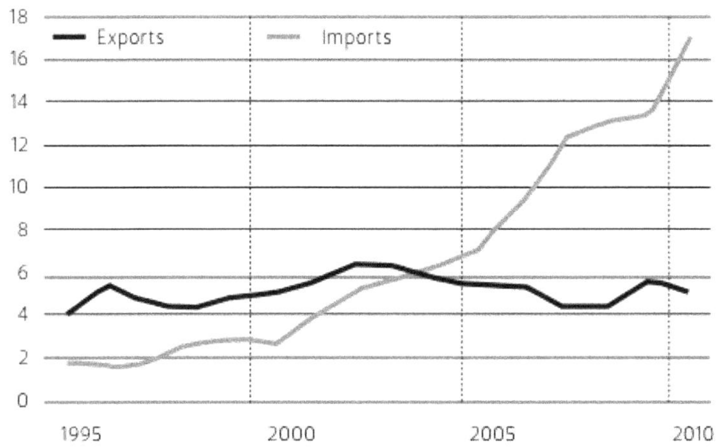

Source: UN Comtrade

Shifts in the Structure of Trade

If you want to know how trade between Russia and China has changed over time, you should not only look at how trade has grown and how market shares have changed. You should also look at how the organisation of trade between Russia and China has changed. In the last fifteen years or so, Russia's trade data with China have clearly shown that high-tech goods have become more important in Russia's imports from China while energy and raw materials have become more important in Russia's exports to China.

It has been said many times by the Russian government that Russia needs to broaden its exports and make more high-tech finished goods. In fact, though, the structure of exports has changed in the wrong way. A private Russian oil company called Yukos began sending oil to China by rail in the first half of the last decade. Energy and raw materials started to make up a bigger part of Russia's exports as prices and amounts went up. About 10% of Russia's exports to China were oil and raw materials (SITC 2 and 3). By the beginning of the 2000s, that number had risen to 30%, and by the end of that decade, it had risen to more than 60%. Russia sent 70% of its goods to China in 2010; most of them were oil and raw materials. A lot of other important types of products, like food, chemicals, and base metals, also include products that haven't been treated very much.

In the second half of the 1990s, machinery and transport equipment (SITC 7) made up a very small part of exports to China. By 2010, it had dropped to just 1%. Overall, it looks like less than 10% of the goods that Russia sends to China are highly processed. It's kind of like how Russia does business with wealthy countries in this way.

The growth of the arms trade, which Russians see as a sign of their country's high-tech potential, makes it clear how Russia and China's stances have changed over time. The Stockholm Peace Research Institute (SIPRI) says that Russia's arms sales to China peaked in 2005 and have been falling quickly ever since. In 2010, Russia sent only 13% of the amount of arms it had sent to China five years earlier. China's share of all Russian arms exports dropped from more than 60% to less than 7% at the same time. Russia doesn't want to sell China the newest military technology, and China has also made progress in its own military production and technology. This is why Russia's arms sales to China have dropped. China has been able to significantly increase its arms exports over the past few years and is now becoming a big player in the international arms trade in this decade.

There have been at least as many big changes in what Russia buys from China as there are in what it sells. It is clear from them that Chinese products are getting more high-tech. Russia's imports of Chinese food goods (SITC 0 and 1) have more than doubled in value since the mid-1990s. However, only 5% of Russia's imports were food products, down from 26% in 1996. Also, the value of imports of various manufactures (SITC 8), which mostly includes shoes and clothes, has grown a lot in the last ten years. They are still very important, but in the last ten years, they have become only half of what Russia buys from China.

Shoes and clothes have to make way for machinery and equipment (SITC 7), which now make up more than a third of Russia's imports from China. Computers, phones, and home electronics make up most of this group of products. As with other items in this group, sales of cars have grown quickly, which worries Russian automakers. The fast growth of imports of base metals and their products (included in SITC 6) shows that Russian companies are facing more competition in this area as well. In fact, Russia has already taken steps to protect its suppliers by limiting imports of things like steel pipes from China.

The last ten years have shown that China's success in the Russian market isn't just due to its low-wage, low-tech businesses. China is now exporting more than just clothes and shoes. It has also expanded its product line and is now sending more and more high-tech goods abroad. They have tried to do this but have not been able to. China has also become a major player in the Russian market, but Russia's part in the Chinese economy has stayed small, except for energy and some raw materials like roundwood.

Table 1.3. Structure of Russia's trade with China, %*

Russian exports to China				
SITC	**1996**	**2000**	**2005**	**2010**
Food and live animals (0)	4.2	7.3	7.2	5.3
Beverages and tobacco (1)	0.0	0.0	0.0	0.0
Crude materials, inedible, except fuels (2)	7.1	18.1	20.5	20.6
Mineral fuels (3)	4.6	13.5	41.3	49.3
Edible oils (4)	0.1	0.0	0.0	0.0
Chemicals (5)	29.5	19.8	13.8	11.0
Manufactured goods by material (6)	32.3	30.1	15.1	12.2
Machinery and transport equipment (7)	17.7	4.1	1.9	1.3
Miscellaneous manufactured articles (8)	3.1	1.7	0.2	0.3
Other items (9)	1.3	5.3	0.1	0.0
Total	100.0	100.0	100.0	100.0
Russian imports from China				
SITC	**1996**	**2000**	**2005**	**2010**
Food and live animals (0)	26.1	6.2	4.7	4.7
Beverages and tobacco (1)	0.5	0.9	0.1	0.1
Crude materials, inedible, except fuels (2)	2.7	1.8	0.7	0.5
Mineral fuels (3)	1.4	2.2	1.0	0.7
Edible oils (4)	0.0	0.0	0.0	0.0
Chemicals (5)	2.4	3.8	3.6	5.2
Manufactured goods by material (6)	6.9	6.8	13.8	18.6
Machinery and transport equipment (7)	5.7	7.2	19.1	35.4
Miscellaneous manufactured articles (8)	54.3	71.2	57.0	34.8
Other items (9)	0.0	0.0	0.0	0.0
Total	100.0	100.0	100.0	100.0

** Data are from the Chinese statistics, as they are believed to convey a more accurate picture, particularly in the earlier years.*

Source: UN Comtrade

Challenges to Russia from China in the CIS Zone

Russia has been an important part of the CIS economy for a long time. It has tried to keep its place by making deals like the customs union between Russia, Kazakhstan, and Belarus. Russia also wants to be a financial hub for the region and for the rouble to be the most important currency in the area. One side of things is that regional trade and banking arrangements can make it easier for countries to do business and trade with each other. There is, however, a chance that regional trade deals will be unfair to third parties, which could hurt the economy. In fact, there are signs that the growing importance of China in the area could be a big reason for some CIS countries to join their customs union. Even so, it has been hard for different countries in the CIS to work together on economic issues and build up their institutions. Even though Russia still has a strong place in the area, trade with other countries shows that things are changing, especially since China is becoming more present.

A lot of the time, the CIS countries' official trade figures are missing or not accurate, and in many cases, a big chunk of their trade happens outside of the reach of the statistics. Despite this, the numbers show some interesting and logical changes in how China and Russia affect the economies of the CIS region. But before we get to the research, we should point out that changes in energy prices have a big effect on how market share changes. In fact, there have been several reasons why energy prices have gone up in the CIS over the last 20 years: 1) The price of oil on the world market went up from about $20 USD per barrel in 1996–2000 to more than $75 USD per barrel in 2006–2010; 2) Natural gas prices in the CIS region have started to follow international oil prices more closely; and 3) The way energy is priced between Russia and the CIS countries has changed a lot as they have started to use prices that are more in line with prices on the international market. If costs were kept the same, all of this means that Russia's loss of market share in the CIS over the last fifteen years would look even worse.

Table 2.2 shows how trade between the CIS countries and Russia and China has changed over the last fifteen years. It shows how different the CIS area is. Trade seems to be mostly affected by geography, such as the distances between countries, transportation lines, and the availability of energy and raw materials. However, there are other factors that play a role as well.

Russia has a big part in the trade with its western countries, Ukraine and Belarus, though its share has gone down a lot. China still only makes up a small part of these countries' trade with other countries, but goods from China have grown quickly in recent years. This is also true for Armenia and Azerbaijan, though Russia is not as important a trade partner for them as it is for Belarus or Ukraine. At the end of the 1990s, a new oil pipeline was built from Baku to Georgian Supsa on the Black Sea. This may have caused Russia's share of Azerbaijan's exports to drop in the early 2000s. After the middle of the 2000s, an oil pipeline from Baku to Turkish Ceihan on the Mediterranean gave Azerbaijani oil another way to get to markets other than Russia.

East Central Asia Kazakhstan is a very interesting country because it is between Russia and China and has a lot of natural resources. China's state-owned energy companies have big stakes in Kazakhstan's crude oil production, refineries, and pipeline transport. Kazakhstan is an important part of China's energy plan. When the oil pipeline from Kazakhstan to China was finished at the end of 2005, it made it much easier for Kazakhstan to sell oil. The finish line for the new gas pipeline from Turkmenistan to China was at the end of 2009. It will also be used to send gas from Kazakhstan to China. Another thing that China does in Kazakhstan is help make other raw products.

One big thing that sets China apart from Russia and its other rivals is its ability to finance energy projects. In the spring of 2009, China's state-owned energy company CNPC bought a majority stake in Kazakhstan's MMG energy company. As part of the deal, China gave Kazakhstan a $10 billion loan. It was also wanted by the Indian and Russian governments to own a piece of MMG.

Even though Russian businesses are still very important to Kazakhstan's economy, Chinese businesses are becoming more and more noticeable. China seems to have been the most busy player in Kazakhstan over the last five years. This is also shown in the trade numbers. Almost a third of Kazakhstan's exports went to Russia in the second half of the 1990s. In the last five years, that share has dropped to about 10%. During the same time period, China's share of Kazakhstan's exports has grown to about 15%. Russia has a one-third share of Kazakhstan's import market. Even though its share has gone down, Russia still has a strong place in Kazakhstan. But the fact that China's part of Kazakhstan's imports has grown from about 2% to almost a quarter in ten years shows how strong the Chinese economy is.

When looking at the trade figures of the other Central Asian countries, the problems are even more clear, and the data often only give a vague picture. Russia and China have both become bigger importers in Kyrgyzstan, but there haven't been many changes to exports. Large amounts of goods are shipped from China to Kazakhstan and other CIS countries by Kyrgyz traders. To keep this business going, Kyrgyzstan wants to join the customs union of Russia, Kazakhstan, and Belarus. Russia and China have both raised the amount of goods they sell in Tajikistan. China has become just as important a trade partner for Tajikistan as Russia when it comes to exports.

	Belarus				Kazakhstan				Ukraine			
	Exports		Imports		Exports		Imports		Exports		Imports	
	China	Russia	China	Russia	China	Russia	China	Russia	China	Russia	China	Russia
1996-2000	2	58	1	56	7	29	2	45	6	27	1	47
2001-2005	2	47	1	65	10	15	8	39	3	20	3	38
2005-2010	2	35	3	58	15	10	24	34	2	23	6	29
	Armenia				**Azerbaijan**				**Kyrgyzstan**			
	Exports		Imports		Exports		Imports		Exports		Imports	
	China	Russia	China	Russia	China	Russia	China	Russia	China	Russia	China	Russia
1996-2000	0	22	1	19	0	15	1	19	6	18	5	23
2001-2005	1	14	2	16	1	5	4	15	5	18	10	26
2005-2010	1	16	8	19	1	5	7	18	3	19	18	37
	Turkmenistan	Uzbekistan	Tajikistan									
	Exports	Imports	Exports	Imports	Exports	Imports						
	China	Russia	China	Russia	China	Russia	China	Russia	China	Russia	China	Russia
1996-2000	0	12	1	13	2	25	2	18	1	15	1	14
2001-2005	0	2	4	15	7	22	6	23	1	10	3	20
2005-2010	7	1	12	15	10	19	15	25	11	9	16	28

Sources: IMF Direction of Trade Statistics, UN Comtrade

When it was finished in December 2009, the gas route from Turkmenistan to China went through Uzbekistan and Kazakhstan. This gave Turkmenistan a big new market to sell its gas. This is clear from the fact that China's share of Turkmenistan's exports went from zero at the end of the 1990s to almost one-third in 2010. This can be seen in Table 2.2, which shows trends over five years, where China's share rose to 7% from 2006 to 2010. At the same time, the amount of goods sent to Russia has dropped dramatically. This is partly because of the blast in the Turkmenistan-Russia gas pipeline in the spring of 2009. China is already as big of a player in the Turkmenistan market as Russia when it comes to goods. Russia is still the biggest trade partner of Uzbekistan, but China is also there and is quickly becoming more visible in both imports and exports.

Central Asia's reliance on Russia has decreased since they can now trade with China. This can be seen in the higher prices of their goods, for example. China's demand has made the market more competitive, but the flood of Chinese goods into Central Asia has already made people worry that these countries will lose some of their ability to make things themselves. Kazakhstan joined the customs union with Russia and Belarus. The government may have wanted to stop too many Chinese goods from coming into Kazakhstani markets and protect Kazakhstani production as part of its policy to do so.

Energy Dynamics in Russia-China Economic Relations

As you can see, energy problems are at the heart of Russia's and China's economic ties. China's growing need for energy and reliance on energy imports make it a perfect fit for Russia's energy industry to grow into Asian markets. In fact, changes in the energy sector show some interesting things about Russia and China's economic ties.

China already gets more than half of its crude oil from other countries, and its reliance on imported oil is growing quickly. China produced 204 million tonnes of oil in 2010 and imported 239 million tonnes. Chinese data show that in the past few years, China has imported about 15 million tonnes of oil from Russia each year. This is about 3-4% of China's total oil consumption and 6-7% of its oil imports. China has done a good job of getting oil from a variety of places. After Saudi Arabia, Angola, and Iran, Russia is now China's fourth biggest oil supplier. In 2010, China bought just over 4% of its oil from Kazakhstan.

The amount of oil that China buys from Russia has slowly grown to 5–6% of all oil sold in the world. But China and other Asian countries are likely to play a bigger part in Russia's energy exports in the future. Based on Russia's energy plan from 2009, 22 to 25 percent of its oil exports will go to Asia by 2030.

The Chinese state oil company CNPC and the Russian state pipeline monopoly Transneft finally came to an agreement in 2008 to build an oil pipeline from Russia to China. The talks had been long and tough. Soon after, in the following year, construction began after the China Development Bank agreed to lend Transneft and Rosneft a total of $25 billion in exchange for future oil deliveries. The new pipeline started sending oil to China at the beginning of 2011. According to the deals that are already in place, Russia will send 15 million tonnes of oil through the pipeline every year for the next 20 years. Up until now, Russian oil has been sent to China by train and through the Kazakh pipeline system. The new route makes it much easier for Russia to send oil to China. But this hasn't yet been reflected in real oil deliveries. From January to March 2011, China bought less oil from Russia than it did during the same time last year. The East Siberian Pacific Ocean (ESPO) pipeline has a branch that goes to China. The ESPO pipeline should be finished by 2013 or 2014.

In addition to the oil pipeline problem, Russia and China have been talking for a long time about building a gas pipeline from Russia to China. However, progress has been slow on this issue as well. While there have been several letters of intent, the final deal has been put off because of a disagreement over the price of petrol. From what we know, Russia wants to tie the price of gas to China to the price of gas to Europe. China has refused to agree to this and has asked for a lower price. Perhaps in 2015, Russian Gazprom could start sending gas through the Altai gas pipeline if they could reach a price deal with China in the summer of 2011. Gas from the Russian Pacific region is also going to be sent to China. Russia's energy plan says that in the next twenty years, Asia will get about one-fifth of Russia's gas exports, up from zero current share.

Even though both Russian and Chinese leaders have talked a lot about energy problems in their speeches over the past ten years, progress has been slow. That's because of a number of things. Russia's energy strategy has been hard to predict, which has made it harder to invest in transport and energy production. Because of interference from the government and state-run energy companies, private oil companies in Russia have not been able to carry out their plans to send more oil to China. High and rising energy prices have also given the Russians some freedom, so there hasn't been immediate economic pressure to speed up energy projects linked to China. Russia is trying to make possible Japanese and Chinese customers compete with each other on different pipeline routes in a very sneaky way. This is slowing down the projects, and this kind of behaviour is known to bother both Japan and China. Obviously, disagreements about business issues like how to pay for projects and how much energy costs have also slowed down energy projects. The Russians have said over and over that the Chinese are not ready to buy their energy at market prices.

People often say that mistrust between Russia and China is at the root of their economic troubles. China is becoming more powerful, and Russia is afraid of it. In the end, economic issues are linked to security strategy. But because Russian leaders can't make up their minds, the Chinese aren't sure if the other side will be able to carry out the business plans that were agreed upon. Energy and raw materials are very important to Russia's economy and politics, as shown by the fact that talks on these topics are hard, especially in the Far East of Russia.

The opening up of Central Asia, which is full of energy, has changed the energy game between Russia and China. China has been able to directly invest in the production and transportation of energy in Central Asia. As a result, China's imports of energy from Kazakhstan, Uzbekistan, and Turkmenistan are growing quickly. In Russia, on the other hand, foreign energy companies have had a hard time getting ahead in the strategic energy sector, which has slowed the growth of the Russian energy sector and China's energy imports from Russia. Russia sees that the fact that China and Central Asian countries are working together more on economic issues has made it harder for Russia to negotiate with both China and Central Asia. Longer term, Russia will have to rethink its current strategy, not just towards China, because of more competition and new options.

Lack of Consistency in Russia's Economic Policy

Russia and China work together on the economy in more ways than just trading things with each other. They are also becoming more economically integrated. These days, it's hard to trust figures on foreign direct investment. However, when put together with other data, they do show that there aren't many investments going back and forth between Russia and China. In 2010, about $52 billion worth of foreign direct investment (FDI) came to Russia. Of this amount, only $300 million came from China. In the same way, Russian companies invested a total of $41 billion in other countries but only $20 million in China. Chinese data also show that Russia doesn't play a big part in China's FDI flows, either coming in or going out.

It's interesting that Russia and China don't have a lot of direct investments in each other. Businesses in both Russia and China have only recently started to go global, and both have a pretty bad track record when it comes to doing business with other countries. Because of this, it is easy to see why Russian and Chinese companies have found markets in third countries more appealing. Also, it's not hard to understand why Russia doesn't invest much in China: there aren't any Russian companies that could fight in the Chinese markets yet, besides those that work with energy and raw materials. The energy market in China is controlled by huge Chinese state-owned companies, which makes it hard for foreign companies to get into the market.

It's harder to understand why China doesn't spend more in Russia. China is already used to making big investments in the energy and raw materials sectors in places that are physically farther away from Russia and have less safe conditions than Russia. So, it looks like there is something strange about the way Russian markets and politics work that might help explain at least some of the reason why China doesn't invest in Russia.

China's businesses that need a lot of workers are less likely to want to invest in Russia because of the country's high wages and low labor productivity. For these areas to get a lot of funding, Chinese workers would have to move to Russia. This is not yet a real option, even though there are probably hundreds of thousands of Chinese working in construction and agriculture, mostly in Siberia and the far east of Russia. There isn't much Chinese investment in areas that need a lot of capital because Russia doesn't like foreign investors in general and Chinese investors in particular. In Russia, there have been a lot of changes for foreign energy companies, and many of them have had to close their businesses to make room for Russian state companies. When foreign companies have had problems with Russian companies, those problems have often affected ties between the two countries at the state level. This could be one reason why the Russian government hasn't let big Chinese state-owned companies buy big shares in Russia's energy industry. When it comes to the strategic energy industry, politics are more important than economics. It's kind of the same with other raw products, too. A few years ago, export taxes on roundwood were raised mostly against China. However, because of concerns about fair trade, the higher taxes were also put in place in Russia's European parts, even though they were bad for business and caused political problems with the EU.

Russia and China both put a lot of weight on strategic sectors and industrial strategies in their economic policies. This could make it harder for the two countries to work together on their economies, though, since their priority areas are mostly the same and have strong protectionist tendencies.

In both countries, shipbuilding, aircraft manufacturing, nuclear power, and telecommunications are some of the most important businesses. China already makes more conventional cargo ships than any other country. Russian shipyards, especially those in the Russian Far East, have to deal with tough competition from Chinese, South Korean, and Japanese factories. It looks like China will soon be able to compete with Russia in the airplane industry, if it hasn't already. This is because China is determined, has access to finance, and works with the biggest European and American parts suppliers. China has made progress in the airplane business, as shown by its work on the jumbo jet and stealth fighter projects. In 2010, a Russian company beat out a Chinese company in a bid to build a nuclear power plant in Belarus. However, China is expected to be able to seriously compete in the international nuclear power business in a few years, thanks to its own technology and lower costs. It was ZTE and Huawei, two huge Chinese phone companies, that came in second and fourth on the list of companies around the world that filed the most foreign patents (PCT) applications in 2010. There were about three times as many foreign patent applications from these companies as there were from all of Russia together.

Figure 1.5. Production of passenger cars in Russia and China, million units

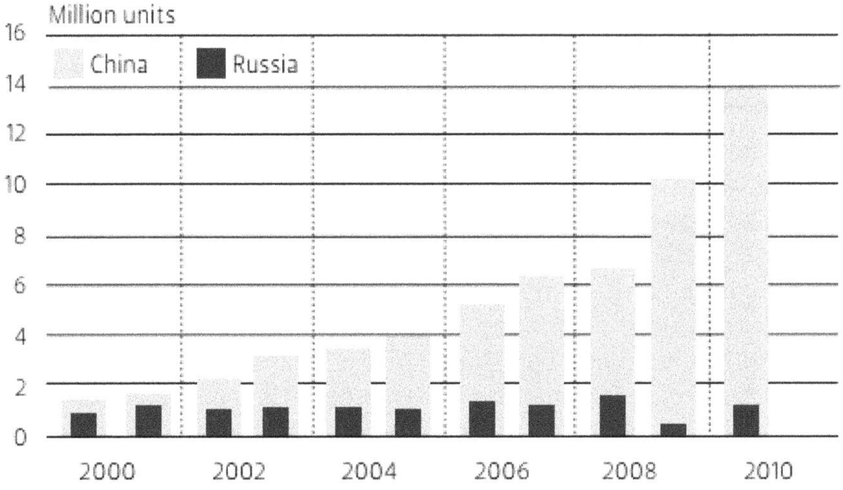

Source: CEIC

The car business is a good example of how well industrial policies have worked in China and Russia. The auto market has grown in both countries because people are buying more cars and their incomes are rising quickly. In Russia, the local auto industry hasn't been able to take advantage of the situation because the rise in demand has been met by imports, and since 2003, more and more foreign automakers have been putting together cars in Russia. Over 1.2 million cars were made in Russia in 2010, but only a few thousand were sent outside of Russia. China has been making a lot more cars and exports are also going up, though they started out pretty low. Chinese car companies have asked for permission to open factories in Russia, but so far Russian companies are only putting together a few Chinese cars on a small scale. This is because Russian car companies have been able to persuade officials not to let Chinese car companies into Russia.

Russia and China have had a slow and hard time integrating in the real sector. The same is true for the banking sector. Even though the rouble and the yuan can be used on the border between Russia and China and there are swap agreements between the Central Bank of Russia and the People's Bank of China, it is still too early to say that there is a lot of financial integration between the two countries. Russia wants to make the rouble at least a regional key currency and Moscow an international financial center. However, China will be a strong opponent to these plans, as the yuan is already playing a bigger role internationally and Shanghai and Hong Kong are better global or regional financial centers than any Russian city. In reality, the lack of strong shared interests—or, more often than not, the presence of competing interests—is also mirrored in the way countries work together across borders. It's hard to see how the BRICS group, for instance, could become a real player in the world economy.

Russia and China both protect and back a lot of the same key sectors. This means that there isn't much room for them to become more economically integrated. China and Chinese companies have been very difficult for foreign businesses to work with in many ways. However, China's cheap labor and large and growing market have made the country an essential business partner. China is truly focused on the rest of the world and wants to join the world economy, which has made cooperation easier. China joined the WTO in 2001, which is a clear example of the country's method. This approach is clearly good for China and the other WTO members. As we talk about strategic sectors and industrial policy, it is important to remember that China's fast economic growth and technological progress are mostly due to activities in the private sector and competitive export production, not because the government protects big state companies.

While China has huge markets that are rising quickly and cheap labor, Russia doesn't have either of those things to make up for its otherwise bad business environment. Russia's economic strategy doesn't really want to open up, as shown by the fact that it couldn't decide what to do during the WTO negotiations. Russia's industrial strategy is mostly made up of protectionism and government meddling. Lastly, it's not clear how much greater integration can happen because both Russia and China seem to prefer working with other countries to talking to each other.

Overview

It took twelve years for trade between Russia and China to pick up speed after the fall of the Soviet Union. It could be said that government ties between the two countries are better than ever, but economic factors have led to the growth of trade. China's fast economic growth, its ability to sell goods abroad, and its need to find new sources of energy and raw materials have all helped trade between the two countries grow. There haven't been many political breakthroughs that directly help economic relations, and decisions have only been made after long, tough discussions. Even though it's easy to name specific investments that both Russia and China have made, their economic unity is mostly limited to trading goods. China has moved much faster with the Central Asian countries than with Russia on important energy problems.

The relationship between Russia and China is a bit shallow and short-sighted, and the chances of greater economic integration are not good. People often say this to show how heavy past is and how much they don't trust each other. In this chapter, we suggest that industrial policies that focus on strategic sectors have made it harder for Russia and China to do business with each other. This has led to a rise in protectionism, especially in Russia. The situation is made more difficult by the fact that many of the players are state-owned businesses that consider political interests of the owner along with business concerns.

At the moment, Russia and China's economic ties are limited to small business projects that don't have a clear goal or framework. The way they work together is similar to how Russia works with other countries, but it is very different from how China and the US or EU do business, which is based on rules and organizations.

China doesn't have to worry about the current situation because it can get the energy and raw materials it needs from Russia, and the fact that the BRICS countries regularly talk about projects and working together is enough to meet their political needs. Furthermore, China's rapidly growing economic ties with other CIS countries give it more negotiating power with Russia over energy problems. From the Russian point of view, things are not at all good, as the relationship between Russia and China in the economy shows how weak the Russian economy is in general. China has been able to modernize and diversify its economy, and Russia has become a pure raw materials supplier, even among developing markets. This is not what the leaders of Russia hoped would happen.

Russian economic strategy is very protectionist, state-centered, and focused on domestic markets. This makes it hard for Russia and China or any other country to work together on economic issues. Russian leaders seem to believe that the economic relationship between Russia and China and Russia's role in the CIS region give it a special place and set of rules in the global economy. However, this is not likely to be the case. As China's economic power grows in Russia and the CIS region, Russia will have to rethink the pros and cons of its current approach. This could take some time. In the meantime, businesses in Russia and China will keep looking for new ways to do business and work together, which will keep the weak integration process going.

The Russian Take on China

Problem

The way Russians feel about China has changed a lot in the last ten years, and this affects both the leaders and the average Russian. China was seen as a "younger brother" and a "strategic partner" during the Soviet era and the first ten years after the fall of the Soviet Union. However, things are not so clear-cut now. The way people and powerful people think about China is quickly changing along with the country's changing place in the world. During the Soviet era, most people, including researchers and experts, had a similar view of China. However, these days, people have very different ideas about how to improve ties between the two countries. These differences are caused by more than just different opinions. They are also caused by the work of the anti-China and pro-China groups in the Russian Establishment, the expert community, and the media. However, the people as a whole is also changing how they feel about the former "younger brother" because of the information pressure.

Over the past few years, Russian experts and the media have talked a lot about ties with China in general and the Chinese threat in particular. There are some good reasons for this, since you can't ignore your relationship with a neighbour that is either already a world star in some areas or will soon be one. The things that are making this kind of talk more heated, on the other hand, are mostly made up. This is what started what could be called "the battle for Russia." There are some experts who say that Russia is special when it comes to China getting resources, even though China gets resources from almost every part of the world. However, most of the raw materials that go to China come from the sea (except for those coming from Central Asia and Russia). This means that if the USA and China start a war, water routes will be blocked because the USA controls the whole ocean. Central Asian supplies go through the unstable region of Xinjiang. The US also has some positions there, at least as long as it stays in Afghanistan.

So, Russia is the only country that can promise stable supplies to China in case of a military conflict between Beijing and Washington or just if the situation in the Pacific Ocean changes in a way that hurts China's interests. Chinese thinkers also agree that Russia plays a unique role in this area. Another well-known Chinese military planner, Dai Xu, who is a senior colonel in the People's Liberation Army Air Force, says that the US is holding China in a "C"-shaped half-circle. From Japan in the north to states that claim part of Chinese land in the south, this half-circle goes. The circle isn't whole because it breaks off at Russia and North Korea, but maybe one day the two ends will meet.

Because Russia is the only country that supplies China with raw materials, the world's biggest players need to work even harder to get Moscow involved in areas that are important to them. The anti-China and pro-China wings are working harder to support a strategic partnership project with a corresponding centre of force. This can be seen in the expert and mass media discourse, as well as to some extent in the scientific discourse. But in terms of how things work, both sides see Russia not as an independent player with its own goals, but as a satellite of one of the spheres of influence. This means that Russia has to follow a set of strategic responsibilities that may go against its own national interests. International policy is moving away from a value-based approach and towards an interest-based approach. Because of this, lobbyists for both sides focus on interests first, playing with different types of risks and possible benefits from different types of strategic partnerships.

The anti-China party

China didn't pay much attention to its public relations in Russia until recently, compared to western countries. Instead, it chose to talk directly with government leaders and businesspeople who are close to the government. This explains why the anti-Chinese party is so popular, though it's not as popular as it was a few years ago.

Alexander Khramchikhin, who is the head of the analytical department at the Institute for Political and Military Analysis, is the most well-known member of the anti-China party and its most powerful alarmist side among experts. Most of the time, Khramchikhin writes about the Chinese danger for major Russian news outlets. Due to his increased activity in the media, it can be said that he sets the anti-China party's trends in the Russian expert community, even though he works alone and other members of his school are rarely seen in the media. As for the kinds of points he uses in his writing, they are pretty much the same; there isn't much new in the last few years. The following points form the main part of his thinking. He uses arguments that are both strong and weak, and he often makes things worse than they really are.

China has a lot more people than it needs, so it needs to add more land to house them. One thing Khramchikhin points out is that the Chinese population is still growing even though they are trying to lower birth rates. The results of the most recent census, which came out in the spring of 2011, somewhat weaken this argument, but they don't fully disprove it. Since the Chinese government started its family planning programme 30 years ago, the population growth rate has slowed down significantly, though the overall growth rate still looks very high. In the last ten years, China's population has grown by 73.9 million, bringing the total number of people living there to 1.34 billion. This is a growth rate just above 0.5%.

Also, the anti-China party representative doesn't think about how the rising living standards and needs of the Chinese people affect the way of China's population growth. In particular, the Chinese government wants to speed up the process of urbanisation in the country. The recently announced goal of shifting the economy from focusing on foreign markets to focusing on domestic consumption will only help this path, since people in cities tend to consume more than people in rural areas.

In 2010, 666 million people in China lived in cities, which was 49.68% of the total population. China is becoming more urbanised faster than ever. From 2000 to 2010, the percentage of people living in cities rose from 36.22 percent to 49.68 percent. In 1978, when China started its economic changes, only 17.9% of its people lived in towns and cities. It wasn't until 1995 that 30% of the population lived in cities.

One area of mining in China where it is possible to meet both local and international demand is the production of rare earth metals, which the country has plenty of. China does, however, lack some resources, which is another reason why it needs new land to produce things. China does have to import a lot of its resources, mostly energy sources. For example, Beijing is a net importer of coal, oil, and, more lately, gas and timber. China is especially asking Russia to send twice as much oil. Although China lacks some resources, this does not mean that it automatically has a problem with its neighbours, such as Russia, which is willing to provide raw materials.

There are problems in China because of its imbalanced population, which is mostly made up of men. Because of the way people in rural areas think and the fact that it is now possible to find out a baby's gender early in pregnancy, there are too many boys born. In rural places, boys are seen as "assets" and girls as "liabilities" in the home. He says that because of this, dozens of millions of young guys in rural China will not be able to find a spouse in the next few decades. In order to make up for this, the government will have to grow, either economically and peacefully through "trekking to find a bride" or militarily through growth. An excessively large number of deaths from war might even be wanted because they would help reduce the number of men in the population.

There is a possible problem in general, but it is not as serious as it used to be. Its effects will become clear in the next twenty years. In China, the gender gap has become less severe, according to the most recent statistics. China had

106.74 men for every 100 women in 2000, and 105.2 women for every 100 men in 2010. These numbers, by the way, disprove Khramchikhin's unproven claims that there are at least 20% more boys than girls in the population. A lot of the extra male population will also move to cities, where single-parent families are becoming more popular, in search of a better life. For someone living in the country, not being able to get married and start a family would be terrible, but for someone with a busy job in the city, having a family might even be a bother. Also, the Chinese government wants to make the state welfare system universal, like it is in Russia. This will make it less important to have a spouse and children when you get old; the Chinese are used to relying on the government for this.

China is slowly getting ready for a military battle with Russia to take over some of its land. At the same time, it is holding military drills and adding to its arsenal. Khramchikhin says that the official Chinese history books now see Russia's actions towards China since the 17th century as aggression and all deals, except for the Treaty of Nerchinsk, as unfair and unequal.

An article from April 3, 1988, in Jiefangjun Bao, an official newspaper of the People's Liberation Army (PLA), helps the anti-China party understand China's military danger. To talk about the idea of strategic boundaries of living space, the article said, "Effective control conducted over a strategic district for a long period of time that is implemented outside of geographical borders will ultimately lead to a shift of geographical borders." This leads us to believe that sooner or later, the Chinese army will take over Russian areas that they are interested in for business reasons.

At least two points are made to support this theory. In the first place, PLA military drills are being held near the Russian border to get ready for battle with the Russian army. China held its biggest military drills ever in 2009, called Stride-2009. The Nanjing military region troops that were in charge of Taiwan did not take part, which would make sense if the military were training for operations that would connect the island to mainland China. The drills did include units from the Beijing, Shenyang, and Lanzhou military regions, which are aimed at Russia, Mongolia, and Central Asia. They also included units from the Jinan military region, which is there in case of an emergency.

The second military point of the anti-China party is about how China's policies are different and how it is re-arming its military. For example, until recently, a lot of people in Russia thought that China couldn't effectively fight Russia in a military battle because it needed Moscow for technology. This was because, until recently, China got most of its weapons from Russia. Russia had an edge because it made these weapons. In case of a conflict, it could either use more advanced weapons or sell old models that would be easily destroyed by Russia's more advanced weapons.

Representatives of the anti-China party say that China only bought military gear from Russia that could be used against the US and Taiwan (as long as Beijing really wanted to take over the island). So, China didn't buy any weapons for its ground troops because these are the ones that would be sent to fight Russia if there was a war. The anti-China party's military and strategic claims are completely disproved by scientists, so they will be looked at in the section that follows based on the views of top experts.

The group that is against China has recently been pushing another word line in the media and among experts. This way of thinking says that NATO doesn't pose a danger to Russia, and Moscow should become an ally of NATO, among other things, to protect itself from the Chinese threat. They say that NATO has become much weaker as a geopolitical alliance and can't even force Russia to do what it wants, let alone overthrow the current government (see the Libyan operation). They also say that NATO's military centre of gravity has moved east, which is a clear reference to the PRC. These claims are meant to calm the growing worries of Russia's leaders about building an anti-missile system in Europe based on the US plan and worries that the Arab uprising will spread to Russia with help from the West.

When it comes to the idea that NATO is not hostile, this anti-China party line of thinking is basically the same as the line of thinking that supports Russia joining NATO. There are people in this school who say that Russia should lean towards NATO without bringing up the idea of the Chinese danger. One person who wants to stop wars from happening is Dmitri Trenin, who is the head and chair of the scientific board of the Carnegie Moscow Centre. He wants to create a EuroAtlantic security community. Treatin said that this should be one of the most important parts of Russia's new foreign policy. As well, he says that Russia needs to tilt towards the United States and its friends, like Japan, Canada, and South Korea, in the east. To put it another way, Moscow is given the same model of foreign policy that aims for a strategic partnership with the West, but the Atlantic is switched out for the Pacific.

For the above study of the anti-China party's stance, we used theses by Alexander Khramchikhin. However, he is not the only expert in this group. But because he has written a lot of books and has access to well-known news outlets, he has a lot more influence on wealthy people and politically active people than his party peers.

The expert Alexander Aladin is another well-known member of the anti-China group and its alarmist side. He is not a member of any expert group like Khramchikhin is, so no one can give him any kind of standing. But he became famous a few years ago when he complained to the Constitutional Court about what the Russian government was doing when they gave part of the land to China as part of a plan to define the state line. He then started to be a regular expert on Russian-Chinese ties in a lot of Russian mass media outlets, mostly nationalistic and patriotic ones that aren't very popular but are meant for a wide audience. Still, Aladin doesn't focus on military and political threats from China like Khramchikhin does. Instead, he looks at threats to society, the economy, and infrastructure.

The Pro-China party

This group of experts doesn't have nearly as much power over the Russian media and other experts as the anti-China group or even its alarmist part. In the expert community, this group is mostly made up of active and former soldiers who worked in the Soviet or Russian army's data and analytical units. This is the Institute of Russian-Chinese Strategic Interaction, which is part of the core of the pro-China party in Russia but doesn't have a website. Director Dmitry Regentov and junior director Andrei Devyatov are public relations people for it.

There are two main areas where this group of experts focuses their work. The first is promoting China and Chinese culture and society in Russia. This includes trying to come up with a kind of common language for Russians and Chinese to use when they talk to each other, a single set of terms and meanings that would help both sides understand each other better and get rid of fears that aren't based in reality. That this group is strong is that they have a deep understanding of the Chinese thought and the facts that shape the policies of this state. Their weakness is that they aren't present in the media enough and can't explain the unique ways that Chinese people think and vote to Russian elites and the general public. The pro-China group, on the other hand, is slowly getting rid of these weaknesses.

Anti-China groups spread false ideas about the Chinese threat, and this expert group's second goal is to dispel those false ideas by describing China's interests and, more importantly, how they plan to achieve those interests. For example, Devyatov doesn't say that China doesn't see some parts of the Far East and Eastern Siberia as important to its long-term goals. However, they probably won't take over by force because Chinese history and traditions value integration more than conquest, which is different from the European and Western pattern of conquest.

Besides the goals listed above, this group of experts has also stated that they will fight against strategic false information that gets in the way of improving ties between the two countries. They say, in particular, that many of the sources that official state groups use for their research give information that is very different from what is really going on. At the same time, it is clear that the anti-China party in Russia is influenced by what happened in the West.

Along with the experts from the Institute of Russian-Chinese Strategic Interaction, there are other groups that support China, such as the Club of Friends of the Military Institute of Foreign Languages of the Red Army. These groups are even less visible in the media, and it's hard to guess how much influence they have behind the scenes through military and related channels.

When looking at what the pro-China party in Russia does, it's also important to talk about some things the Chinese are doing that are becoming more and more common and fit Western ideas of "soft power." The first one has to do with what the Russian-Chinese Centre of Trade and Economic Cooperation does. This group was created in the late 1990s at the request of the Russian Union of Industrialists and Entrepreneurs, a strong lobbying group for Russian companies. It is now having a bigger impact on relations between the two countries. The Centre works to promote Chinese interests in Russia. Before, most of the lobbying was about economic problems. But lately, the Centre has been focusing more on the humanitarian side of its work, like improving China's image in Russia and stopping the anti-China group from spreading false information. Sergey Sanakoyev is the executive chair and major spokesperson for the Centre. He has been in the presidential HR reserve since 2009, which shows how powerful he and his allies are as lobbyists.

The humanitarian side of Sanakoyev's and the Center's work can be broken down into a number of linked parts that can be studied. The first is to make China look like Russia's most important and strategic partner. This goal has been the focus of a lot of articles and conversations. Another thing he does is say that the West, especially NATO, is Russia's biggest danger. Third, this member of the pro-China party often disproves claims that China is a demographic danger and is growing. It's not the Chinese who are moving to Russia, even though it's said that the northern parts of China are empty. Instead, Sanakoyev says that Russians are slowly moving to China because it has better infrastructure, which has been mostly true over the past few years.

The work of the Confucius Institutes in Russia is another important part of the Chinese part of the pro-China party. Based on where they are located, it seems that the Chinese would rather have these kinds of groups in big towns or in almost all of the big regional centres in Siberia and the Far East. These organisations say they want to promote Chinese culture and language. This means that their work to advance Chinese interests is more indirect and over a longer period of time than the Centre for Trade and Economic Cooperation's related work. Russian police, on the other hand, found a threat to national security in the work of these groups. For example, in 2010, the Yakutian branch of the Federal Security Service (FSB) stopped an attempt to open a Confucius Institute in Yakutsk because the institute's goal was "to promote the spread of Chinese ideology and economic growth in Russian territory."

That being said, it's important to note that stopping the spread of Chinese ideas into Russia is not the official stance of the government as a whole, but only of one law enforcement agency. For example, high-level representatives from the United Russia Party, which rules Russia, often go to China to meet with representatives from the Communist Party of China and talk about their experiences. The most recent visit was in the middle of May 2010, and Russian members gave the Chinese experience of setting up a party system good reviews.

In closing, when we talk about what the pro-China party in Russia does, we must say that popular culture is where the growth of Chinese culture in Russia is most obvious. In Russia in the past, Chinese feature films were shown in theatres and sold on video tapes and DVDs, but only a small group of people who were interested in Chinese history and culture went to see them. These days, there are also more Chinese blockbusters that put special effects and story twists ahead of historical accuracy. But it's not likely that this is because of a Russian plot, since China can easily join the US in expanding its culture and use Hollywood methods if it wants to.

Researchers and Academicians

When looking at how the academic community talks about how it affects making foreign policies, it's not as interesting as looking at how the media and expert groups talk about it. This is because of a simple reason. As was already said, the Russian government views bilateral relations through the lens of economics. On the other hand, academics who were trained in Soviet practises think in terms of foreign policy concerns. That is, foreign policy plans aren't used to make strategic choices; instead, the needs of big Russian companies are taken into account. For example, Rosneft and Transneft needed credit during the economic crisis.

Russia's focus on Europe until recently is what led to this economicization of its eastern foreign policy direction.

Because of this, the Russian elites were even willing to give up some of their gains to become full-fledged members of the European "board of directors." For example, many asset swap deals between Russian and European companies were not very profitable. Political planning organisations, including those that have worked with academics in the past, played a big part in pushing for these kinds of policies. In Russia's eastern direction, which includes China, policies are shaped by a business-like approach. This is a big reason why Russian leaders don't need to bring in university experts to help them make plans.

These experts have written a lot of articles that argue against people who are against China. Scientists, who care a lot about truth, are often furious about how facts are picked and sometimes outright lies are spread. Consider Yury Morozov, a candidate in military sciences and a leading research fellow at the Centre for Strategic Problems of North East Asia and SCO of the Institute of Far Eastern Studies of the Russian Academy of Sciences. He wrote a series of articles called "Chinese Threat in Khramchikhin's Head" in which he harshly criticised the main ideas of the alarmist wing of the anti-China party's military and strategic doctrine as well as other things.

According to Morozov, China does not have as many people living in it as is said (per sq km). In terms of coal, iron, manganese, copper, tungsten, tin, aluminium, gold, and other minerals, the country has the most or the second most stocks in the world. The author also says that non-military means are mostly used to reach goals in the modern world, which is a bit of a stretch. But he makes it clear that a military conflict with Russia and the Central Asian states would not be good for China. This is because a military conflict would do a lot of damage to the mining infrastructure and take a very long time to fix. Making use of numbers based on military theory and strategy, Morozov also strongly disagrees with Khramchikhin's idea that Russia could be attacked with weapons in one of his writings.

There were also public statements from other academics about their feelings about the most well-known anti-China party leader. Sergey Kazennov, who is in charge of the geopolitics group in the strategic research section of the Institute of World Economy and International Relations of RAS, put out some information that disagrees with what his opponent said about how likely it was that China would attack. While the writers agree that Khramchikhin showed where the Russian army was weak, they don't think that China would easily win a war between Moscow and Beijing. Along with their coworkers, they also doubt the idea that China wants to expand to the north and that China is ready to use violence to solve all of its issues. Lastly, it is emphasised that Russia has strategic nuclear deterrent forces that it could use to make up for any unbalance in conventional arms. On top of that, the US probably won't do nothing if China decides to use force to expand its area into Russia.

Public View

It also makes sense to take a quick look at the main trends in Russians' views on the relationship between the two countries and how they see China. This will be one of the most important factors in the end because it has a secondary effect on the policy content in this direction (in the future, not now). Even though Russia's political system is very formal and decisions are made behind closed doors, both the anti-China and pro-China parties try to change public opinion as well as the opinions of the ruling class.

In general, the way Russians think about China has been changing quickly over the past ten years, with some factors moving in a sinusoidal pattern. People's views on China are negatively related to how well they get along with the West. When relations with the West get worse, people think better of China, and when they think better of China, relations with the West get worse. As an example, in mid-2001, when Russia was still feeling anti-Western after NATO's attack on Yugoslavia in 1999, 31% of those polled thought that China would be Russia's friend in the 21st century, while only 3% thought it would be an enemy. The residual junior brother effect should be taken into account, since it wasn't totally gone from people's minds after the fall of the Soviet Union by 2001.

By 2005, the number of people who supported the allied method had dropped to 22%, while the number of people who supported the opposite view had barely changed, rising to 6%. The rest of the people who answered had more general opinions. The number of people who had positive views on China rose to 28% in 2007, when anti-Western feelings were at their highest (see Vladimir Putin's speech in Munich, for example). At the same time, the number of people who saw China as an enemy dropped to 4%. But by 2009, only 20% of people still believed that China was an ally.

Another interesting trend is how people in different parts of Russia think about China and how they feel about the possibility of working together with China. About 66% of Russians who answered the survey think it is unsafe for Chinese companies to work on developing natural resources in Siberia and the Far East. Their share is 71% in the Far Eastern Federal District and 81% in the Siberian Federal District. This is the biggest percentage of any federal district. There are about 21% of people in Russia who think that China should become Moscow's main partner in Southeast Asia. In the Far Eastern Federal District, however, that number is almost double that, at 36%. In other words, the people of the Far East already do business with China and are aware of the threat that China poses, so they don't see any other option but to continue doing business with and becoming part of China.

Russia's Stance

The way Russia handles its foreign policy towards China doesn't match up with what experts and scientists are talking about. A simple way to sum up the relationship between the two countries is "Russian natural resources in exchange for access to Chinese financial resources, such as tied loans." In line with the 2001 framework agreement on neighbourliness, friendship, and cooperation between the Russian Federation and the People's Republic of China, this position of the Russian government was written into the agreement that the leaders of the two countries signed in New York in 2009. This is officially about the cooperation between the regions of the two countries across borders. It's about the plan of cooperation between the regions of Far East and Eastern Siberia in the Russian Federation and northeastern China from 2009 to 2018. Though, in reality, this is a great example of the kind of structure that the Russian elites don't really have a problem with right now. For example, when Dmitry Medvedev went to the PRC in the autumn of 2010, many agreements were made at different levels. Most of these agreements were about trade and economic problems. Also, more concrete agreements have been made between the governments of both countries and businesses with ties to those governments in the past few years. In particular, Rosneft and Transneft got loans backed by long-term oil sales to China (Rosneft) and finishing the building of the pipeline from Eastern Siberia to the Pacific Ocean (Transneft).

It's interesting that the signing of this strategic document was almost forgotten by Russian government-run news outlets, but in the Far East, headlines read things like "Moscow gives up the Far East to China." After this paper was signed and talked about in the Russian media by the middle of 2001, two different views on how to carry out the project came to light. According to the first, Russia and China have very different ideas about how to improve their cooperation. This is because almost all of the projects in Eastern Siberia and the Far East are focused on producing raw materials, while in China's northeastern provinces, plans are being made to build processing plants. One of China's main goals in its strategy is to get access to energy and natural resources and to set up long-term ways for trade and economic cooperation to benefit China.

The other point of view says that it is not possible to say that more unity will only be bad for Russia. Russia depends on exporting natural resources, and its location as a transit country makes it easy to build up its infrastructure for shipping, storage, and maintenance. This is why China is seen as Russia's natural partner in Asia: it has both cash and labour, which are needed to make things. But if you look at the overall nature of the two countries' relationships, you can say that the trade in raw materials will be the main focus of their cooperation and will continue to be so for a long time. So, the actions of the anti-China party that were big in the Russian media until recently didn't really change the minds of the Russian elites.

But economic ties between the two countries aren't the only thing they have in common. Russia and China try to work together in at least two other foreign groups: BRICS and the Shanghai Cooperation Organisation (SCO), which celebrated its 10th anniversary in 2011. At first, the SCO was meant to be a tool for regional security, mostly in Central Asia. But in the last few years, it has become a tool for boosting China's power, which made things hard for the Russian government, which was one of the founders of the bloc. There is a notable difference between the SCO and the Collective Security Treaty Organisation in the Russian media over the past two years.

When it comes to BRICS, the goal is not to coordinate working together on security issues, but to work together to destroy the West's absolute dominance in international matters. Recently, this group has been used to organise the needs of developing countries before G20 summits. This is different from G7 meetings, where western countries agree on what to do. But Russia's joining both the G8 and BRICS at the same time makes things more complicated, especially when it comes to how Russia and China can work together in the world.

Yet, over the last six to twelve months, the Russian leaders have had the feeling that their country is becoming more and more politically dependent on other countries. This is not something they are against economically. The Russian Establishment is worried that the Asia-Pacific area is becoming more and more important in world politics and strategic decisions. There were times when the Russian government tried many times but failed to get involved in the decision-making process in the old, post-Soviet world order, which was dominated by the West (mainly the USA and to a lesser extent, the EU). The way its economic ties with China are set up now, it may miss a similar chance to get a seat on the world's "board of directors" in the Asia-Pacific region.

In this area, the Russian government often acts in a random way to show that Russia is interested in the area. One example is when President Medvedev (for the first time in history) and later a number of ministers went to the Kuril Islands. It's likely that these visits were made for domestic political reasons and not to make things worse between Russia and Japan. However, they made things much worse between the two countries and showed that Russia doesn't have a clear plan for how to join the processes going on in the area. There are also moves being taken by experts and academics to end China's monopoly on Russia. More specifically, the ASEAN Centre opened at the Moscow State Institute of International Relations (MGIMO) in 2010. And in the spring of 2011, ISEAS and the ASEAN Centre held their first joint meeting at MGIMO.

When you summarise this chapter, you should pay special attention to the following points. For starters, talks about Russian-Chinese relations in the media and among experts have a bigger impact on public opinion than similar discussions in the very closed academic community. At the same time, the state officials make choices without being involved in either discussion. Instead, they are guided by the very practical economic needs of the moment. However, the media and talks between experts, which affect both the elites and the public, might be noticed by the government when they begin to make a comprehensive plan to advance Russian interests in the Asia-Pacific region. Also, Russian elites are starting to realise that their economic dependence on China, which hasn't bothered them so far, is turning into political dependence as the centre of power moves to the Asia-Pacific region. This must be a cause for worry.

A U.S. Outlook on the Crossroads in Russia China Relations

Russia and China don't have a "American" view of each other. Obviously, the US government doesn't usually talk about how other countries deal with outsiders in public. There are some differences between Russia and China, though, because they are the only two countries that could really hurt the US. Additionally, these connections are fundamental in Asia and have a big impact on how everyone is connected to Russia, China, Central Japan, and Northeast Asia. Because of this, they have big effects on the politics and strategies of most of Asia and the world as a whole. So, while some US experts have talked about these connections, a lot less have than one might think. Given how important their relationships are to both Moscow and Beijing, this lack of attention is strange. President Medvedev actually said that China is Russia's most important foreign partner and that relations are improving in every area. He even suggested a new security system for Asia.

Reason of Concern

The "normative convergence" of these two states, their almost identical views on North Korea (as seen in the crisis caused by North Korea's nuclear and missile tests), their calls for a new international financial, political, and economic order, and their criticism of US policies that promote democracy and other policies, such as NATO's operation in Libya, all point to the possibility of even closer convergence in the future, often at the expense of the US. Not only do these countries have similar goals, but their relationships are also based on similar values, which is something that US analysts often miss. At the moment, both sides say that these relationships are at their best and that they should be used as a model for other countries' relationships. They also say that things can only get better, as recent conversations between them show. Ong's claim that "the basis for China's strategic partnership with Russia lies in countering the global export of America's liberal values" would be supported by this. He also says that Russia's political ideals, which include sovereign democracy, are more in line with "Asian values" than with European ones.

In fact, Professor Ouyang Wei at China's National Defence University's Crisis Management Research Centre said that this relationship could be a strategic partnership or even a quasi-alliance, since both sides usually use the word "partnership." When talking about the "Peace Mission 2009" military drills between China and Russia in July 2009, he said this to show the difference between this kind of relationship and an alliance:

> *The natures of joint military exercises are different when the relations of countries are different. If the relations are of a coalition or alliance nature, joint military exercises are similar to those conducted in their respective countries. Such exercises have strongly defined objectives in mind and are strongly marked with actuality. There are also such relations as strategic partnership or quasi-alliance, under which joint military exercises bear a strong symbolic and political nature, with less clearly defined targets in mind. There are relations between friendly countries, which conduct joint military exercises in specially designated spheres, such as providing disaster rescue and humanitarian aid. This will help strengthen mutual understanding and mutual trust.*

So, there is a real chance that their ideological and strategic competition with Washington could turn into a hostile, polarised, and two-way split of Asia into blocs, with a bloc of China and Russia facing off against a US alliance system led by alliances with Japan, South Korea, and Australia. As early as the 1990s, well-known world politics experts like Richard Betts and Robert Jervis, as well as later CIA studies, said that an alliance between Russia and China would be the biggest security threat to US interests. Some people who study East Asian trends think that the current energy crisis and other international crises are making the Russian and Chinese union against American power and ideas stronger in Northeast and Central Asia.

The Discourse on the True Nature of Relations

These two states' current closeness is incontestable. Marcin Kaczmarski's 2008 analysis of Russia's Asian policies observes that:

> *The scale of cooperation between Russia and China is reflected in the extensive infrastructure of dialogue between the two states. Regular contacts are maintained at nearly all levels of central Authority. Political dialogue takes*

> *place within an extensive framework for bilateral consultations, including meetings of Heads of State held several times a year (at least once a year on a bilateral basis, and also during several multilateral meetings); meetings of prime ministers and foreign ministers; consultations on strategic stability (at the level of deputy foreign ministers); consultations on military cooperation (at the level of defence ministers); and consultations on security issues (between national security advisors since 2005).*

Western and US writers, on the other hand, tend to play this option down and assume that Russia and China don't have enough common strategic interests to form a lasting alliance or pose a threat to the US. Kaczmarski says that since 2006, these relations have been stuck in a strategic rut that has made problems they still haven't fixed and a lack of trust between them worse. James Bellacqua says that this relationship is mostly practical and based on shared interests, but there are clear signs of trouble in it. In the same way, Gilbert Rozman says:

> *There exists no cause for alarm about a Sino-Russian alliance or a renewed split marked by hostility. Efforts to check direct challenges to the existing world and regional order by each country can continue without serious concern that they will be driven into each other's arms.*

Others, including Richard Weitz, Rajan Menon, Kaczmarski, Bobo Lo, and Rozman, stress the differences between Russia and China that make it impossible for the two countries to have a connection deeper than a partnership and definitely not an alliance. They say that links between Russia and China are mostly utilitarian and instrumental. This is the view that most critics agree on, and it has become what most people think. There are real problems in the relationship between the two countries, so we need to give them a fair evaluation. But Weitz, Menon, Kaczmarski, and Lo disagree in that Lo thinks that the relationship between Russia and China is changing in a way that will give Beijing a lot more power over Moscow than it did before. This will change the partnership into something very different, with China as the rider and Russia as the horse, to use Bismarck's example of an alliance. In that case, Russia will rely on China more and more to protect its interests in Northeast Asia, even if they don't have a formal alliance. And so, China would basically set the rules for those interests and protect them in exchange for Russia agreeing to some kind of control. There isn't much difference between this and the traditional Chinese tribute system that ruled Asia until modern times. Some writers see this as a trend that is already happening in Asia. In fact, China is now seen as the way for Russia to get accepted in Asia from other countries. This author has also said in other places that we are at the start of making such a Chinese-dominated order in Asia and has looked at what went wrong for Russia in Asia and what happened after it. In longer chapters and upcoming books, this author has also tried to look into the growing signs of military tensions between Russia and China, which go against what the elites say about how close the two countries are and show that Russia is becoming more uneasy about China. At the same time, it is clear that Russia is becoming more and more dependent on China for energy and economic reasons.

Some Russian writers and writers born in Russia who now live in the West make similar points. Dmitri Trenin writes, "China is becoming the state that sets the agenda for the two countries." China is stronger and more active than Russia for the first time in 300 years, and it can back up its economic and security goals with large amounts of cash. Similar points are made by Fyodor Lukyanov, editor of Russia in Global Affairs: "Neither Russia nor the United States knows how to structure relations with China, or more accurately, they are structuring them to China's Diktat." In the same way, Andrei Tsygankov writes:

> *Overall, Russia is increasingly unable to resist China's economic and political influence. Both in state action and on the level of national discourse, China's importance has considerably expanded, which has translated into the growing prominence of Russian Sinophiles in national debate. Russia's relative economic and administrative weakness will continue to challenge its ability to fully preserve political independence and other attributes of a great power. Although the nation has largely recovered from the chronic malaise of the 1990s, gaining greater confidence and preserving important attributes of a great power, in the foreseeable future it cannot act on a par with the West and China. Despite the rhetoric of Russia's resurgence, Russia has not become and is not in a position to become a rising great power in the face of growing international challenges, such as the continued expansion of the Western and Chinese influences in Eurasia. The fact that Russia continues to muddle through is not a guarantee that it will be able to do so in the future; the economic crisis narrows the Kremlin's options still further.*

He also says that the pro-China group in the elite is taking over policymaking and public speech more and more. Lastly, Sergei Karaganov, who runs the well-connected Council on Foreign and Defence Policy, says that Russia is moving away from Europe and towards China, which it sees as a "younger brother" but one that it respects. Karaganov may have been fooled by how smart China has been dealing with Russia in this situation.

By looking closely at recent changes in this relationship, we can see that Lo's, Karaganov's, Tsygankov's, and Trenin's ideas are correct. We are now in the beginning stages of a trend that suggests China is better than Russia in Asia, which has important strategic implications for Russia as an Asian power.

Similarly, both Bellacqua and Rozman think that the relationship between the two countries is becoming more competitive. In fact, Bellacqua calls Russia a "junior partner" to China, which is the exact phrase that Russia doesn't like when talking about the US and that Russian writers like Trenin openly fear. Putting this trend forward keeps us from getting stuck in the pointless conversation about whether or not this relationship threatens US interests in some way. The more important question is whether or not a new Chinese order is taking shape in Asia, and if so, what does that mean? It could be bad for the US, as many people worry, but it could also be bad for Russia.

Chinese Framework

This part can only make you think or sound the alarm. There is, however, a lot of proof for this point of view. Russia's main goal in East Asia is clear and simple: it wants to return to its previously recognised position as a great independent system-forming power that could change the security situation in Asia (especially Northeast Asia) on its own. In addition, Medvedev wrote in November 2009, "Russia wants Siberia and the Russian Far East to be directly involved in regional integration." Despite its best efforts, Russia is failing to reach its goal due to both bad policy choices and events beyond its control. It has no choice but to let China create a new Asian order based on Chinese economic power. The first signs of this order can already be seen, both in and outside of Northeast Asia, for example in Central Asia. Russia has also failed to reach its goal, which can be seen in its foreign and defence policies, as well as in its energy-focused economic policy towards Asia. These problems can also be seen with China, Japan, and the two Koreas, which are the main countries involved, especially with the six-party process about North Korea's nuclearization. These failures are very important for Russia's "Ostpolitik" because Russian leaders know, even if they won't say it out loud, that they need support and recognition from other countries in order to play a part in Asia. In his 2008 annual review of Russia's Asia policy, for example, deputy foreign minister Alexei Borodavkin says that all of Russia's Asian-Pacific neighbours want it to become a part of the Asia-Pacific region (APT), seeing Russia as a source of strategic stability and long-term economic growth in the area. If this were true, everyone would see it right away and think it is clear. The fact that this has to be said shows how much Russia depends on another party or parties to make sure it is fully accepted as an Asian power, and how it has failed to do so.

So, Russia will still need help from other countries to fully enter Asia. But because it has failed in the past with Japan and the Korean peace process, it still relies too much on China's help to get the status it wants so badly. So, the most important effect of those failures can be seen in Russia's relationship with China, which has been its most important partner in Asia since 1992, when it chose to work with China instead of Japan. This choice was made because Russia didn't like Japan's liberal values and liked China's authoritarianism more, as well as for geopolitical reasons.

The following business and energy areas show that China is leading the way. In the middle east Turkey and all of Central Asia's gas will soon be bought by China more than by Russia. Russia has no choice but to let China make huge investments in Central Asia. China was able to successfully stop the Shanghai Cooperation Organisation from recognising Abkhazia and South Ossetia as independent states. Lastly, it worked with Uzbekistan to stop Russia from getting involved in the racial killings in Kyrgyzstan in 2010.

In Northeast Asia, Russia has had to build an oil pipeline that only goes to China. They hope to finish the planned East Siberian Pacific Ocean (ESPO) pipeline in the future with money from other countries. China had to take out huge loans, so even if the oil sells at market price, it will still get 15,000 tonnes of oil a year for twenty years at a big discount. We are sure that Rosneft, Transneft, and their leaders were paid a lot of money "under the table." This deal also makes it possible for China to spend a lot of money in Russian oil and gas companies in the Russian Far East (RFE), which it couldn't do before.

Even worse for Russia, it had to admit in 2009 that all of its plans had failed and that it would have to tie its regional development plan to China's regional development plan for Heilongjiang, making it a raw material extension of China. This was despite years of trying to develop its Far East on its own or to attract as much foreign investment as possible. Because Moscow didn't have any other options, Medvedev pretty much admitted on May 21, 2009, that Moscow's big plans for growth in the Far East could not come true unless China invested in big projects there. Medvedev was honest when he said that the Far East's economic growth would rest less on Russia's relationships with Europe and more on its relationships with its main Asia-Pacific partners. Besides that, he said that the RFE's plan for regional growth must work with China's plan to revive its old industrial base in Northeast China, like in Heilongjiang province. The news agency TASS said, "Basically, China now has the power and the ability to pick and choose the fields of cooperation and projects of cooperation with Russia. It also has the initiative to choose." That plan also works for energy purchases, since China has a lot of different energy sources and can often get energy for less than Russia wants to charge. It's clear that Russia wants to sell gas to China more than China wants to buy gas from Russia. Because of this, China and Russia still haven't agreed to sell gas to each other as of May 2011. In the meantime, China's deals with Australia and Turkmenistan have made it unnecessary for it to buy gas from Russia or agree to pay Russia's price for it. In this case too, too, Russia depends on China more than China depends on Russia. Accordingly, China's desire to increase the number of projects it works on with Russia is mostly due to Beijing's effort. Analysts in China also seem to think that the fact that Russia depends on China as a gateway to the Asia-Pacific makes China less worried about Russia becoming a threat to China again in the future.

Because of this, Russia has had to ask China to help its economy and accept Chinese economic power in ways that have forced it to change long-standing Russian policies in the RFE. Moscow's Vneshekonomobank (VEB), which is the Bank for Development and Foreign Economic Affairs, had to borrow money from China. And since China now owns a lot of Lukoil stock, it has indirect power over both the bank and the oil company. Second, Moscow had to let Chinese, South Korean, and Kazakh miners and refiners back into the bidding process for the huge Udokan copper mine in Southeast Siberia after previously excluding foreign companies. Another foreign owner that Moscow had to make welcome was Shell, which had to sell its share of Sakhalin-2 two and a half years ago. All of these actions are a total change from what Russia did for energy and mineral investments starting in 2003. Bloomberg News also said that Russian companies may invest in oil exploration and natural gas distribution in China, even though they don't have the money to do so right now. On the other hand, Chinese companies, which have a lot of money to invest, may also invest in developing oil and gas fields in Russia and building liquefaction plants. China also made this point in its 2009 deal with Russia to trade oil for loans, which happened almost at the same time.

Chinese companies are buying up large areas of farming land in the Russian Far East (850,000 acres as of mid-2010) that the region's shrinking population has left empty. They are also trying to get Chinese people to move there and work there seasonally. The Chinese are also pushing hard for deals on the terms of trade between the RFE and China. As the New York Times' Andrew Kramer wrote:

> *The Chinese are pressing for discounts from world prices because of the remoteness of the border region. They argue that the Russian commodities should be cheap because of their abundance - and because without China as a near and ready buyer, the vast reserve in eastern Siberia would be far less valuable. The Russians, on the other hand, argue that without their commodities, buyers in northeast China would have to pay much higher prices to suppliers from farther away.*

In the same way, China seems to be pursuing its own competitive goals, such as a trans-Asian railway. Moscow has long supported the idea of connecting the Trans-Siberian Railway to the planned Trans-Korean Railway (TSR-TKR). This railway would be an important part of Moscow's policy towards both Korean states, and if it is built, it would have a big impact on the growth of Asiatic Russia, especially Primorskiy Krai (the Maritime Province, the easternmost province of the RFE). The TSR-TKR also shows how the four biggest powers in Northeast Asia are competing for control over what happens in Korea. Each of them has important things at stake in the country. Russia and China are often said to be competing for power in Pyongyang and Seoul. In 2002, Putin said that "our beloved neighbour, China" would build the train that would connect the two Koreas and Asia to Europe if Russia didn't. This was a sarcastic and telling reference to this competition.

Russia also has a big plan for a goods service that would go along the Trans-Siberian train from China to Europe. This would be possible once the ESPO is finished, which will free up space on the railways. China does not, however, plan to work with Russia on a Far East high-speed train at this time. At the same time, China has started an offensive around the world to build cheap high-speed railroads, including in Russia to compete with Japan and possible Russian rivals. Officials are also not afraid to say that these railway investments will not only help Chinese goods reach more people, but they will also improve the image of Chinese brands. When these projects are finished, they will "heighten China's political influence in the importing countries." These kinds of projects help show why leaders like Xi Jinping say Russia is an important market for China's "going global" business plan. A recent article in the journal International Affairs from the Russian Ministry of Foreign Affairs said that the economic growth of other countries in the Asia-Pacific region is a threat to Russia because it leads to an unchecked competition for power in the world's politics. This may be because the authors knew what the effects of the current trend could be.

Since Russian officials made it clear that the RFE's development was tied to Russia's ability to play this "system-forming" role in Asia, the fact that the area hasn't been developed and is now tied to China's regional development plan is a sign that Russia's "Ostpolitik" has failed. This failure also has effects on strategy. It has already been said that Russia is becoming more worried about its defence and that we will be writing more about this soon. In the last bit of room, we should say that we think Russia will also not be able to handle Chinese intellectual theft and the competition that will come from that in third-party arms markets. In the meantime, Russian-based systems are still being put in place. Moscow now knows that these systems could easily be used against the RFE. China only buys 10% of the arms that Russia sells, but it still wants and sometimes gets high-tech, top-of-the-line Russian weapons, even though Russian arms sellers are wary of it. Even though the government is angry, they won't cut the link to China. This means that Russia is now fully aware that it is backing its most likely enemy in the Far East.

It is strange that Russian officials keep saying that their goals and interests are so similar to those of China, even though the relationship is getting worse. But besides selfish financial concerns (which do play a part in energy, if not elsewhere), the most likely reason for this harmful behaviour is a dislike of America and the ideals it stands for. The director of Russia in Global Affairs, Fyodor Lukyanov, says the following:

> *The mentality of Russian politics is such that relations with the United States remain at the center of universal attention and virtually any problem is seen through an American prism. This is partially a reflection of inertia of thinking which is finding it hard to break with perceptions of Cold War times. It is partially a demonstration of a hidden desire to have a sense of our own significance. There is still a desire to compare ourselves specifically with the only superpower.*

The same thing was said by Leonid Radzhikhovsky: "the existential void of our politics has been filled entirely by anti-Americanism"; giving up this rhetoric "would be tantamount to destroying the foundations of the state ideology." So, it is very dangerous for us to ignore the ideological and value-based parts of Russian foreign policy thought. In international relations, Moscow may say it is a pillar of the Church of an Atheistic Realism, and in some ways it is. But Russia's foreign policy has a history of ideological posturing and a heavy focus on values, even before the Soviet revolution. Even though it is denied, that tradition goes on, and the Kremlin's policy towards China shows it the most. Even though Russia wants to get along with China, they don't want an identity of interest because of China's policies that have become more and more aggressive since 2008. But Moscow keeps supporting it, even though it's strong, or maybe even because it is. Beijing definitely has every reason to try to get Moscow to side with China against the US. But do Russian leaders really want to be China's liars, even if it means giving China oil and gas instead of bowing down? Unless China makes a big change, this, not partnership, seems to be Russia's future role in Chinese strategy. That job is completely unpleasant for everyone, but especially for powerful people who are still proud of their imperial past.

Military Frictions

Rising worries about China's military power in the Far East are a big reason why military tensions between Russia and China have grown. Since 2009, there have been more signs that the elite are aware that China is not only ahead of Russia economically, but that it has also built a modern, highly-intelligent military that could be dangerous. Russian leaders are impressed by China's model because they have so far failed to follow it, and their current efforts to reform their military are having trouble. As a result, people are showing more and more open concern about China's armed power. These skills can be used against China as well, even when Moscow makes public moves against Japan or the US in Asia, like moving Borey Class subs to the Pacific in 2008 or making the Kuril Islands stronger in 2011.

China's Great Stride exercises in 2009 were the first time that the Russian military talked openly about the possible danger. They also likely influenced some of the planning for Russia's Vostok-2010 exercises in Asia, which ended with a simulated tactical nuclear strike against the People's Liberation Army. Russia said that these Chinese drills included "about 50,000 Ground Force and Air Force servicemen who participated in the exercises, which were held on the territory of four military districts and tested the newest weapons systems and the national satellite navigation system." From 2006 to 2007, the combined-arms divisions' push went from 1,000 km to 2,000 km". Soon after, Chief of the Ground Forces Main Staff Lieutenant General Sergey Skokov talked about dangers in the East for the first time in public. "If we talk about the East, this could be an army of millions of soldiers who fight in a traditionally straightforward way, with a lot of people and weapons concentrated in a few areas." In 2009, General Nikolai Makarov, who was Chief of Staff, gave a briefing. One of the slides "showed that it is, after all, NATO and China that are the most dangerous of our geopolitical rivals."

By the time Russia's defence policy came out in 2010, China's rise was being seen as both a model to follow and a possible threat to Russia's southern regions. This policy brought up the NATO threat again, as it had done before, but it also added new threats that seem to be aimed at China, albeit in a more general way. "Show of military force with provocative objectives during exercises on the territories of states adjacent to the Russian Federation or its allies" is what it talks about. It also talks about "stepping up the activities of the armed forces of individual states (groups of states) involving partial or complete mobilisation and the transitioning of these states' organs and military command and control to wartime operating conditions." Commentators in Russia and other countries saw this language as emphasising that Russia saw China as a bigger danger because of China's efforts to modernise its military and the 2009 exercises that seemed to be a sneak peek at operations aimed at the RFE.

The improvements in China's power that worry the US could also be aimed at Russia. This is what Russia did. Experts say that one of the main jobs of the

Russian Navy's four new operational-strategic commands (directions in Russian) and its new modernization programme is to keep Russia's access to its oil, gas, and other mineral reserves on its continental sea safe. By 2020, 36 subs and 40 surface ships will have been added. But these plans do more than just this main goal and future naval construction. They also shift Russia's naval focus to the Asia-Pacific to meet China's challenge and make up for the fact that Russia's ships are far less numerous and of lower quality than China's in the RFE.

Nuclear problems are no different. China's new DH-10 cruise missile, along with the operationalization of several cruise missile brigades and the DF-16IRBM, is a big step forward in its tactical nuclear weapons (TNW) capacity. China's military planning still sees Russia, the US, Japan, and India as possible threats, even if Taiwan stays the main focus. This means that China is planning for possible nuclear attacks on these countries. Vostok-2010 shows that the role of TNW in Asia will grow, not shrink. This is supported by the practise launches of TNW and Tochka-U precise missiles against China.

A general designer at the Moscow Institute of Thermal Technology named Yuri Solomonov says that China is 10-15 years behind Russia when it comes to rocket technology, but that China will catch up in 5–10 years. Taiwan, the US, and Japan are still the main places where China is building up its military:

> *Within the jurisdiction of No. 51 military base, the 810th Brigade (96113Unit) stationed at Jinzhou District of Dalian and Ji An City is at a very high level of combat readiness. An instruction unit of this brigade is located at the Dalijiazhuang Township of Dalian. Among all the intermediate range ballistic units of the PLA Second Artillery Force, the 810th Brigade is the only one that has the capability to strike the whole of the Far East region of Russia and the Pacific Fleet nuclear submarine base on the Kamchatka Peninsula. This also indicates how seriously the PLA Second Artillery Force regards nuclear deterrence upon Russia. 96113 Unit was originally armed with DF-3 intermediate range ballistic missiles. Further observation on whether it has started to deploy DF-21c Missiles is warranted.*

This could be the reason why Russia believes that all six nuclear powers should be involved in any new talks about arms control.

In October 2010, Admiral Vladimir Vysotsky, who was in charge of the Russian Navy, said that the Pacific and Northern Fleets would continue to be built up in the Arctic. He also said that work would continue to be done to build up the Air Forces and the coastal reconnaissance monitoring system. In the same way, submarine searches will still happen in the Arctic. They may also send more Ilyushin IL-38 and TU-142 planes to patrol the Arctic. However, Vysotsky, who was likely speaking with permission from above, picked out China as a threat to

Russia in the Arctic because China has questioned Russia's Arctic land claims. It was Vysotsky who said:

> *There are a lot of people who wish to get into the Arctic and Antarctic from an economic point of view. ... We have already been observing how a number of states, which are not members of the Arctic Council, are setting out their interests quite intensively and in various ways. In particular, China has already signed agreements with Norway to explore the Arctic zone. We know about the economy and infrastructure that exist in China today, which is becoming our serious partner from both positive and problematical sides. . Therefore Russia needs to form its rational position and, at the same time, not give up any of its interests. . There are not long-standing relationships, overt opponents, or overt allies in the Arctic yet. But I believe the most problematic relations will be with those countries which are not traditional members of the Arctic Council.*

Moving Toward a U.S. Policy Response

Based on what we now know, Washington has a reason to fix things and the tools to do so. China wants to protect North Korea and keep the US from getting to it. In 2011, there were signs that US views were changing, as the US military policy now sees Russia as a possible partner in East Asia. The Russian government and press have also noticed this acceptance. But for this plan to work, Russia, our allies, and I must all work together, take steps that benefit each other, and most importantly, think strategically. The real threat is not an alliance between the Soviet Union and China, but rather a partnership led by China with Russia and North Korea as minor players that poses a threat to Japan and South Korea, who are becoming more and more worried. This means that an agreement has already been made after a lot of talks with Japan and South Korea about important problems that affect them. First, the US needs to come up with a plan to reach out to Russia that will help it join the US side in the Six-Party Talks on Korea. This means that the US will have to work with Pyongyang a lot more, which is what North Korea wants. Conservatives will be against this, but their policy of ignoring North Korea has mostly failed because Pyongyang knows that Sino-Russian policy will keep any costs for its actions from getting too high. We can't count on North Korea giving up or falling apart, so the only ways to solve this problem are through a war or a peaceful solution.

This process isn't just about getting North Korea to give up its weapons. Instead, it's about making a new, legal, long-lasting, and peaceful order in Northeast Asia where everyone can safely take part. Despite severe crises, the regime has survived and is now going through a succession shift. Even though the change in leadership may be a big reason for North Korea's erratic behaviour, it doesn't have much of an effect on outside sources, so the country has become somewhat stable. Also, the fact that it has nuclear weapons makes people more interested in its security rather than its collapse. Another bad idea that hasn't come true is the thought that China will put pressure on North Korea on Washington's behalf. Because of this, Washington should try to change the East Asian order so that it works better for it instead of Beijing. If allies don't come up with a plan that makes sense, North Korea will end up as China's economic colony, just like Russia did. This will make it hard to have peace in Northeast Asia for a long time.

At the same time, Russia gains a lot from having an American option to deal with China. That offer could help it move away from being completely in line with China's Korea policy, even though it wouldn't be a friend or even a full partner with the US. As an example, Moscow would be very happy if the US promised to pay for the cost of sending energy from Russia to North Korea as part of any future deal. This kind of action might also make North Korea pay attention to the fact that the talks have gone from being three-way and three-equal to four-way and two-two against it, which China does not like. China does not like being left with North Korea. Also, the US can only positively affect the future of both North and South Korea by directly interacting with North Korea. Otherwise, the US would be leaving the field open to a Russian-Chinese partnership led by Beijing, with Pyongyang as a Chinese satellite. That method would work well in South Korean politics and give Seoul more control over what happens in North Korea than it would have otherwise. At the same time, Russia could add its weight to a US plan to talk to North Korea within the Six-Party Framework, which is what China and other countries have suggested. Then it might be possible to start talking to North Korea again, this time with terms that work for everyone and with the promise of more direct US involvement, which is a must for any long-term peace process.

The second part of this plan has to do with ties between Russia and Japan, which are currently stuck. Before the March 2011 earthquake, Moscow seemed to think it could force Japan to agree to the postwar settlement of the Northern Territories or the Kuril Islands, while also getting a lot of Japanese money to invest in Russia. This is despite the fact that Russia insults Japanese feelings and refuses to change its economy to attract more investment. Now, Russia is giving Japan emergency energy supplies to help the RFE grow, get Japan to invest there, and get Japan to agree to Russian political conditions. So, Moscow sends cabinet ministers to the Kuril Islands to please its own people, even though it is starting a plan for growth and building up its military there. But it looks like Russia's plans will not work out. Japanese experts don't think that Russia's energy fields can be developed on a big enough scale to meet Moscow's hopes of selling a lot of energy in East Asia. Japan can't change its mind about claiming all four Kuril Islands because of its own politics, and the US's support for this stance makes it even less flexible. Japan, on the other hand, can't do anything about Russia's chauvinistic policies other than stop investing in Russia. Japanese companies would like to invest in Russia if they knew they would make money, but they won't until Russia changes its policies. Neither will the government of Japan push them to do so until the territorial disputes are resolved.

The US needs to take the lead here too. We might be doing Japan a favour if we could get it to agree that Putin's revival of Khrushchev's 1956 offer of two of the four Kuril Islands is the best it can get for now. This is because the risks of a nuclear North Korea and a rising China that defends it outweigh the benefits of domestic posturing for territories that aren't possible otherwise. In fact, that's the only idea that has any chance of making things better between Russia and Japan. It would also give Russia a way to invest in the RFE and finish a pipeline to the Pacific coast, which would free it from being too dependent on China's energy market and even making it independent. These steps, especially if they are coordinated with US partners, would make it harder for China to change the balance of power in East Asia in its own favour. They would also help solve two long-standing problems. First, the urgent need to find a way to lower North Korea's nuclear threat while also integrating it into a stable, legal system in the region. Second, the strange connection between Russia and Japan. If these kinds of efforts don't happen, Russia will almost certainly lean towards China. In fact, some experts say that Russia agreed with China's position on the disputed Senkaku (or Diaoutyi) Islands with Japan in order to get China to back its position on the Kuril Islands. In this way, Russia and China have formed a diplomatic alliance against Japan. So that it can get even more angry with Japan, Russia is also trying to get China to invest in the Kuriles. We have been trying to stop this kind of bloc since 1949, and it shouldn't be able to form because too many people here aren't paying enough attention to the trends in Sino-Russian ties.

Russia will benefit from these moves in more ways than one. For example, it will no longer have to depend on China as its only way to get involved in Asian diplomacy or deal with a possible military threat from China. Russia would be able to do what it needs to do in order to be successful in Asia, which is to spend. This could be done with a lot of help from other countries in Siberia and the RFE. But for these efforts by the US and its allies to work, Russia can't just sit back and take advantage of the changes that are made. It must also do something to bring these projects to its attention and give Washington, Tokyo, and Seoul long-term reasons to believe they will work. Russia needs to clear up the heavy load of past doubts that came from its actions. To stay a big Asian power and be seen as a partner in East Asia, Russia must also change its policies to keep up with the huge changes happening there. But Russia needs to make more than that to take advantage of these deals, stay alive, and even do well as an independent Asian power.

The changes that need to be made will allow foreign investors to come into the RFE, if not Russia as a whole. The amounts needed to complete these projects are huge, and they won't come until Russia can promise, like China has since 1978, that foreign investments will be safe and profitable, without being taken by the whims of local or central government elites. Basically, this means that there will be no more Khodorkovsky or Magnitsky cases, which are two of the most famous cases of the Russian government raiding businesses. Russia will only be able to get the investments it needs to grow the country and the RFE in particular if it changes its laws and policies to protect property owners' rights and make sure that only legal processes are used in disputes.

We shouldn't be afraid to say that we know these changes will have big effects on Russian politics and the economy, hopefully for a long time. Moscow wants to rebuild the RFE and play a useful independent role in East Asia, but these changes are the only ones that can make those goals come true. We have to admit that if Russia doesn't make these moves, which we think is very likely, they will give up on their foreign policy goals and the RFE will automatically become a Chinese economic colony. In fact, Russian leaders know and say that progress is necessary for any strategy in Asia to work. Asean and the Pacific Rim will not have "a worthy economic partner" in Russia, said Aleksei Kudrin, who is the deputy prime minister and finance minister. "China and the Southeast Asian countries will steamroll Siberia and the Far East." After that, China would also beat Russia badly in Central Asia. In the same way, Putin told Russians in 2000 that they would have to learn Chinese, Japanese, and Korean if Russia didn't change. The leaders of Russia are very aware of what will happen if China doesn't put a lot of money into the RFE.

A US plan to treat Russia as a serious East Asian partner, talk about security threats in East Asia, and make it clear that the US is willing to invest in the RFE in exchange for real guarantees of that investment, along with efforts to get Japan and South Korea to invest there at the same time, could get a positive response from Russia. That being said, this is a big change in Russian strategy that has a lot of effects that you should not underestimate. So, it's possible that the Russian government will miss the chance in East Asia, just like it has every year since 1970. Since the beginning, the relationship between Russia and China has been mostly hostile towards the United States and liberal ideas. It keeps going because it supports Russia's economic and political system, which has pushed the country to the edge of Asia's centre stage but gives its leaders a lot of money. It's not just in the interests of the US and its partners to change that system and the mindsets and even the crazy economic and political actions that go along with it. They are mostly for the good of the people of Russia. In terms of Asia, they work for the Russian government because if they don't, only China will be interested in the RFE. It will be China, not Russia, who benefits if that happens.

The US should start these projects because it needs help in Asia to keep China from becoming too powerful and hostile. In this way, Russia's decision to get more satellites is a blow to a plan that has been used since John Hay came up with the Open Door policy in 1898. Also, Russia's inability to grow on its own or get out of the situation its leaders see as being cut off from everyone else in Asia only helps China and threatens the balance or stability in East Asia as a whole. Washington should make the offer after giving careful thought to how its national interests in East Asia are changing. But even if it starts these plans and Russia doesn't accept them, it will still be able to handle strategic trends in East Asia with the help of its friends. But Russia's interests won't be at risk if it doesn't take advantage of the chance that might be given to it now. Since this is now being talked about, its very existence as a major Asian power will be in danger. We should let Russia know about these offers, even if Moscow doesn't fully understand them. That's the very least we can do. But Russia controls its own path in Asia as well as everywhere else. An old American joke says, "How many psychologists does it take to change a light bulb?" One, but the light bulb has to really want to change. So to speak, the US is the doctor in this story. But Russia needs to change if it wants to stay alive in Asia.

Conclusion

The way ties between Russia and China have changed since the fall of the USSR has been and still is a success story. Without mentioning their tough shared history or current problems, this is an amazing example of how two large and powerful states have been able to not only work out their differences but also form what is called a "strategic partnership." Many people are worried about the current situation, while others are more interested in what the future holds. However, almost everyone agrees that ties between Russia and China are important for the future of Eurasia, Asia, and the global political order.

But it's normal to wonder how long or even if the partnership pattern can last between the world's biggest and most populous states. People may think the relationship between Russia and China is solid because of the practical reasons behind the question, but it is not. Every day, the relationship between China and Russia's power changes because China is growing much faster than Russia could possibly hope to in the near future.

The need for Moscow and Beijing to depend on each other is not the same for both countries, which is another important thing about this relationship. As a percentage of its total sales, China's trade with Russia is very small, and the country will not become too dependent on Russian energy sources any time soon. As a rising power, it is expanding its impact around the world. This is happening on top of, not in place of, its flexible economic cooperation with Western countries. Beijing is even actively looking into ways to strengthen its presence in the post-Soviet space. These words mean that it can move around freely and has many choices. At the moment, Russia depends more on China's goodwill than on China's own. This is because Russia's exports are mostly based on energy, the Far East is losing people, its relationships with the EU and the US are unstable, and Russia is clearly not able to remain the only centre of gravity for the CIS countries.

Most people in the West think that the relationship between Russia and China is good for China overall. In some way or another, this point of view is also held in Russia. For example, a group of well-known analysts just put out a report saying that "Beijing's growing power is causing concerns regardless of its course, which has been cautious and peaceful so far." The report also warns that Russia could become "an energy and raw material appendage" and, in the future, "a junior political brother" of the rising China.

The idea that Russia could handle China's rise on its own is not a very good one. In the most general and imaginary sense, if that's the case, there are two very different decisions that Russia could make in this situation. One option would be to join forces with China and let the idea of a "junior brother" come true, while maybe also trying to work out the best terms for the partnership. There is also the idea of keeping China in check by relying on Western powers. This idea would work well because of the "reset" in relations between Russia and the US and Europe's backing for Russia's plans to modernise.

However, this is constantly a hypothetical picture that only shows that an alternative exists. There hasn't been enough research and analysis into which choice, if any, is most likely to be made, whether the US and Europe want this choice to be made, and whether they are willing to push Russia in one way or the other.

This study from the Finnish Institute of International Affairs tries to fill in some of that gap by looking at the different trends that are happening in relations between Russia and China and the different paths that these relations could take in the future. FIIA hired a group of foreign scholars to write a book. Each scholar presented their own ideas in a separate chapter, while the editors did research and interviews in Moscow, Beijing, and Shanghai.

What the project found and what it concluded are shown below.

To begin, it's important to note again that Russia and China seem to have found a way to work together that works. Speaking positively about ties as "best historically", "best in the last 40 years" or "best among China's strategic relationships" is reasonable, as is easy to see. Trade is growing, and the fact that countries that send both energy and manufactured goods can help each other out is a good thing, even though it's not enough to explain the trend by itself. It is in both Russia and China's best interests to get along with their neighbours, keep the area safe, and fight terrorism and religious extremism in Central Asia. China recognises that Russia is a great power, even if it is on the decline. China doesn't want to talk about Russia's internal order and doesn't publicly question Russia's claim to have special rights in the post-Soviet space.

Most importantly, this relationship is valuable in and of itself for both countries. It is not directly linked to their relationships with the West, which is something that needs to be thought about when predicting how Russia might act. It is clear that both Moscow and Beijing want to limit the US's influence in Central Asia. This, along with their strong opposition to the US's global dominance or the creation of the infamous "unipolar world," was a major driving force behind their actions. However, it would be wrong to say that there is or could be a real geopolitical triangle. Russia and China work together with the West in different ways. China's cooperation is mostly economic, while Russia's is mostly military. Luckily, this means that a closer relationship between the West and one of the two states won't automatically hurt the other.

That being said, it's also easy to see the signs of mutual dissatisfaction. It's probably not possible to give a single number that shows if the contradictions are getting worse or not, but Russia's efforts to make things a little better show that people are unhappy to a point where it can't be ignored any longer.

Russia is unhappy with the way trade between the two countries is going. It may be good that the turnover is going up, but Moscow can't stand the deficit, the small amount of manufactured goods that Russia sells, and the fact that China will only buy Russian energy if it is priced very low. On the other hand, China shouldn't just buy goods from a "strategic partner" even if they aren't as good as other choices on the world market. As a non-member of the WTO and centre of the Customs Union, which also includes Kazakhstan and Belarus, Russia can't afford to be openly protectionist towards China. However, it can take steps to limit imports from China, which would hurt individual Chinese businesses. On the other hand, China is likely to be cautious about Russia's development, since Chinese businesses would have more competition if it worked. It's not likely that the politically-driven economic agreements, like using national currencies in trade with each other, will work out. This is because if Moscow and Beijing really tried to make the rouble and yuan foreign currencies, they would be competing with each other.

China is always getting stronger in the military balance in the area, which worries both the people of Russia and its forces. In Russia, this trend puts the question of what will happen to the Far Eastern regions at the top of the political agenda. Even though Beijing has been trying hard to calm Moscow's fears, it is still possible for Russia's edges to become China's edges. To see this, one only needs to visit certain business areas in Beijing or cities in the north of China.

The unity in foreign policy has also shown its limits. The Shanghai Cooperation Organisation (SCO), which will be 10 years old in 2011, doesn't look like a group that is growing and changing right now. The SCO has done its job of making it easier for China to come to Central Asia for political and economic reasons. It has also found its place in the world of regional cooperation, but it doesn't look like it will be able to become even more important and influential. China probably won't let India become a full member because it has a complicated relationship with that country. This means that the SCO probably won't grow. On the other hand, Russia has been paying more attention to the Collective Security Treaty Organisation lately since it is the only leader in that group. BRICS is still and probably will stay a place where people can share their thoughts because the member states are too different in size and interests to have a comprehensive common agenda.

It's true that ties between China and Russia in Central Asia are pretty stable and balanced, but China is still upset that Russia "allowed" or "welcomed" the presence of Western troops in the area after 2001. At the same time, Russia will not like how China is becoming more active in other parts of the former Soviet Union. Beijing may say that its main reason for wanting to be in the Western NIS region is to find new markets, but when China comes in with all its resources, Russia will automatically lose some of its power. Belarus is a good example of this because its leaders are always looking to China for economic and political help while keeping the country in balance between the West and Russia.

The cultural gap between the two countries doesn't seem to be closing, even though both governments are trying to teach more about their cultures and more people are meeting each other. Both are also getting more and more worried about the possible rise of nationalism and racism. This makes people less confident in general, which is a problem. Russia did not keep some high-level agreements, especially those related to energy, the Chinese said, and Russia either provided the promised goods too slowly or not at all.

Lastly, China doesn't seem to believe that Russia will become an effective country in the future or that it will be stable in the long term. This view makes it harder to work together. Chinese experts have a lot of negative things to say about Russia's corruption, lack of legal control, and population problems. These are all things that Western experts also talk about. It's no surprise that China has a very low opinion of Russia. It's only normal for a country that is growing and doing well to look down on its weaker neighbour.

So, what do you think Russia will do? Is there anything it can do to improve its own situation? First, it looks like the above-mentioned tough choice between joining China and keeping it in check by making an agreement with the West is not really a choice at all. This country can't voluntarily become China's junior partner for cultural and political reasons, even though there is a strong push for this choice in Russia due to unclear economic interests and lingering anti-Western feelings. In the same way, Russia can't move too far towards a partnership with the West either. A union that looked like an anti-China alliance, especially if Russia joined NATO, would put it on the front lines and take away some of its independence and freedom to play a big role in international affairs, which it values a lot.

The tough choice wouldn't have to be made if Russia were to or could become a Euro-Pacific power, that is, if it could be part of the system of international relations in Asia as a country with good ties to the West, starting with the US, and lots of room to interact with Pacific countries. In this direction, the talk among Russian experts seems to be going, and the formula "Lean on the West, stabilise the South, and go East" sums it up. It is clear that this choice would be good for Russia because it would help Asia grow without doing anything that would make China dislike Russia.

The problem with this approach is that it is not realistic for Russia and its leaders to use today, even though it makes a lot of sense and isn't controversial on paper. Again, the economy is very important. As long as Russia can only export energy and weapons, it won't be a good partner for India or other big countries in the area. As long as it doesn't improve relations with Japan—and things got worse around the Kuril Islands in 2010—it won't be possible to work together on security with the US, and Japan won't be able to invest in the Russian Far East, which is important to counteract China's economic influence. As long as Russia doesn't fix its internal problems, which are hurting its image around the world (as the Chinese discussion shows), it will be hard to stop Russia from going downhill. It will be hard to build a strong alliance with the United States, which is the main Western representative, as long as Russia sees the West as a part of the problem and not a part of the answer when it comes to security.

In the middle term, it's much more possible that Russia will do nothing about its policy towards China. China likes the way people live together now better than Russia does, but Russia needs vision and leadership to change the pattern. Russia lacks these things on too many problems, including its relationship with China, which doesn't seem to be seen as a top priority. Even though this choice might not be the best in the long run, Russia would have to make a big change in its politics in order to get off the road dependence it is currently on. This change does not seem to be happening any time soon.

The West doesn't need to worry about Russia's likely "nondecision" right away. Russia and China don't seem to want to form a real anti-Western union, and the political rapprochement between the two countries has reached its limits, albeit not in words. Adding another pipeline or making more trade happen won't change the big picture that includes both the places where people can work together and the ones where they disagree.

In general, ties between Russia and Europe and relations between Russia and China don't seem to have much in common. Because of this, people in the West, especially Europeans, shouldn't think that China's rise will instantly make Russia want to work with the EU. And the other way around: Russia can't send energy to China instead of Europe, and Russia will be interested in Europe's financial resources and technologies no matter how promising the Chinese direction looks.

So, Europe should stick to its strategy of interacting with Russia, even though China is a factor. When the EU talks to Russia about a value-based plan, it won't make it more likely for Russia to form an alliance with China, even though this kind of talk is getting stronger. The EU wants Russia to make a change that will make their moral differences smaller. They should also try to build a relationship with Russia based on clear rules that both sides accept and follow. Specifically, when it comes to matters like Russia's membership in the WTO, Europe's stance would likely not be too different from China's.

From the US point of view, things might look different. If, in a made-up situation, Russia did become China's junior partner over time and not a separate political player in Asia, the US would have a lot more trouble with the Asian security order. At the time, Americans aren't very worried or wary about such a situation, which shows that they aren't paying enough attention to Russia. But this could change. A serious conversation between the US and Russia about security threats in East Asia could save the "reset" process and slowly make the US and its allies in the area more interested in investing in the Russian Far East. A big step like this would bring Russia a lot closer to the best case situation that people in the country have been talking about.

To get the most out of a possible repositioning of the United States in East Asia, as argued for in this report, and Europe's interest in modernising Russia, Russia should be willing to make changes within its own country, make foreign investment safe, and get rid of the naturally anti-Western views of its foreign policy elite. If they don't do this, it will have effects that go far beyond Russia's influence over China or its place in Asian politics.

Chapter 2
Dynamic Alliances: Exploring the Complex Tapestry of China-Russia Relations

The Russian Federation (Russia) and the People's Republic of China (PRC or China) have a strategic relationship that includes a lot of military, political, and economic ties. China and Russia have had a past together that goes back longer than the fall of the Soviet Union in 1991. There have been times when they worked together on security and diplomacy, times when they were rivals, times of crisis, and even a border war in the 1960s. Many experts say that the relationship has become more active since 2014, when the US, the EU, and some other countries responded to Russia's first invasion of Ukraine with sanctions. This made Moscow want to improve its ties with China and other countries.

Because China and Russia seem to get along, some U.S. policymakers and lawmakers are worried that Beijing and Moscow are really working together, and they want to find ways to fight their power around the world. The PRC and Russia don't have a mutual defence deal. Instead, they have more of an unofficial alliance based on their shared dislike of what they call the U.S.-led international order. This shared resistance has made the two countries work together, but it hasn't changed their long-standing mistrust of each other's strategic intentions. Since Russia started invading Ukraine again in 2022, it has become more dependent on China's economic and political backing. This gives China an edge in the relationship.

Key Points

The 2001 Treaty of Good-Neighborliness and Friendly Cooperation built on the 1991 Sino-Soviet Border Agreement. It said that both Beijing and Moscow were happy with border issues and set up broad areas of cooperation in areas like trade, economics, and fighting terrorism. The fact that the treaty will be renewed in 2021 shows that ties are generally getting better.

The course of the two countries' relationship seems to be affected by the fact that Presidents Xi Jinping and Vladimir Putin are very close personally.

Since 2013, Xi and Putin have met many times and set up ways to talk to each other regularly at lower levels. In 2019, leaders of the PRC and Russia said they wanted to create a "Comprehensive Strategic Partnership of Coordination for a New Era." They said they had a "high degree of political trust" and would work together in every way.

There is a lot of military cooperation between the PRC and Russia. They share information and work together to make new weapons systems. They also do exchanges and drills. The two sides signed a Road Map for Military Co-operation for 2021–2025 in November 2021. This will help them work together in this area. The PRC and Russia are two of the founder members of the Shanghai Cooperation Organisation (SCO), an intergovernmental group based in Eurasia that mainly deals with security issues.

The PRC and Russia also have close business and financial links. They work together to try to "dedollarize" the world economy, which they see as being tied to the US. (See CRS In Focus IF11885, Efforts to Lower the Value of the Rouble in China and Russia.) Both countries say they don't want unilateral sanctions to be used as a policy tool.

In international settings, such as the UN, the SCO, the BRICS grouping, and the Group of 20 (G20), the PRC and Russia often work together and coordinate. In 2022, the PRC and Russia both vetoed a draught U.N. resolution led by the United States that would have put more penalties on North Korea for its missile launches. The PRC and Russia have tried to make the goals of projects that cross, like the Belt and Road Initiative (BRI) and the Eurasian Economic Union (EEU), more compatible so that they don't clash.

The PRC and Russian Standpoints

China and Russia are at what officials in the People's Republic of China call a "historic high" in their relationship right now. Both countries back each other's views on national sovereignty, security, territorial integrity, and economic growth. One of the PRC's main goals in the relationship seems to be flexibility, which is clear from its call to "form partnerships, not alliances." By taking this stand, it has been able to separate itself from some of Russia's actions in the world. China values its access to the US and European markets, including their capital markets. Russia's role as a strategic partner in world events has sometimes caused problems for the PRC.

Russian worries about China's economic edge are often overshadowed by the need for and benefits of working together more in business, politics, and the military. Russian leaders are wary of China's leaders and don't trust them, even though they know that having a close relationship with the PRC would be good for business. This means staying away from the binding responsibilities of a formal alliance, especially ones that could lead to a fight over Taiwan. Russian officials don't seem to want to be called a "junior" partner and want to handle the relationship in a way that is good for both sides.

Prominent Issues

Concerns for Global Order

Officials from the PRC and Russia see each other as allies in their fight against the U.S.-led global order. "In a changing and turbulent international environment, it is important that China and Russia remain true to the original aspiration of cooperation, maintain strategic focus, enhance strategic coordination," and "continue to be each other's development opportunity and global partner." This was said by Xi in a phone call with Putin on December 30, 2022.

A lot of experts say that even though both the PRC and Russia seem to be against the current world order, they may not agree on what should come next. A lot of experts think that the PRC is a "revisionist" power that wants to change some parts of the current order, maybe with the goal of replacing it in the long run. Officials from the PRC often say that China's vision for global order is based on the principles of state sovereignty and not meddling in other countries' affairs. They compare this to the present order, which they say puts human rights and meddling in other countries' affairs ahead of these principles. Russian leaders say that the current global order doesn't take into account the position and sovereignty of other great powers besides the US and doesn't give those other powers what Russian leaders see as acceptable spheres of influence. So, Russian leaders try to fight back against what they see as excessive U.S. unipolarity and to remind the U.S. of Russia's status as a great power and its place in the world order.

Defence Cooperation

It is important for both countries to work together on defence and security issues. In the past, the PRC has bought a lot of Russian weapons to update its forces. As the PRC's defence industry has grown more complex, defence trade has become more complicated as well. This is said to have made Russia more worried about technology transfer and intellectual property violations. China provides Russia's defence industry with important parts and money for the creation of advanced weapon systems.

The two countries work together on military drills to make their armies more compatible and to improve cooperation in the defence sector and joint arms development. Russia has tried to take part in more military drills with the PRC, both at the strategic and tactical levels. Russia has also wanted to take part in more navy drills and air patrols in the Asia-Pacific region. It's possible that Russia holds these drills to improve its ability to work with PRC troops and to show that it is still a player in the area. In August 2023, a fleet of ships from the PRC and Russia did a maritime patrol in areas near Alaska.

Energy and Economic Matters

There are imbalances in the economic relationships between China and Russia. China's economy is much bigger and more active than Russia's. Once again, China is Russia's ninth biggest export market, and the EU is its first. One thing that makes the relationship between the two countries unique is that Russia is a major source of energy imports for the PRC. According to statistics from the PRC's customs, Russia tied Saudi Arabia as China's biggest source of crude oil in 2022, sending about 17% of all the oil that China bought. China wants to move away from coal, which could mean that Russian hydrocarbons, like "green coal" and natural gas, play a bigger part. It is believed that the Power of Siberia Pipeline will be fully operational by 2027. This could make China one of the biggest buyers of Russian natural gas.

Aftermath of Russia's 2022 Invasion of Ukraine

The invasion of Ukraine by Russia has made the relationship between Beijing and Moscow more public. There are questions about how willing and able China is to ease the pressure of sanctions on Russia. China has not publicly criticised Russia's actions, even though some people think that Russia's attack made things more difficult between the two countries. These people say that China didn't know about Russia's plans and still doesn't want to get involved in the fight. Russia, on the other hand, seems to be looking to China to get around Western sanctions. For example, Russia is selling oil to China and buying important parts for its defence industry. The PRC has become "an even more critical economic partner for Russia" since Russia invaded Ukraine in 2022, according to a report released by the Office of the Director of National Intelligence in July 2023.

Some trade data shows that some PRC companies may be giving Russia goods that can be used for more than one purpose, which could be helping Russia win the war. But it's not clear if and how much these actions are directed by the government. According to the news, the PRC government only engages in certain activities that are good for China, like getting oil at a discount, but not when it comes to providing lethal weapons.

The Biden Administration has told China many times not to help Russia invade Ukraine. We've been very clear with the PRC, even in private, about any costs that would befall the PRC if they decide to help Russia avoid U.S. sanctions or provide security assistance that would then be used against the Ukrainian people in Ukraine. This was said by Ned Price, a spokesperson for the State Department, in January 2023. Executive Order 14024 says that sixteen Chinese companies have been punished because of Russia's attack.

Congressional Challenges

A top national security goal for U.S. policymakers, including those in Congress, is to stop coordinated PRC and Russian threats to the current international order. In their national security plans, both the Trump and Biden administrations used this kind of wording. According to the James M. Inhofe National Defence Authorisation Act for Fiscal Year 2023 (P.L. 117-263), there needs to be a report on whether and how the PRC has helped Russia with its war against Ukraine. The Countering PRC Influence Fund got $325 million and the Countering Russian Influence Fund got $300 million from the Consolidated Appropriations Act, 2023 (P.L. 117-328). The 118th Congress might look at how these funds are being used to fight the stories being told by the PRC and Russia. It might also think about how sanctions, including those against companies based in the PRC, might affect relations between China and Russia.

China-Russia Ties Amidst a Shifting Global Order

China and Russia announced a strategic cooperative partnership in 1996. This partnership was later solidified in the Treaty for Good Neighbourliness, Friendship, and Cooperation, which was signed in 2001. Both countries signed off on an action plan to carry out the pact in 2008. In 2011, the relationship was upgraded to a "comprehensive strategic and cooperative partnership," which is China's idea of the top level of cooperation. More than 50 other agreements have been made between China and Russia since the treaty in 2001. In 2009, when Russian President Dmitry Medvedev went to the Shanghai Expo, he said that relations between Russia and China had reached the "highest point in history." High-level leaders have visited each other a lot, cooperation in energy is growing, trade is growing, Russia is selling more arms to China, and people are talking to each other more. There is also some diplomatic cooperation over the Middle East and other problems.

China and Russia work together because they both don't like some things about the way the world is set up now and they need to get things done. In terms of world order, both countries want to end what they see as US dominance and replace it with a system with more than two major powers. This means that the UN Security Council (UNSC), which is made up of Russia and China, would have to deal with important security problems in a more powerful way. It is somewhat ironic that the "liberal" United States has doubts about the United Nations while China and Russia support it. A more multipolar world order with more power for China and Russia would raise their status and better protect states like Iran, Syria, and North Korea that the West doesn't like but where China and/or Russia has important interests. In March 2014, Russia used its veto in the UNSC to stop a draught resolution that would have condemned the vote in Crimea to join Russia.

The liberal focus on human rights and minority self-determination, along with the loss of power that comes with them, is another part of the current world order that China and Russia want to change. Russia and China think that state governments should be in charge of human rights, not the whole world. This point of view comes from politics at home. Russia wants to be able to handle Chechnya, the Caucasus, and most recently, Ukraine in any way it sees fit. China wants to get back Taiwan and stop any opposition in Tibet, Xinjiang, and other troubled areas. Also, both China and Russia believe in keeping their spheres of power. By "near abroad," we mean the states that are part of the former Soviet Union. For Russia, this means having a big say in the foreign policy of these states. This is good for China because it gives its rights to land in the South China Sea more weight and helps North Korea keep its friendly government. A top goal for both China and Russia is to stop revolutions in Central Asia and other former Soviet republics that would bring in democratic, pro-Western governments.

Reforming international institutions is another problem that matters to both Russia and China when it comes to the world order. It's interesting that this doesn't include the UNSC. There is no desire in either country for the Security Council to grow or for its veto power to be taken away. Some changes are made to financial institutions like the World Bank and the International Monetary Fund (IMF), which gives non-Western states more power in those organisations. It also includes the growth of multinational groups that don't include the West, like the Shanghai Cooperation Organisation (SCO) and the BRICS (Brazil, Russia, India, China, and South Africa).

Still, Russian and Chinese views on world order are also very different in important ways. China may not know what kind of world order it wants in the end, but there are many voices in China today talking about foreign policy, and they all have different ideas about where it should go. Hu Jintao said that China's growth would be peaceful, but China's neighbours aren't so sure after seeing its recent aggressive actions in the East and South China Seas. Some people in China, like some soldiers in the People's Liberation Army (PLA), want China to be the most powerful country in the world. Other thinkers want to go back to a "all under heaven" system with a hierarchical world order ruled by a good Chinese empire. Most of these ideas about how the world should work see China becoming more powerful on the world stage, which could hurt important Russian interests.

Putin has a narrower view of how the world should work, but he also questions the way things are now. Putin wants the world to see Russia as a major power. Russia is trying to get closer to Europe, but it still wants to keep the former Soviet states close to it. This is seen as imperialism by some and the Monroe Doctrine by others. With Russia's military action in Ukraine and Georgia, this has mostly messed up the international order in Europe. It also goes against Chinese interests in Central Asia.

The relationship between China and Russia is also based on very real problems. These will be quickly talked about here, but in more depth later. The first one is about money. Russia and China both put a lot of importance on growing their own economies. Because of this, trade and business between the two sides are important. The energy trade is a good way for both Russia and China to make money because Russia has a lot of oil and other natural resources and China buys them. The Russian Far East (RFE) also has a weak economy that Moscow can't afford to grow on its own. The goal of Russian-Chinese partnership in the RFE has been economic growth, but this goal has not been met as well as hoped. In general, trade and investment levels outside of the energy industry have been disappointing.

Another important thing is safety. Threats and fights at the borders brought the world dangerously close to war in the late 1960s and early 1970s. By the 1980s, both China and Russia were focused on problems at home. Both Russia and China needed to make sure their border was safe. The last border conflict was settled through talks in 2008, and the border was no longer armed. Also, the Russian defence industry was eager for orders and money in the 1990s and early 2000s. China wanted more modern weapons, and Russia sold China fighter planes and submarines, which was good for both countries.

The "comprehensive strategic and cooperative partnership" between China and Russia is based on shared interests, not love. This is true in politics, economics, and security. Well-known Russian political expert Dmitri Trenin says, "There has never been a spirit of camaraderie about Russo-Chinese summits." They don't take off their ties or call each other by their first names. It's also been a while since there were real strategic talks. But the meetings are always serious and focused on getting things done. For the same reason, Andrew Kuchins says that Russia feels "profound ambivalence" towards China but acts in a practical way. A study by Trenin on the relationship between China and Russia found that "both countries need each other and would benefit from a stable political relationship and close economic ties, but both Moscow and Beijing lack the long-term strategies to create such a bond."

The relationship between China and Russia might not last for a long time. As China gets stronger, its view of the best way for the world to work is going to become more different from Russia's. As an example, Leszek Buszynski says that China has become more powerful than Russia in the Asia-Pacific area. Russia is being pushed to the edges, and its relationship with China has not been good for it. Also, China and Russia may be getting into more trouble because their areas of influence overlap, especially in Central Asia. To sum up, world order is based on both values and power. As China's power grows compared to Russia's, different people will have different ideas about what that order should be.

Things that are useful can change over time. China's growing military might make Russia rethink how it protects its borders. Russia's worries about China taking over the RFE and Russia being mainly a source of resources for China could hurt business ties. So, it's important to look into different issues to see where China and Russia agree to work together and disagree.

Russia's takeover of Crimea in March 2014 showed that the Chinese and Russian worldviews are at odds with each other, which also affects everyday life. China was put in a tough spot by Russia's action. China has long said that it doesn't want other countries to get involved in other countries' internal issues, even if that doesn't always mean that they do. The United States has been criticised by China for breaking this principle many times. Russia clearly broke this principle in Ukraine. Also, China has important reasons to be interested in Ukraine. It buys weapons and defence technology from Ukraine, has agricultural interests in Ukraine, and sees Ukraine as the key to its investment plans in Eastern Europe. Most importantly, the Crimean referendum sets a bad example that people in Taiwan, Tibet, or Xinjiang could use to call for similar votes in the future.

China, on the other hand, sees Russia as a key strategic partner, and Putin knows that China will back him. The Chinese government thought that a loss for the West would be good for them, and the Chinese press praised Putin for being tough and staring the West in the face. Also, China had a lot to gain from a fight between Putin and the West, which would have made Russia more reliant on China for money and oil.

China wouldn't commit to either side in the end. It didn't vote on a draught UNSC resolution that would have condemned the Crimean poll. It made vague, noncommittal comments and tried to find a way to get things done that wouldn't anger either Russia or Ukraine. But it was clear that realpolitik and practical concerns were more important than a strong moral stand.

Sino-Russian Engagement

As was already said, the relationship between China and Russia is affected by a number of very practical problems. The most important ones are economy, safety, and shared and/or competing interests in Central Asia.

Economic Matters

Energy is the most important thing that Russia and China trade with each other. China buys more energy from other countries every year, while Russia exports a lot of it. China has also turned into a profitable market for Russian oil. Still, building the necessary energy infrastructure and coming to solid deals on energy supplies and prices have not been easy. This is because Russian energy companies are fighting with each other, and China and Russia don't trust or understand each other. People are angry about this, especially in China.

Russia tried to play China off against Japan for years before starting to send oil to China through the East Siberia-Pacific Ocean (ESPO) pipeline in January 2011. A deal made in 2009 allowed this to happen. China lent $25 billion to Russia's Rosneft and Transneft oil and pipeline companies in exchange for Russia sending China 300 million tonnes of crude oil over 30 years. However, Russians said that the Chinese National Petroleum Corporation (CNPC) was paying too little for oil by $100 million in the first two months that the pipeline was open. The disagreement was solved the following year. Also, during his trip to Moscow in June 2013, Chinese President Xi Jinping signed an extra $270 billion crude oil deal with Russia.

But natural gas from Russia to China hasn't started to flow yet, even though Gazprom and CNPC agreed in 2006 to send 30 billion cubic metres of gas to China through a western route and 38 billion cubic metres through an eastern route. They also agreed to do this in 2009. China and Russia have very different ideas about how much gas should cost, which is why the pipes that are needed have not been built. Part of the reason for this is problems in Chinese politics that have to do with the CNPC. Some analysts thought that a loan deal with Gazprom would finally solve the problem, just like the oil deal did. But it looks like Gazprom will no longer be the only company that can ship gas. Rosneft now wants to sell liquid natural gas (LNG) to Japanese companies from a terminal on Sakhalin. At the same time, Novatek, a separate gas supplier, has teamed up with CNPC to sell LNG from the Arctic to China. Finally, during the meeting between Vladimir Putin and Xi Jinping in May 2014, China and Russia agreed to a 30-year gas deal. Gas will start flowing from Russia to China in 2018 after the necessary infrastructure is built. In business, the price of that petrol is known as a "commercial secret."

In a related matter, Russia has clear economic and political reasons for developing the RFE even more. It wants to regain control of the area and build a stronger base for its foreign influence in the Asia-Pacific region. Some of these goals have to do with energy, but there are other parts to this task as well. The RFE wasn't given much attention after the fall of the Soviet Union while Russia's new leaders tried to put the country back together. The number of people living in the area has dropped by 20% since 1991, to 6.28 million. By 2025, that number is expected to drop even more, to 4.7 million. But in the last few years, Russia has paid more attention to the RFE. This is partly because China is growing and economic growth based on trade and business with Europe is looking less likely. Like this, the Russian government passed the "Strategy for Socio-Economic Development of the Far East and the Baikal Region until 2025 (Strategy 2025)" in 2009 to help the eastern parts of the country grow. Moscow became interested in Vladivostok after the 2012 Asia-Pacific Economic Cooperation (APEC) meeting. The Russian government is said to have spent over $20 billion to improve the city's infrastructure.

As Russia works to improve the RFE, it faces a problem. At the same time, it needs help from China and other Asia-Pacific countries to grow its economy. The Russian government doesn't have the means, and large parts of its work are slowed down by corruption and inefficient bureaucracy. Russia, on the other hand, doesn't want the RFE to merge with China. There is no guarantee that Russia will be able to walk this queue. The Chinese State economic Bank said in August 2013 that it might spend $5 billion in the RFE to help pay for Russian economic projects. Also, it is said that Chinese workers now farm 40% of the arable land in the RFE's Jewish Autonomous Region. In 2012, 90% of the veggies sold in the RFE came from Chinese farms. In conclusion, the RFE opens up a lot of economic prospects for both China and Russia that are good for both countries. It could be dangerous for Russia to let go of these chances, though, as it tries to take control of its eastern regions.

China and Russia are also finding ways to work together on business and trade. In 2010, China became Russia's biggest trading partner. To make trade less reliant on the dollar, China and Russia started trading the yuan and ruble on Russia's Micex exchange. Still, Russia's role in China's general trade is still small. IMF statistics on China shows that from 2005 to 2012, Chinese exports to Russia more than tripled, from $13.21 billion to $44.07 billion. Still, estimates show that

China's exports to Russia only went up from 1.7% of all exports in 2005 to 2.2% of all exports in 2012. So that you can see the difference, in 2012, China's exports to Russia were only 12.5% of its exports to the US. China's imports from Russia went from $15.89 billion in 2005 to $43.95 billion in 2012, but they still only made up 2.4% of all imports.

The amount of Russian goods sent to China increased from 5.4% of all Russian exports in 2005 to 6.8% of all Russian exports in 2012. In 2012, only 36% of Russia's goods went to the US. The rest went to China. From 2005 to 2011, Russia's imports from China more than five times increased, from 5.2% of all imports in 2005 to 14% of all imports in 2012. That is, Russia depends on trade with other countries more than China does. The amount of trade grew only 2% from 2012 to 2013 to reach $90 billion.

Both countries will benefit from more trade, but Russia is worried about the kind of trade that will happen. Over-the-top trade with China was a big problem for Putin in 2006 because Russia doesn't want to just give China natural resources. Chinese onlookers often complain about problems with the structure. One writer, Qiu Huafei, says that most of the trade between China and Russia is for the needs of border towns and not enough high-tech goods. Qiu also says that trade is slowed down by breach of contract, a lack of formal ways to settle disagreements, unfair treatment of Chinese businesspeople in Russia, a widespread belief that China is a threat, and unpaid Russian bills. Other Chinese experts, on the other hand, are more positive. They see the chance for Russia to sell high-tech goods to China and think that China will move towards a more consumer-based economy, which will give Russia more chances to sell its goods abroad.

Security

After fighting between the two sides in 1969, wanting to keep the border safe was a big part of getting along better in the late 1980s and early 1990s, and it still is. As a defence, Russia looks at the US and NATO. It also sees terrorism coming from the south as a big threat today. At the same time, China is in a fight with Japan and Southeast Asia, and it wants to stop trouble among its minorities inside its own borders. Each side needs to know that the shared line won't cause any problems.

The new shift in power between the two countries is an interesting part of the security relationship. The Soviet Union was the most powerful country in politics, the economy, and the military during the Cold War. Today, China is in charge of the relationship, even though some major weapons systems are very technologically advanced and have nuclear weapons. In fact, the fast growth of the PLA might make someone think that Russia will become more protective towards China.

'Though there are some signs that this is happening, Russia does not really see China as a big security threat right now. The rise of China has made the world more multipolar, which gives Russia more room to move. Russia also thinks that China is focused on its east and south, and it knows that China has many problems at home that require its leaders' time and resources. Russia wants to keep a good relationship with China for its own safety. From China's point of view, having strong links with Russia keeps Russia from getting closer to NATO, which would cut China off from the rest of the world. Also, many people in China saw Russia's takeover of Crimea as a victory over the West. Based on a number of reasons, one Chinese analyst says that the US, Russia, and China are all playing defence against each other.

One important part of China and Russia's security partnership is the sale of arms. China has been steadily and for a long time building up its high-tech weapons since the 1990s. Because the US and Europe won't sell China most types of military gear since 1989, Russia has become China's main source of arms from other countries. Eighty-four percent of the weapons China bought from 2006 to 2010 came from Russia. From Russia's point of view, the years after the fall of the Soviet Union have been very hard on the economy, though oil exports have helped. So, selling weapons to China has been a welcome and sometimes life-saving way for Russia to make money. Russia has sold China a wide range of weapons. These include fighter planes like the Su-27 and Su-30, surface-to-air missile (SAM) systems, destroyers of the Sovremenny class, helicopters, cargo planes, antiship missiles, torpedoes, radars, and jet engines.

Still, Russia's arms sales to China peaked in 2005 and have been going down since then. Sales have gone down from $3.13 billion in 2005 (based on prices that stayed the same in 1990) to $679 million in 2012. In 2005, 60 percent of Russia's arms exports went to China. By 2012, that number had dropped to 8 percent. By 2009, Russia had sent most of its major weapon systems to China. Since 2006, Russia has only sent jet engines, fire control radars, transport planes, and helicopters as major weapons. There are several possible reasons for this drop in sales of weapons. According to China, many of the weapons it used to buy from Russia can now be made by its own defence companies. Some people were also unhappy with the way Russia sold weapons. Russia often wouldn't sell China its most advanced technology, but it was happy to sell India more advanced things. China doesn't like this at all. China wanted more licenced production of systems in China and to share information. They were not happy with the quality of Russian arms or the delays in delivery.

The Russian point of view is more complicated. On the one hand, people are worried that China is taking Russian technology apart and using it to make its own weapons, which is cheaper than Russia's. Russia says that China's J-11B fighter plane is a copy of the Su-27, but China is putting a lot of effort into selling the JF-17 fighter plane, which was made with Pakistan. While the Russian government was ordering a report in 2011 called "The Strategies and Tactics of Chinese Exporters of Arms and Military Equipment," the head of the Mikoyan (MiG) and Sukhoi design bureau wrote to Roxoboronexport asking them not to send a lot of RD-93 engines to China because the MiG-29 is competing with the JF-17 for export sales and the JF-17 uses that engine.

A number of Russian leaders are also worried about what China's growing military power means for Russia's future. There are different views among Russian leaders on this issue. Kevin Ryan says, "From Moscow's point of view, military relations with China look different depending on the person's organisation." Strategic managers and people who make weapons see things differently. It's hard for Russia because China wants more and more advanced weapons, which could change the balance of power in the Asia-Pacific area and between China and Russia. This could make the US less friendly with China.

The way Beijing and Moscow sell guns to each other will need to be closely watched to see how well they work together on defence. There have been talks recently about Russia selling more weapons to China, especially the Su-35S fighter and the 400-kilometer-range S-400 SAM system. These are Russia's most powerful weapons. News magazine Jane's 360 said in December 2012 that Russia will also give China four Lada-class diesel submarines. Even so, these deals are not firm.

Joint military drills are another sign that China and Russia are working together on defence. Peace Mission 2005 was the first military exercise. It was put on by the SCO with the claimed goal of fighting terrorism. This drill took place in the RFE and China's Shandong province. It included both naval and land operations. There were 10,000 soldiers, as well as submarines and strategic bombs. This made people think that the drills were about a lot more than just fighting terrorism. China wanted them to be seen as practise for an attack of Taiwan. There have also been a number of other Peace Mission drills. But most of the time, these kinds of workouts don't really improve coordination.

Recent navy manoeuvres showed that the military is working together better. Joint Sea 2013 was the name of the huge naval drills that Russia and China held together from July 5th to July 12th, 2013. China sent seven ships, including a guided-missile destroyer and two frigates. Russia sent eleven warships, including the Varyag, the leader of the Pacific fleet, a guided-missile cruiser, and a Kilo-class submarine. The drills were mostly about surface warfare, antisubmarine warfare, air defence, and freeing a ship that was being held hostage. The political message was just as important as the military parts of the drills. As a message to the US and Japan, China wants the drills to be seen as a sign that Russia stands with China in its many maritime disputes, especially those over the Diaoyu/Senkaku Islands. Russia, on the other hand, has not taken sides in these disputes, so the exercises may not accurately show Russia's real stance.

Just as if to balance things out, Russia started its own armed drills soon after the Chinese left. Reports say that 160,000 soldiers, 500 tanks, 130 combat aircraft, and ships from the Pacific fleet took part in the largest military drill since the fall of the Soviet Union. As part of the exercise, Russian troops sent to the RFE had to respond quickly. It was meant to show Russia's Asian neighbours how strong its military is and how quickly it can move troops to protect its eastern areas. So, the naval drills at the beginning of July showed that Russia and China worked well together, while the exercises later in the month showed that Russia was independent and could defend itself against any possible Chinese invasion.

Central Asia

Central Asia, which includes Kazakhstan, Kyrgyzstan, Tajikistan, Uzbekistan, and Turkmenistan, is a place where weak states with small populations try to run large areas. The area is ideally placed between China, Russia, and the Middle East, and it has a lot of energy reserves. It can also help keep Afghanistan safe, but it is also open to violent ideas and extreme ideologies that spread outside of Afghanistan. In this way, Russia, China, the US, India, Pakistan, Iran, and Turkey are all trying to gain power in the area. Of course, the people of Central Asia want independence and room to move, so they play the different forces against each other. Besides that, they fight with each other. Russia and China are both at odds with each other and working together in this situation. So far, the helpful side of their relationship has been stronger because they both want the region to be stable and for the US to stay out of the area. One interesting thing that Charles Ziegler says is that "surprisingly, these two powers have found that their interests coincide remarkably well in Central Asia, at least in the short term."

In 1997, Zbigniew Brzezinski said that Russia's problem in Central Asia is that it is not strong enough politically to control the area and not strong enough economically to grow it. This is still true now. Central Asia is in Russia's "near abroad," which is a vital part of the old Soviet Union. Russia thinks that Central Asia is in its area of control. Russia cares a lot about the safety of Central Asian states and the kind of government they choose. It does, however, have business goals. Russia has tried to take over Central Asia's energy infrastructure by buying energy at low prices and then selling it to Europe for a profit. It also uses its power to protect Russian-speaking people who stayed in the area after the Soviet Union broke up.

There are three main goals that China wants to achieve in Central Asia. The first is to keep the Xinjiang Uyghur Autonomous Region in the northwest of the country stable. To keep rebellion alive in Xinjiang, China does not want Central Asia to be used as a base. Second, China wants to have stronger business and transportation ties with Central Asia. Beijing thinks this will help its general goal of fast economic growth and keep Xinjiang stable. Third, China wants to get more energy from Central Asia. It plans to do this by getting energy contracts and building the facilities needed to bring oil and gas to China. China thinks this is an important part of a plan to get different types of energy. It also thinks that pipeline paths through Central Asia are safer than sea lanes from the Middle East, which the US Navy could block.

The "three evils" of "terrorism, separatism, and religious extremism" are something that both Russia and China want to get rid of in the area. Some of the things they do to try to lessen US power in Central Asia are to stop new "colour revolutions" that might bring more democratic government to the states in the area and to limit US military bases in the area.

China has been working to improve Central Asia's infrastructure. For instance, the China Road and Bridge Company won a bid to build a road from Osh in Kyrgyzstan to the Irkeshtam Pass with China. The Chinese government will help pay for some of the costs. China is building rail lines that will go through Tajikistan and connect Xinjiang to Afghanistan. At the same time, Chinese telecom and internet companies are connecting the area electronically. China has taken part in the Central Asia Regional Economic Cooperation (CAREC) programme run by the Asian Development Bank (ADB). CAREC is meant to boost economic growth and lower poverty. Also, China is working hard to boost its "soft power" and "people-to-people" knowledge in Central Asia through Confucius Institutes, which are government-funded groups that spread Chinese language and culture outside of China. Russia has lost ground in this area to China, but people in the area still have doubts about China because of its size and possible power.

As part of his trip to Central Asian countries in September 2013, Chinese President Xi Jinping signed business deals in what he called the "Silk Road Economic Zone." These deals showed that China's strategy was working. President Xi went to Kazakhstan, Uzbekistan, Turkmenistan, and Kyrgyzstan. Xi and Nursultan Nazarbayev, the president of Kazakhstan, signed $30 billion worth of deals and opened a 700-mile gas pipeline as a sign of goodwill. This pipeline, along with others, will bring gas from the Caspian Sea to the coast of China. Through CNPC, China also bought an 8.4 percent share in Kazakhstan's Kashagan oil field in the Caspian Sea, joining a group of other oil companies from around the world. Xi opened Galkynysh, the world's second-largest gas field, in Turkmenistan. This will cause China to receive three times as much gas from that country. During his time in Uzbekistan, he made energy deals worth $15 billion. With China making big investments in the area and starting new "strategic partnerships," Igor Morgulov, the deputy foreign minister of Russia, felt he had to say, "Our Chinese friends recognise the traditional role our country continues to play in this region, so we do not see any regional rivalry problems." This was said in a way that wasn't entirely convincing.

The SCO is the group that brought Russia and China together to work on problems in Central Asia. China, Russia, Kazakhstan, Kyrgyzstan, Tajikistan, and Uzbekistan are all part of the SCO. The Shanghai Cooperation Organisation (SCO) was created in 2001 and has a history of successful border negotiations. It gives Russia and China a way to work together on problems that affect Central Asia and, as we already said, it's how they do military drills. China helped to create the SCO and sees itself as the organization's leader, making it a special group for the country. The Shanghai Cooperation Organisation (SCO) is a proud example of China's "new diplomacy" that is based on trust, equality, respect for variety, and a focus on development.

From the founders' point of view, the SCO has been very successful in some ways. An expert from China says that the SCO has been able to keep things stable during the global economic crisis that started in 2008, and there was no "Arab Spring" in the area. There have been no big terrorist attacks in the area, and ties between China and Russia are good. Also, the countries in Central Asia are working together. Also, other groups in the region have been eager to become monitors at the SCO.

But Russia and China do not agree on everything about the SCO. Russia isn't sure how it feels about the organisation. It wants the Eurasian Economic Community or the Collective Security Treaty Organisation to be in charge of security and trade in Central Asia. Both of these groups are controlled by Russia and do not include China. Russia also wants the SCO to focus on working together on security and strategic problems, while China wants it to focus on working together on economic issues. China thinks that Russia doesn't do much to work with China in the SCO but doesn't stop Chinese initiatives either. There have also been disagreements about adding more members. One Chinese analyst says that Moscow has apparently backed Iran, India, and Pakistan joining the SCO. However, China doesn't want this to happen because it would take attention away from Central Asia and make the SCO more anti-Western, which is something China doesn't want. It's also hard for the SCO to carry out its cooperative deals, in part because Central Asian member states don't have the tools they need. Even though these things are different, the SCO is still an important organisation for building relationships between Beijing and Moscow.

Consequences for the United States

The US does not and should not try to stop Russia and China from getting along. Europe and Asia will be more stable if these two nuclear powers can get along. In the 1960s and 1970s, China and the Soviet Union were very close to going to war. That time was very dangerous. The US also thinks that better relations between Russia and China are good for many US goals. For instance, if Russia and China work together on energy issues, China may become less reliant on oil from Iran over time, which could weaken its ties with Iran's government. Working together with Russia and China is good for growing Central Asia and keeping the area from being dominated by one country. Russia and China may also need to work together more to help stabilise Afghanistan after the US leaves.

There is, however, a competitive side to the relationship between the US, Russia, and China, with each side using different hedging tactics. Even though a lot of what Beijing says says otherwise, one expert in Beijing made it clear that the US's shift towards China is not a containment strategy but a hedging strategy. In the same way, China is protecting itself from the US by having a good relationship with Russia. Russia protects itself from both China and the West. Each country is afraid that the other two will get too close, though the US may be less likely to be affected by this fear than China or Russia. For instance, Russia is highly against the idea of a G2 between the US and China because it would keep Russia from having a say in how the world works. Most multilateral platforms, like the G8 and BRICS meetings, show that Russia is not as important as other, stronger countries. In the same way, China is afraid about the possibility of Russia becoming closer to NATO. In particular, China does not want Russia and NATO to work together on missile defence. However, China does not want the US to think that it has joined forces with Russia in a way that would be harmful to US interests. In the same way, Russia looks to the West for progress and growth. It doesn't want a relationship with China that would cut it off from the US or Europe.

What is the best way for the US to handle this foreign policy triangle? First, it needs to understand how this triangle works and think about how decisions about problems that are important to either Russia or China affect the triangle.

When the US backs policies that China and Russia don't agree with or promises to back policies that are aimed at China or Russia, it brings those two countries closer together. This doesn't mean that the US can't disagree with Russia and China on any issue, but it does mean that the US needs to be aware that Russia and China will work together more on problems of world order. Syria is one case in point. Some people think that the US's choice not to attack Syria with armed force was the right thing to do from a Middle East policy point of view. Still, the choice to make peace with Russia did solve a world order problem that was making Russia and China more like each other and less like the US. One more example is the war in Ukraine. China and Russia now have better economic ties thanks to new economic sanctions from the West against Russia. When making decisions about regional policies, policymakers should look at them from both a local and a global point of view.

Second, Russia wants to be a major player in the Asia-Pacific area again. In the past, the US has wanted to make sure that no one country controls the area. Once the Ukrainian crisis is over, it might be good for the US for Russia to play a bigger part in Pacific affairs, which would be helped by the RFE doing better. Because of this, the US should work for better ties between Japan and Russia and between South Korea and Russia in the long term. This means pushing for Russia to send more energy to South Korea and Japan and for Japan and Russia to end their disagreement over the Kurile Islands. If it makes financial sense, the US should offer benefits for US companies to invest in the RFE. Russia and the US Pacific Command have talked to each other through port calls and Russian involvement in RIM-PAC exercises. However, more could be done to improve military-to-military cooperation.

Third, it might be time to get three-way nuclear talks going soon. China has always kept a small nuclear arsenal, and the exact number of these weapons is a closely guarded secret. They say that the US and Russia need to significantly lower their forces before China will talk about arms control. But both the US and Russia have lowered the number of nuclear bombs they have on hand, while China has likely been building more weapons. As a result, Alexi Arbatov and Vladimir Dvorkin say, "It is possible that China's reasons for keeping its nuclear forces secret are not because they are "weak" or "small," but because China's real nuclear arsenal is much stronger than what can be seen from the weapons it has on display." Plus, China has the economic and technological power to quickly build up its nuclear arsenal. This is more of a threat to Russia than to the US because Russia relies more on nuclear weapons to protect itself. So, it might be time to finally push for trilateral talks on arms control, even though there are still big problems with that right now. There are new problems between the US and Russia, China is still keeping its nuclear arsenal and policy secret, and China wants both Russia and the US to disarm even more before it will start real talks about reducing its nuclear arsenal.

Fourth, the US leaving Afghanistan makes it possible for three countries to work together to make Afghanistan and all of Central Asia safer. Russia and China both said they didn't like that the US had troops in Afghanistan, but now they are afraid of what will happen if the US pulls out. China doesn't think it has the tools to deal with Afghanistan, and a lot of Chinese experts think the Afghan government will fall when the US pulls its combat troops out in 2014. China is very worried about the security of its own country and what a possible state of chaos in Afghanistan could mean for what it sees as its Uyghur problem. So, it is clear that all three countries want Afghanistan to have a strong government after 2014 so that violence stays low in Afghanistan and terrorism and terror don't spread outside the country's borders. The United States, Russia, China, and maybe even the SCO can work together to make policies that will help all of these countries. So, the fight in Afghanistan and the areas around it is between organised states and nonstate players, and the states have reasons to work together.

To sum up, the friendship between China and Russia is strong and has been getting stronger for almost twenty years. Russia and China want to see a world order based on classical Westphalian values instead of liberal ideas that question the value of state sovereignty. They also want to see the SCO grow and work together on economics, energy, security, and issues affecting Central Asia. Still, this is not a union against the US. In order to reach their own growth goals, Russia and China need the US and Europe. China thinks that its progress in development is fragile and that unrest at home is a threat, while Russia hasn't been able to significantly grow its economy beyond energy production. Russia and China can work together in some ways that are good for the US. Also, each of the issues this chapter talks about has places where people disagree. China's power will keep growing compared to Russia's over time. This will make these clashes worse because Moscow doesn't want to be seen as Beijing's junior partner. With smart policies, Washington can use the strategic triangle to protect its most important interests.

Chapter 3
Collaboration Between Russia and China in Multilateral Organizations

A Tactical or a Strategic Partnership?

Several writers have talked about the idea of a strategic alliance between Russia and China for a number of years. Some have called this growing relationship the "dragon bear." This alliance is part of a number of regional groups that meet to talk about security and, increasingly, business cooperation. It can also be seen more and more around the world. Cooperation in multilateral forums and foreign organisations is one thing that needs more attention.

When people talk about how the way Russia and China work together in international organisations affects them, they often talk about how they work together in the UN Security Council. But it's worth taking a closer look at other multilateral meetings, especially the ones in Geneva, where you can see how some interesting trends have changed over the years. This article will look at how both countries work together, especially in the UN Human Rights Council (UNHRC), the World Health Organisation (WHO), the World Trade Organisation (WTO), and Geneva-based Standard Development Organisations (SDOs) like the International Telecommunication Union (ITU). It won't look at how Russia and China have worked together in the past, nor will it look at how they vote and where they sit on the UN Security Council, which would probably be a good topic for a separate piece. Instead, this analysis will look at the two countries' current goals and how they try to change things in some of the most important multilateral forums in Geneva. It will also look at what the two countries have in common and what makes them different. After that, it will focus on some key areas of cooperation and answer the question of whether or not Russia-China cooperation in these platforms is more tactical (defensive) cooperation or a strategic alliance to (re)define the norms of multilateral cooperation. At the end of the chapter, ideas will be made for how the West can deal with the challenge.

Agendas, Shared Features, and Disparities

The Focus Areas of Russia and China in Geneva Forums

Russia and China are both regular members of the UN Security Council, so it goes without saying that they are big players in the multilateral bodies in Geneva. People also think that multilateral organisations are good places to raise one's standing on the international stage. It is also an important place to get (positive) "social markers" to improve the legitimacy or standing of a country. So, the goal is to get praise for what you do at home and in your foreign policies and avoid criticism. Russia and China may use similar tools to reach this goal, but when they focus on Geneva-based forums, they have shown that their goals are different.

Organisations that have to do with security policy are still very important for Russia. Also, the United Nations Office at Geneva (UNOG) is seen as important and prestigious. Moscow thought it was important that Tatiana Valovaya, a Russian citizen, was named director general of UNOG in 2019. From Russia's point of view, Geneva is also an important place for mediating conflicts, where a lot of background talks happen about situations where Russia is a major player. One example is Russia's participation in the Syrian Constitutional Committee, which hasn't led to any results. This way of thinking about security also works for other international forums: Russia is a big part of the International Telecommunication Union (ITU) because it thinks that internet security is part of the ITU's job.

China's geopolitical and economic interests strongly shape its priorities, and the Belt and Road Initiative is often a good way to look at them. This is why China pays so much attention to SDOs in Geneva, such as the ITU, the International Organisation for Standardisation (ISO), and other forums. People think that building the groundwork for future global economic leadership means having a strong voice in setting technical and digital standards and norms. This is also true for organisations that work on infrastructure and other economic bodies like the UN Economic Commission for Europe (UNECE).

Even though both countries joined the WTO late, they have different weights in the organisation. China is an important member of the group. It has used the WTO's conflict resolution system more often and has also joined 18 other WTO members in a system of interim arbitration. Russia doesn't belong to as many WTO groups as China does. China's tools for influencing the world are more economic than Russia's, which may explain why it participates more in international economic forums. Neither country has a full market economy; instead, they use a state-capitalist model. This makes them ideal allies whenever there are calls for new and stricter rules on state subsidies. Even though many differences in the WTO have nothing to do with US-China hostility, China has often been seen as an enemy of the US and the West. China's strategy on hiring and firing shows how important the WTO is to them: keeping one of the deputy director general positions is seen as very important for China.

China has been more involved in global health over the past few years, especially in the WHO, where it is seen as a key player and where its impact has grown a lot. This is in addition to its involvement in organisations that work on economic development and trade.

The UN Human Rights Council is a very important group for both countries because it is where they try to answer criticisms of their human rights records. The fact that both countries are always members of the UNHRC shows how important it is to them. China has been a member of the HRC for 12 of the 15 years since it was founded. Russia has been a member for 9 of those years. Each country can only be a member for a total of two 3-year terms in a row.

China is working with a number of groups to make it harder for Taiwan to get help from other countries. Even though this isn't possible in all Geneva-based organisations (Taiwan is a member of the WTO, where it is called the Separate Customs Territory of Taiwan, Penghu, Kinmen, and Matsu [Chinese Taipei]), it has stopped Taiwan from joining the World Health Assembly, even as an observer, for the past few years.

Migration and humanitarian issues get less notice, which I find interesting. For example, neither the UN Refugee Agency (UNHCR) nor the United Nations Office for the Coordination of Humanitarian Affairs (UNOCHA) seem to be a concern for China or Russia. This is shown by how little money they put into both organisations: About 900 times more money came from the US than from China to the UNHCR. In 2021, neither country was one of the top ten donors to UNOCHA. The same is true for the International Committee of the Red Cross (ICRC), where neither Russia nor China are among the top 23 donors.

When it comes to humanitarian or migration policy, the differences in financial involvement are very clear. However, in many other international organisations, neither Russia nor China's financial contributions even come close to the impact that the US, Germany, the UK, or the EU as a whole have on those organisations. Even though China's contributions to the UN and a few other foreign organisations have grown a lot over the past few years, it is still a long way behind the countries above in many UN agencies.

Disputing the Narrative

As seen in the joint statement by Russian Foreign Minister Sergey Lavrov and his Chinese counterpart Wang Yi, both sides want to tell a different story about democracy, human rights, and international law. The goal is to change the "hegemony" of the Western view of human rights and democracy, as well as the role of international organisations. Both sides also say, "We noted the growing importance of Russia, China, and a wide range of other countries working together to keep the current system of international law in place, especially as the West tries more and more to promote its idea of a rules-based international order."

Since the US left some multilateral forums, like the UN Human Rights Council (UNHRC), it has given China more confidence. As a result, China has stepped up its efforts in recent years, especially in the UNHRC, to change the way people talk about human rights so that they focus less on individual rights and more on collective rights. This new way of talking also puts a lot of stress on a human rights dialogue that focuses on the state and the respect of state sovereignty. Lastly, the speech talks about how the right to growth and the fight against poverty are important parts of human rights. All three of these things are seen as moves to weaken the way the UN usually talks about human rights. In the past, China has often put forward a motion on "mutually beneficial cooperation in the field of human rights" in order to reach this goal. The title of a resolution may seem innocent, but it hides parts that would change the way most people think about human rights. When the resolution was first brought up in 2018, it had wide support. Since then, opinions have become more divided, but that hasn't stopped the resolution from being passed. So, China has taken a much more active role in shaping and promoting a different way of talking in international organisations, instead of just criticising rules or methods it doesn't like.

Russia's efforts to change the story and normative discourse have been less obvious than China's. However, Russia's speech in the ITU tries to get global approval for highly controversial practises by "disguising" them with words like "information security." Referring to the value of rules "in the field of information security" is often seen as an attempt to go after all actions that could make states less stable, including free speech.

Tactical Workforce Strategy

Russia and China use personnel strategy as a major tool in their work with international groups. Overall personnel strategy can be done on three levels: promoting the placement of junior staff in UN organisations, securing key roles in UN organisations, and making sure that diplomatic staff rotates between major UN locations. Over the last few years, China has used the UN's Junior Professional Office (JPO) programme more and more to get young workers to join UN organisations. Both countries, like other big players, have shown that they want to put their own people in key UN positions. For Russia, it was Tatiana Valovaya's successful campaign for the UNOG. In 2021, Russia also put forward a candidate to replace the current secretary general of the ITU. China has four of the 15 secretary general or director general positions in specialised UN agencies, and it has tried to get the job of director general of the World Intellectual Property Organisation (WIPO) in 2020. Lastly, especially compared to other countries, China and Russia tend to hire UN staff at their missions who are experts in UN affairs and who only move between UN locations (and the appropriate ministerial unit at home) and don't work anywhere else. The effect of this should not be understated: it takes time to get used to the often very technical discussions in the UN and its related bodies. Half of the writing is over by the time the diplomatic staff not only understands what is being talked about but also has strong things to say. Not only in technical UN bodies, but also in the UN Human Rights Council, it can be very helpful to have people who are very experienced and know a lot about how things work.

Experts and people who spend a lot of time in Geneva often say that China's power at the UN has grown a lot in recent years. Some people have even said that, despite all the work Russia has done over the past few decades, it has never had as much political power in Geneva as China does now. Diplomats think that Russia's approach to some UN meetings is both confrontational and defensive. China, on the other hand, has tried to go further and more actively try to change the story in some policy areas. Russia's partial isolation in a number of places will make China's role as boss of the autocratic alliance even stronger.

Collaboration of Russia and China in Geneva Forum

An in-depth look at how Russia and China work together in each Geneva-based UN agency would be outside the scope of this study. But there are four things that can be pointed out. As was already said, both sides often work together to dismiss complaints of their policies in UN forums. China is usually the main force behind efforts to change the way things are told in UN organisations, while Russia backs these ideas. Both sides work together to stop foreign bodies from changing. Last but not least, Russia and China have behaved as "authoritarian gravity centres" in multilateral bodies, forming the core of countries that protect other authoritarian regimes from criticism and argue for a state-centered "dog doesn't eat dog" approach.

Reaction to Criticism

Russia and China often work together to answer critics of their domestic and international policies. The UNHRC is the place in Geneva where this is most clear. Both Russia and China were elected to the Council from 2021 to 2023, and the first session of the Human Rights Council in 2021 shows that they will work closely together. Of the 30 resolutions passed in February and March 2021, 15 were controversial votes, and Russia and China voted the same way in all of them. Both countries successfully pushed for a resolution that criticised the effects of sanctions. The resolution was passed by a vote of 30 to 15, with two countries not voting and all African countries voting in favour. China was also one of the few countries that agreed with Russia's move to end the Human Rights Council session because one special rapporteur didn't turn in his report on time (see Figure 3.1).

Both have also usually been on the same side when they have made a joint statement. For example, in July 2020 and 2021, Russia backed joint comments made by Belarus that were very critical of people who criticise China's policies in Xinjiang. Figure 2 shows how many people accept the plan as a whole. When Russia was criticised for its aggressive actions against Ukraine, China would either back Russia or do nothing.

Shaping Narratives

Cooperation isn't just a way to defend against international criticism; in some cases, it also leads to the promotion of a shared goal and set of stories. In 2021, Russia backed the Chinese position on "mutually beneficial cooperation" at the UN Human Rights Council. This is a resolution that supports a different, more state-centered, and collective view of human rights.

With the US's return to the UN Human Rights Council, China and Russia have joined forces to attack not only the US, but also other Western countries in general, accusing them of meddling too much in their own matters and using two different sets of rules to talk about what they say are human rights problems in Western countries. The most recent example was when China started a joint statement criticising Canada for "serious human rights violations against the indigenous people in Canada." This was right after Canada started a joint statement criticising China's policies in Xinjiang, Hong Kong, and Tibet. Both sides have used promoting government-organized non-governmental organisations (GONGOs) in NGOs-only meetings as another way to make it hard to tell what each side is saying about human rights. Several observers in the Geneva area say that this has made it harder for truly independent human rights NGOs to be heard.

Figure 3.1 Voting behavior regarding the proposed suspension of the UNHRC by Russia, Venezuela and China during the 46th UNHRC session, February/March 2021

Figure 3.2 Support within the UNHRC for Canadian and Belarussian joint statements exercising and dismissing criticism of Chinese human rights abuses, June/ July 2021

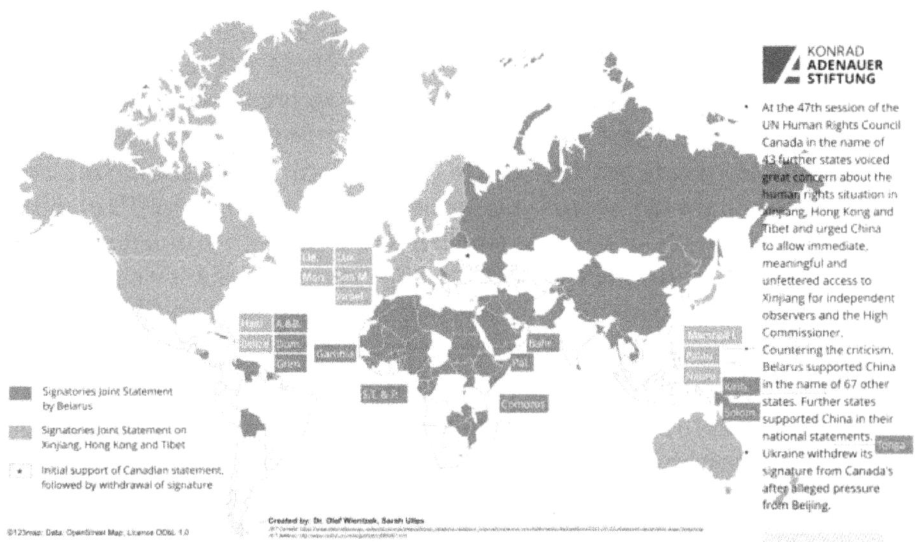

Figure 3.3 Voting behavior in the UNHRC on a Chinese resolution on the role of human rights in the UN system, February/March 2021

When it comes to talks about setting rules for digital technologies, Russia and China also seem to be on the same page. As a result, there is more and more cooperation in foreign organisations that set standards. This is true for things that are very sensitive, like the need to set global norms for facial recognition. China is pushing for global standards in this area, which the EU and Western countries strongly oppose for ethical reasons. China is pushing for global standards for facial recognition and surveillance technology, most recently in the ITU in 2020, to get global approval for certain practises that don't fit well with the right to privacy and can lead to discriminatory practises. On the other hand, Russia wants to talk about cyber security issues as part of the ITU mandate, which some people see as a way to limit freedom of speech in online platforms. In general, China agrees with Russia's positions in the ITU, but it would be hard to call this a full-fledged strategic partnership. While Russian officials pay a lot of attention to cybersecurity, Chinese experts prefer to talk about artificial intelligence and new intellectual property rights at these meetings.

When it comes to policy about people, Russia and China work together. One example is the new talk about who should take over as the ITU's next director general. Rashid Ismaylov, the Russian candidate to replace Chinese national Houlin Zhao, can probably count on China's backing, even though his chances of being elected have gotten much worse since Russia attacked Ukraine. Observers think that the choice of the next option is important for how the organisation that sets standards will move forward in the future.

But a recent example shows that cooperation doesn't always work: in 2021, both countries opposed the nomination of the Ambassador of Fiji, Nazhat Shameem Khan, as the new chair for the UN Human Rights Council, because she was known for having a strong and outspoken position on human rights violations. In a similar way, the fact that China lost the race for the post of director general of the WIPO to a candidate from Singapore with a fairly clear vote in the last round in 2020 shows the limits of the Chinese-Russian union on personnel policy. In some cases, open backing from China or Russia could even be seen as harmful. This may be one reason why China was very careful not to say who it wanted to be the next director general of the WTO and the ILO when they were looking for a replacement. China's support for WHO Director General Dr. Tedros was important for his election in 2017. However, this support has become a problem during the COVID crisis, as some countries have accused him of being too easy on China after the COVID-19 outbreak. In the spring of 2022, the limits of the partnership became clear when resolutions were passed in both the UNGA and the UNHRC condemning Russia's attack on Ukraine. Russia was kicked off the UNHRC against the wishes of both Russia and China. In the same way, the ILO chose to work less with Russia.

Stance on Reform

Both countries have similar views on how the UN should be changed. They both support an approach that puts an emphasis on state authority and is wary of putting in place monitoring or even punishment systems. This can be seen in the ongoing discussions about the reform of the WHO: both countries have resisted calls from other countries to make the WHO more politically independent or to change the International Health Regulations, and neither is in favour of stronger external scrutiny during outbreaks, as suggested by some reform proposals, let alone mandatory and immediate access for outside observers or punishments for non-compliance. Observers also worry that if the UN Human Rights Council is reformed, Russia and China might work together to try to lower the standards that are already in place.

Beacons of the Autocratic Alliance

In multilateral groups, Russia and, especially, China have also played the role of "authoritarian gravity centres." Overall, China has been the main focus and has done a lot more to bring people together. This can be seen in a number of places, such as the Human Rights Council, WHO, and the SDOs based in Geneva. Pakistan, a country with which China has deep economic (China-Pakistan Economic Corridor), political (joint containment of India), and military ties, has been one of China's most important allies in a number of places. With Islamabad's help, resolutions in the UNHRC that were critical of China's policies in Xinjiang were avoided.

Russia and China have both stood by dictatorships like Cuba and Venezuela, as well as Eritrea and other authoritarian states like Egypt, Cameroon, and Belarus. Several decisions at the UN Human Rights Council's last meeting show that China and Russia are at the centre of the "autocratic alliance" in the UNHRC. Figure 4 shows which countries' votes in the UNHRC in 2019 were most in line with China's.

Recently, Svitlana Tsikhanouskaya, the leader of the opposition and a presidential candidate in Belarus, made a virtual appearance at an important debate on Belarus. This was an example of how dictators support each other. The people from China and Russia tried to stop the discussion by speaking up over and over again.

China and Russia also protect the terrible human rights records of authoritarian states, such as Syria, Saudi Arabia, and Belarus. They do this by regularly ignoring criticism of these countries. During talks on resolutions about Belarus, both Russia and China often put forward a lot of changes to make the language less harsh. Several cases have shown that protecting other autocratic or semi-democratic states from criticism leads to a "unvirtuous cycle," which means that the countries in question become more loyal to Russia or China, in particular. In response, the countries involved make joint comments that say criticism of China is unfounded. Cuba, Venezuela, Belarus, or Cameroon usually put forward statements or votes on behalf of China. In the same way, China is able to use the support of countries with which it has close economic ties to change how people vote, sometimes even weakening the camp of countries in the West that are in theory on the same side. Joint comments from the UN Human Rights Council show how much support there is, or how little support there is. Many Central and Eastern European countries that are part of the 17+1 plan chose not to sign a joint statement that was critical of China's policies in Xinjiang and Hong Kong in 2020. This statement was started by the UK.

Even though it has had some important wins, the "autocratic alliance" on the UN Human Rights Council is often on the losing side and can't count on backing for its own ideas. So that its resolution wouldn't be voted down at the last Human Rights Council meeting of 2020, China pulled back a resolution about how human rights should be interpreted and defined when it wasn't sure it had enough votes.

Figure 3.4 Percentage of alignment with Chinese voting behavior in disputed resolutions in the UNHRC during 2019

China, with help from Russia, has tried to change the way things are told, especially in the area of human rights. It is interesting, though, that both sides rarely come up with real multilateral plans. So, it is surprising that, for example, in the COVID-19 crisis, both sides used vaccine diplomacy a lot, but China and Russia only play a minor part or none at all in the ACT Accelerator or the COVAX initiative, which are both important examples of ad hoc multilateral instruments. In speeches, China has often talked about how important multilateral solutions are. However, both countries have shown that they prefer bilateral support, which lets them find and reward "reliable allies."

Cooperation between Russia and China is not enough for either country to be successful in foreign settings, though. The results are mixed as a whole.

But a number of reasons favor the effect of the Chinese-Russian cooperation.

a. West fatigue: among many (particularly developing) countries, one can sometimes detect a certain "West fatigue" and the perception of a disproportionate role Western countries play in multilateral forums not only financially, but also in shaping narratives. China—with partial success, particularly in the WTO, but also in the WHO and in the UN Human Rights Council—has managed to portray itself as an advocate for developing countries and has at times successfully managed to rally the African group or the Organisation of Islamic Cooperation (OIC) to its side. This is facilitated somewhat by the membership of China in the G77. Russia seems to benefit from this effect to a lesser extent, although in some cases the G77 have supported Russian candidacies in multilateral forums.

b. A slow West: in several cases—be it on personnel questions or on substance— Western countries were either not united, managed to unite too late or did not manage to build alliances quickly enough beyond their own camp. The election of the director general to the Food and Agriculture Organization (FAO), during which Western disunity resulted in the election of a candidate from China, is just one example. Similarly, complaints about the lengthy internal EU coordination process—which leaves little time to acquire further allies aside from the "usual suspects"—can be heard in Geneva.

c. A lack of willingness of many states to challenge China or Russia for fear of repercussions. The relatively timid (and regularly unsuccessful) support for Taiwan's participation at the World Health Assembly seems to simply be a recognition of the fact that crossing blades with China in multilateral forums is simply not worth the fight. Even EU countries prefer not to position themselves too clearly on the side of Taiwan. Usually only the US, sometimes Canada and Australia as well as a dozen countries that recognize Taiwan, argue decisively for the inclusion of Taiwan in the WHA.

The influence of Russia's and China's cooperation has, however, also shown its limits for several reasons:

a. Good knowledge of procedures and instruments, the ability to build alliances and leveraging economic and political influence are important, but the (still) relatively small financial footprint in multilateral arenas in Geneva somewhat limits the impact and—this should not be underestimated—the credibility of the commitment of Moscow and Beijing to multilateral organizations. There continues to be a stark discrepancy between strongly-worded commitments to multilateral solutions and the absence of financial support for truly global initiatives.

b. In most cases, the cooperation had a primarily defensive character: dismissing criticism, and avoiding reform of multilateral organizations. However, only in a few cases did China and/or Russia manage to bring forward constructive proposals or initiatives to address global challenges. For example, during the COVID-19 crisis, most of the initiatives to combat the pandemic on a multilateral level were initiated by Western or Latin American countries—and not by China or Russia. The joint attempts to redefine narratives, particularly on human rights, are notable and should not be underestimated, but are not part of a strategy that covers all organizations.

c. While a sizable number of countries may sympathize with Russia or China, both countries fail to gather majorities for their positions among the countries that may not belong to the Western camp but are not autocracies either.

d. Disillusionment: Among at least some states, there is a certain disillusionment as to China's intentions. The pressure China exerted on Ukraine following its support for a critical joint statement on China's policy in Xinjiang and Hong Kong during the UN Human Rights Council in June 2021 served as another eye-opener that help from China does not usually come without a price tag. This was also mirrored by the weakening support for China's candidacy for the UN Human Rights Council. This is even more true for Russia since February 2022: Several states from Africa, Asia or Latin America that usually tend to abstain on country resolutions or controversial issues, strongly condemned Russia's actions in Ukraine.

Overall, the relationship between Russia and China doesn't seem to be a full-fledged, coordinated strategic alliance with a unified vision applied across multilateral groups. Instead, it seems to be more of a tactical alliance that is becoming more regular.

Choices for Western Nations

The West faces a task when China and Russia work together in UN forums. Even though both countries are needed as important partners to deal with world problems like climate change and disarmament, they both have a very different view of multilateralism that is very different from the way the West sees it. This isn't just about the UN Human Rights Council; it's also about what international organisations should do. By breaking the normative hegemony of the West on the values and rules of multilateralism, China and Russia are trying to reduce Western power in general and in countries they see as their zones of influence in particular.

This should be one of the West's biggest worries: if China and Russia decide on morals and standards, it will hurt the West's political and economic power. Two examples: If IT standards are set by China instead of the West, it will hurt companies because the rules will be based on what Chinese businesses need and not on a non-market economy model. Also, being able to talk about a "ITU standard" is already a key way to get into third-world markets. If China and Russia change how people around the world think about human rights, this could make people question some values at home in the long run. But liberal societies do have ways to deal with this:

Enhanced Participation in Multilateral Forums

Because they don't seem to be able to change or deal with the problems of a changing global environment, the US and some Western think tanks are talking more and more about alternatives to the UN Human Rights Council, the WHO, and the WTO. In the present situation, these thoughts are kind of understandable, but they still don't make sense. Even though the US left the Human Rights Council in 2018, for the vast majority of states, this did not make the organisation less legitimate. In fact, it just made China take a stronger stand. So, to stop China and Russia from having too much power, Germany, Europe, and the West as a whole need to get more involved in these organisations, even though they aren't perfect and have their own views.

Stronger involvement should also be looked at in terms of how much it costs. China and Russia may not give enough to some of the organisations in Geneva, but especially China's donations have been going up. If, on the other hand, Western countries decide to cut back on their donations, it will hurt these organisations' ability to do their jobs and make them more open to authoritarian control. As outlined in the Franco-German WHO reform paper in August 2020, it is a step in the right direction for the EU and, especially, Germany to invest more money and push for a rise in assessed contributions. This will give the organisation more political independence. Recent cuts to the UK's payments are a more worrying sign, since the UK is one of the UN's most important countries in a number of policy areas.

Investing more money in these groups doesn't mean you have to ignore the problems they have. Instead, what would be needed is a "tough love" method that ensures political and financial engagement while also pushing harder for change. In this situation, it will be important to agree on common proposals. For example, there are many plans to change the WHO, but the push for reform will be more likely to succeed if countries with similar goals can agree on a single plan.

Initiatives like the "Alliance for Multilateralism" (started by France and Germany) or a future "Alliance of Democracies" (suggested by US vice president Joe Biden) can help with this goal if they can bring together countries with similar goals, work in tandem with these forums, or push for change in these UN groups. For these initiatives to reach their higher goals (stated in joint general statements), they would need a clear set of criteria for who can join and who can't, as well as a shared view of the rules and values of multilateral cooperation in the future.

Russia and China's desire for bilateral support, which produces not only economic but also political dependencies, could be countered by strong multilateral bodies and projects that can actually get things done.

Optimized Workforce Policy

Some painful examples from the past few years have shown that Europe and the West as a whole will need to move faster, be more strategic, and work together better when it comes to personnel policies. There should be a clearer joint policy, not just among EU countries but also with key allies with similar views, like the UK, Canada, Australia, Japan, Ukraine, New Zealand, and the US, whose positions are seen as very important. More importantly, building alliances with other groups (like the African Group, countries from Latin America, and Southeast Asian countries) is very important if you don't want key positions where norms are set to be held by people from countries like Russia or China that want to change policy and talk the way they do. The fact that the campaign for the WIPO Secretary General election in 2020 was able to bring together partners with similar goals, including but not limited to Western countries, should be seen as a good thing. The next problem will be the ITU polls, where a candidate from the US is running against a candidate from Russia. Aside from the top positions, it will be important to help and urge one's own diplomatic staff to get jobs in international organisations. It might also be important to think about changing the policy for sending staff to permanent missions, giving more weight to people who have already done useful work in multilateral or regional forums.

Forging Alliances

Since most organisations are based on the idea that "one country, one vote," it is important to make relationships with people outside of your comfort zone or group of people who think like you. Neither the authoritarian union nor Western countries with similar views have a majority on their own in multilateral groups. This is especially true of the African Group, which is very well organised on many issues and is often the key to making majorities or at least putting more pressure on countries that are blocking progress. Authoritarian players' power can be limited in a big way by reaching out more to the African Group or other countries in Asia or Latin America that are similar to them. This will also mean giving up some long-held beliefs, though. Some of these agreements will hurt, but getting to the "neutral middle" is important if they don't want to be pushed into the arms of Russia and China. Even touchy topics like agriculture or health problems that are controversial around the world shouldn't be off-limits in this context. If they were, China or Russia couldn't pose as the defender of the developing countries. Even though a large number of African countries agreed that Russia should be kicked out of the UNHRC, this should not be taken for granted. Some African officials' claims that Western countries have different rules for different people should not be taken lightly.

Exemplifying Leadership

Important pillars include personnel policies and building alliances, but the most important thing will be to not only talk the talk, but also walk the walk in each organisation. To (re-)gain credibility and in many cases support, it will be important to back efforts to improve the global public good, such as the COVAX project, humanitarian efforts, and practical steps to make it easier for developing countries to take part in global trade. Russia and China, as was clear at the last UN Human Rights Council, like to point out the West's flaws and lack of solidarity, whether they are racist incidents in the US or alleged serious human rights violations against indigenous people in Canada. Even though many, if not most, of these accusations can and should be seen as (sometimes rather crude) attempts at "what a boutism," this doesn't mean that the West shouldn't try to follow the highest standards and work as closely as possible with the UN Human Rights Council's different representatives and instruments.

If the West is not united and loses the chance to build strategic alliances with countries other than the "usual allies," the effects of Chinese and Russian cooperation in multilateral forums will grow and may, in the long run, change the way multilateralism works. Aside from the change in norms, this would have a big impact on what Germany, the EU, and the West as a whole want most.

Chapter 4
Sino-Russian Connections in Central, Eastern and South-Eastern Europe

In recent years, the relationship between China and Russia has become the biggest threat to the rules-based international order that came after the Cold War. This story says that the problem isn't just China's rise or Russia's comeback, but a rising strategic convergence: a "axis of authoritarians" that helps each other. It has become normal to talk about forming a group. The "comprehensive strategic partnership of coordination for a new era" between China and Russia has become the most dangerous thing in the world. This feeling of worry has been made worse by the tense situation in the world, which is ruled by rivalry between the world's biggest countries and the terrible effects of the COVID-19 pandemic.

One area, on the other hand, hasn't been talked about as much. Central and Eastern Europe (CEE) is still a backwater in the relationship between China and Russia, so Western responses have been low-key. Still, the area is a good way to see how the relationship works.

a. It highlights the extent to which Beijing and Moscow pursue their own foreign policy agendas. The usual self-serving rhetoric about partnership is absent. Here, more than anywhere else, it is all about individual national interests.

b. In the longer term, greater Chinese activity in Central and Eastern Europe could expose latent tensions in the partnership, given Russia's perception of the region as a sphere of special interests.

But so far, there doesn't seem to be much trouble between them. Russia and China have come to an unspoken agreement about how to get along. Their relationship isn't about working together or competing with each other. Instead, it's about putting things in their own boxes and giving each other space. It helps that the area isn't very important to Beijing, and Moscow doesn't feel threatened by how much China is doing there. For both sides, success is mostly measured by how well they avoid bad things.

The Framework of Strategy

The relationship between China and Russia is one of the most interesting things to happen after the Cold War. Beijing and Moscow have gotten past ages of distrust, imperial hangovers, national humiliations, and big differences in culture to work together in a way that has never been seen before. Their partnership has many different parts. They have close political and institutional ties, are working together more on defence and security, agree on many international problems, and have different but complementary economies.

But the partnership is also a classic one between two independent great powers, each with its own ideas, objectives, and goals. It is not based on love, principles, or even trust. Instead, it is based on what happens. Both sides see big political, security, military, economic, technological, and technological benefits from working together. This helps them get the most out of the gains, keep their goals in check, and get over differences.

Russia and China agree on a number of important ideas: the United States' "unilateralism" is not acceptable, great powers have a special place in the world, the Security Council of the United Nations is the most important group for making decisions about world affairs, and state autonomy will always be important. They agree on a "sovereign internet," don't want "interference" from the West in their own business, and don't want to be punished. They have solved any problems that could have come up between them, such as the Belt and Road Initiative (BRI) of Chinese President Xi Jinping being expanded into Central Asia and China becoming more interested in the Arctic. There is also a change in how they talk to the people.

So, many Western policymakers think that Russia and China are working together for a bad reason, which adds to the dangers they each pose to Western interests and ideals. But things aren't that simple in real life. We don't understand what makes them different and how fiercely they protect their strategic independence and room to move. We also think too much about how much their relationship is based on the West.

China plays by the rules. It is a revisionist power, but its changes are small and not all at once. It also tends to be less strategic and more opportunistic. Far from trying to create a new authoritarian world, it uses the strengths and weaknesses of the current order to its benefit, taking advantage of global and regional trade, investment, norms, and institutions to make money. Beijing knows that a stable outside world is important for China's economic growth and the security of the government.

Russia is a disrupter of systems. From the Kremlin's point of view, the U.S.-led post-Cold War order destroyed Russia's economic and geopolitical interests in the 1990s. Today, President Vladimir Putin not only thinks that liberalism is out of date, but he also thinks that the liberal international order should fall apart quickly to make way for a Concert of Great Powers in the twenty-first century. In the meantime, he has shown that he is willing to use force to help Russia. Instability around the world is good for Moscow. The more chaos there is, the more opportunities Russia has to change things.

These gaps in how Beijing and Moscow see the world are not too big of a deal. But they make it harder for them to work together strategically. Every big foreign policy move China or Russia has made in recent years has been done on its own. Before sending troops into Georgia (2008), Ukraine (2014), or Syria (2015), Putin did not tell or even talk to the Chinese. The actions of the Chinese People's Liberation Army (PLA) Navy in the South China Sea, Beijing's growing hostility towards Taiwan, and "foreign influence" operations are also seen as China's business. Xi started the BRI in Astana, Kazakhstan, in 2013 without even getting permission from Moscow. The 2015 agreement between the Silk Road Economic Belt (SREB) and the Eurasian Economic Union (EAEU), which is run by Russia, was the first time Beijing tried to make Russia happy. Even now, Russia's actual participation in the BRI is not very big. Beijing looks out for Chinese interests, not those of some made-up group.

The CEE Region in the Foreign Policy Outlooks of Russia and China

Central and Eastern Europe is not a single place in terms of geography or politics. It includes Central Europe, the Baltic states, the countries of the Eastern Partnership, and the Balkans. Neither Russia nor China has a single plan for the area as a whole. The countries are all different in terms of how important they are and how much policy attention they get.

Still, Russia and China's policies are based on facts that won't change. Most of all, the CEE area is more important to Moscow. Some countries, like Ukraine and Belarus, are very important from a political, cultural, and moral point of view. Some, like the Baltic states and Poland, are right next to each other. Russia has also been connected to the Balkans for a long time through history, language, and religion. In a broader sense, the Kremlin sees a lot of the area as the front line of its long conflict with the West.

This has nothing to do with China. Beijing doesn't have a strong reason to spend a lot in Central and Eastern Europe's economy, politics, or security. The countries in the area are mostly important because they are a (secondary) way for China to get its goods and services to its main export markets in Western

Europe. Unlike Central Asia, Indochina, Africa, and Latin America, they don't have many important natural resources. Even if the BRI, which has had many setbacks so far, spread across the area, China would still be an outsider in every way except the economy. Even though Beijing's 17+1 framework has made a lot of fuss, it hasn't changed much in the real world. In fact, it has hurt Chinese interests by building up people's hopes and then letting them down.

The region isn't very important to China, so Beijing doesn't want to risk hurting the Sino-Russian relationship. This is especially true now, when China is facing increasing pressure on many fronts. Also, Russia's feelings are hurt more here than in Central Asia, which is at least in the same area. Because of these things, we need to be careful. For China's leaders, not upsetting the Kremlin is much more important than taking advantage of small business possibilities.

So, there isn't much communication between China and Russia in the area. There's no other place where their strategic partnership is more official than here. Each side does its own (not very interesting) thing with almost no mention of the other. In 2015 and 2017, Chinese ships took part with the Russian navy in combat drills in the Mediterranean Sea and the Baltic Sea. But other than that, most defence cooperation has been focused on Asia. Beijing's lack of support for Moscow's annexation of Crimea and de facto occupation of the Donbass, as well as its general refusal to attack the EU and NATO, are both striking. Keeping a low profile helps China keep its choices open with the West and keep Russia on its side.

The Unusual Group: Serbia, Hungary, Belarus, and Ukraine

Two things stand out for Serbia, Hungary, Belarus, and Ukraine. The first is imbalance. They care a lot more about their ties with China than Beijing does. Second, events and how the Russian and Chinese media report on them don't show much or any sign of conflict between the two outside powers.

Serbia is the best place to see how China has affected the CEE area. In 2008, there was a global financial crisis that made the country need more help from other countries and hurt the reputation of the European economic model. It also led to "enlargement fatigue," which made people less interested in joining the EU in the future. Western countries tend to think of the Western Balkans as a backwater, but China sees opportunities for logistics growth in this neglected and dangerous area.

China and Serbia have strong diplomatic ties, and Xi went there in 2016. China's most important goal in foreign relations is to get Serbia to stop not recognising Kosovo. Aleksandar Vucic, the president of Serbia, says that ties with Beijing are "iron" and that Xi is like his "brother." "Thank you, brother Xi" was written on billboards in Belgrade when Chinese help arrived at the start of the pandemic in 2020. The Comprehensive Strategic Partnership Agreement shows how close the two countries are to each other. There are many outward signs of close cooperation, like the Confucius Institutes in Belgrade and Novi Sad and the media collaboration agreement that allows for many exchanges and sharing of material. This makes it so that China looks very good in state-run television.

Vaccine diplomacy has shown the most clear signs of unity in recent years. Serbia, which was hit hard by the pandemic, was the first European country to accept Sinovac's coronavirus vaccine. It has gotten a million doses of the vaccine and has the second-fastest vaccine rollout in Europe. But technology and the business world have also been successful. Serbia is now a member of the "Digital Silk Road." There are two deals with the Chinese telecommunications company Huawei. One is for "smart cities" in Belgrade, Novi Sad, and Nis. The other is for high-speed internet and a regional data centre. Serbia is a place where Chinese spying technology can reach Europe.

Other notable projects in Serbia that involve Chinese investments include:

- The Smederevo steelworks , was purchased by China's state-run HBIS Group, or Hesteel Group, in 2016 for €46 million. It is now Serbia's largest exporter ;
- At least €800 million of planned investment in the Zrenjanin tire factory, €486 million in the Kostolac coal-fired power plant, and a €730 million investment in the Zijin Bor copper mine ; and
- The Pupin Bridge over the Danube River in Belgrade, which was constructed by China Road and Bridge Corporation (CRBC) with a €145 million loan and completed in 2014 .

China's sales of weapons to Serbia are also very important. China's first sale of military aviation equipment to Europe (CH-92A combat drones) included not only new weapons but also more basic knowledge and technology. This was a test to see if China should try to get into the European defence market in the future. In the Balkans, Serbia has become the country with the most drones. Serbia also agreed in August 2020 to buy the Chinese FK-3 anti-aircraft missile system instead of the Russian S-300 system.

Still, China's $4 billion in investments and $5 billion in loans and infrastructure projects add up to only 6.6% of all foreign direct investment (FDI), which puts it behind the EU (72.3%) and Russia (11.2%). Under the surface, things don't look as good.

- The Budapest-to-Belgrade high-speed rail line, announced in November 2013, is the flagship of the 17+1 and the BRI in Europe. But the €2.89 billion (original budget, now €4 billion), 350 km (220 mi) project is behind schedule and over budget .
- Under US pressure, Serbia apparently excluded Huawei from its 5G rollout .
- Chinese workers at the copper mine in Bor complain of slavery-like conditions; locals there, in Smederevo, and elsewhere complain about environmental damage.
- For all the fanfare over Chinese weapons sales, between 2008 and 2018 the United States was the largest provider of military hardware to Serbia .

After Kosovo declared independence on its own in 2008, links between Serbia and Russia got stronger. The Kremlin doesn't want the rest of the world to recognise Kosovo, and it also supports Bosnia's Republika Srpska, which is run by Serbs. Western intelligence thinks that the humanitarian emergencies centre in Nis is a base for espionage and special operations. This shows how close the two countries are. It is the only military-like building that Russia has in Europe outside of the old Soviet Union. Russia has given Serbia MiG-29 fighter planes, T-72 tanks, Mi-35 helicopter gunships, battle patrol vehicles, and the Pantsir air defence system. When these shipments go through the land of NATO countries, it causes diplomatic problems.

Energy is where Russia and Serbia work together the most. Gazprom Neft, a division of the Russian energy company Gazprom, bought a controlling stake in the Serbian oil and gas company Naftna Industrija Srbije (NIS) in 2008. The deal was worth more than $450 million, and Gazprom Neft promised to spend at least $600 million more in NIS. When it opens in January 2020, the Turkstream gas pipeline will make Serbia even more dependent on Russia, which sends two-thirds of the country's gas and oil.

In terms of building infrastructure, Russian Railways (RZD International) is helping to build the part of the Budapest-Belgrade line between Stara Pazova and Novi Sad.

Serbia's links to Russia, like those of other countries in the Western Balkans, are more practical and showy than based on deep loyalty or shared beliefs. There are a lot of irritants and bumps in the relationship, but the leaders of Serbia don't want to burn their bridges with Brussels or Washington. Relations with the Kremlin got much worse after Vucic went to the White House in September 2020. At the time, the Trump administration was trying to broker a deal between

Serbia and Kosovo but failed. A crude personal joke made by Foreign Ministry spokesman Maria Zakharova got a lot of attention, but it was just the latest turn in a downward trend that started three years ago. Earlier in 2020, the Serbian government used state propaganda to say that political turmoil was caused by Russian agents (since the nationalist opposition is very pro-Kremlin). They also stopped taking part in the annual "Slavic Brotherhood" military drills between Russia, Belarus, and Serbia.

For its part, Serbia doesn't have to choose between Moscow and Beijing. Instead, it uses both to counteract pressure from Brussels and Washington. China is more useful to Belgrade than the other one.

Hungary is the second most important example of how China has affected CEE.

Hungary's relationships with the West have gotten worse since 2010, when Viktor Orban was re-elected as prime minister. The European Commission wants the government to limit freedom of the press, civil society, political competition, and the rule of law. As a result, Hungary has strengthened its economic and political links with Russia and China. It is now seen as China's biggest supporter in the EU. Hungary started its "Opening to the East" programme in 2011, and in May 2017 it signed a comprehensive strategic partnership with China. In 2015, Hungary was the first European country to join the "One Belt, One Road" initiative.

This has led to some results, especially in the area of vaccine diplomacy: stocks of the jab made by Sinopharm, a Chinese state-owned pharmaceutical company, may help Orban's chances in next year's elections. In 2017, Hungary blocked an EU statement that said China was breaking human rights. In February 2021, it was the only EU country that didn't sign a Canadian statement against locking up foreigners as a way to settle international issues. It did not try to stop the EU from signing the statement, though.

China's Fudan University opening a controversial campus in Budapest is a sign of ties. The China-CEE Institute is China's first think tank in Europe. It is based in Budapest, the capital of Hungary. And Budapest has a big Chinese population and the only Chinese-Hungarian kindergarten school in the area.

Business ties are good, especially for Hungary, which has $5 billion (2020) in direct investments from China, more than any other EU member state in the CEE region. Lorinc Meszaros, a close friend of Orban's, is building the 150 km Hungarian part of the Budapest-Belgrade railway. It should be finished by 2025. Details about the $2.1 billion project will be kept secret for the next 10 years. China is Hungary's largest trade partner outside of the EU. In 2020, rail freight will be ten times bigger than it was in 2020. In 2021, a 100 MW solar power plant built in China will start to work. The Chinese and Hungarian central banks signed a deal to switch currencies in 2013. The deal will be renewed in 2016 and 2020. This is part of China's plan to make the renminbi more international and weaken the dollar's hold on the world economy. The Bank of China's office for Central and Eastern Europe is in Budapest. Huawei's biggest supply centre outside of China is in Hungary, which is also where the company does research and development.

But the connection with China is more about how it looks than how it works. Since 2010, there have been no big investments, except for the deal to pay for the train. It's not clear if Hungary will let Huawei work on its 5G network even though other EU countries have banned it.

Even though as a young man Orban was very against communism, he has avoided Western criticism of the Putin government. In 2015, after the attack on Ukraine, he asked Putin to come to Budapest. At the time, Putin was seen as a pariah in other Western cities. Hungary was the first country in the European Union to test the Russian Sputnik V covid-19 vaccine.

Notable controversies include:

- **Energy**: In 2014, Hungary picked the Russian atomic energy corporation Rosatom (without a tender) in a €12.5 billion deal to build two 1200 MW reactors at the Paks nuclear power plant. Russia is financing 80% of the cost. Hungary has signed up to the Turkstream natural gas pipeline and will begin receiving supplies in late 2021 . Cheap gas underpins Orban's popularity.
- **Espionage**: Hungary controversially agreed that a Soviet-era financial relic, the International Investment Bank, should open its headquarters in Budapest, and granted the staff of the institution wide-ranging diplomatic privileges. Western intelligence agencies believe the bank is a cover for clandestine operations .

Hungary is still a part of the EU and NATO, though. It hasn't stopped either organisation from making decisions on things like putting sanctions on Russia or making plans for the military to protect frontline states.

Like Serbia, Hungary's ties with Russia and China are based on practical concerns. They help the government in political and economic ways, which helps the government stay in power. Decision-makers in Berlin, Brussels, and Washington know how important Hungary is because they play with it and try to stop it. Hungary may sometimes repeat what Russia and China are saying (usually with bad effects). But neither a foreigner nor any other country has much of an effect on the country. He has the right to do that.

Alyaksandr Lukashenka's government in Belarus has worked hard to build ties with China. This is partly to help the economy, which depends heavily on cheap energy from Russia, and partly to counteract the Kremlin's strong political and diplomatic power. After 2014, China saw Belarus as a good option to Ukraine, which was in a lot of trouble.

In the past, there have been many outward signs of friendship. In 2010, Xi went to Belarus to open the Great Stone industrial park, which he has since called the "pearl" of the BRI. In 2015, he went back to open another industrial park. In Minsk, China is building a new mission. There are five Confucius Institutes in Belarus. China pays for aid projects like a new football stadium, a swimming pool that meets foreign standards, and housing for the poor. There are signs in Chinese at the international airport in Minsk. But most of what comes out of the relationship is depressing. The trade gap is huge: Belarus sent $675.5 million worth of goods to China, but China sent $3.8 billion worth of goods to Belarus. Chinese purchases and transfers of technology have been small. Belarus does not want to sell its industrial "crown jewels," like its potash and nitrogen fertiliser companies. Several plans to make money have failed. For example, Geely stopped making cars in 2020. Lukashenka said that "sloppy" work by Chinese businessmen was to blame and that he would talk to Xi about it. The building of a battery plant in Brest was stopped because of protests about the environment.

Belarus is cut off from the rest of the world. The government has threatened to block the transit of German exports, and rail travel between Poland and Belarus could be stopped. Words like "iron brotherhood" and "all-weather partnership" don't match up with actions.

Even though Xi congratulated Lukashenka on his rigged election win, China has not given the government in Minsk any diplomatic or other help against the pro-democracy protesters. This may be the most frustrating thing for Lukashenka.

China has made it clear that it doesn't want to be Russia's strategic balance in Belarus. Its main goal is to make it easier to ship goods to Europe by road. Ukraine could be a more interesting place for China to invest in the future if its relations with the West get better. China's role in Belarus is fine with Russia. In fact, Russia favors it because it would prefer east-west freight routes to take a northern route (through Russia and Belarus). Lukashenka's dreams of geopolitical balancing are just that: dreams, indulged by China and ignored by the Kremlin. What happens in Belarus is up to Russia.

China's relationship with Ukraine looks better on the surface. The government in Kyiv is looking for all kinds of ways to fight Russia, which is their only enemy. The people in charge in Beijing don't like changes in borders or separatism.

They didn't like it when Russia took over Crimea or helped separatists in the Donbass. Ukraine is the largest country in the CEE region and an important link in east-west transit. Notable features of the relationship include:

- **Trade**. China was, by the end of 2020, Ukraine's largest trading partner, accounting for 15% of foreign trade . Key Ukrainian exports are iron ore, grain, sunflower oil, arms (air-to-air missiles, aircraft, and tank engines).
- **Technology**. Huawei has had a presence in Ukraine since 2000. In 2017, it set up an R&D center in Kyiv. The company provides scholarships and supports Ukraine's flagship e-government program .
- **Covid Vax**. Ukraine signed up for Sinopharm's Covid-19 vaccine after expressing disappointment with its Western partners, the EU and the United States, for failing to provide help during the pandemic .

Still, Ukraine's politics are still geared towards the West. Under pressure from the US, the Kyiv government put sanctions on three Chinese people and four legal organisations that were involved with the Motor Sich company. The pro-Kremlin news service Regnum was happy to report that China responded with "thunder" by stopping the purchases of agricultural goods and metal products. Motor Sich is also a source of tension between Moscow and Beijing. When China bought the company, Russia lost its valuable role as a middleman in sales to China. In 2021, the Ukrainian government put four Chinese companies and three Chinese people on a blacklist because they were involved in a deal with the Ukrainian aerospace business Motor Sich. Motor Sich is one of the biggest manufacturers of engines for helicopters, jets, and missiles. Under pressure from the US, Ukraine is also moving away from Huawei and switching to Cisco as part of the "smart city" programme for Kyiv. China recently surpassed the U.S. as Ukraine's biggest trading partner, with high exports of $7.1 billion and imports of $8.3 billion. Ukraine's pro-Western attitude, which had never been questioned before, has been put to the test. Ukraine left a group of countries that backed a US-led move that criticised China at the UN Human Rights meeting in Geneva in June 2021. Since then, it has signed a trade and business deal with China, and President Volodymyr Zelensky spoke to Xi Jinping on the phone in a very friendly way.

China-Led Multilateralism: The Case of the 17+1 Format

The 17+1 framework, which started in 2012, is the main way that China works with countries in the CEE area. It is made up of Albania, Bosnia and Herzegovina, Bulgaria, Croatia, the Czech Republic, Estonia, Greece, Hungary, Latvia, Lithuania, Macedonia, Montenegro, Poland, Romania, Serbia, Slovakia, and Slovenia.

From the beginning, the project has been a source of debate. In addition to what seemed to be an uncontroversial goal of boosting trade and cultural ties, it was seen in Brussels and Washington as an attempt to split the EU into East and West and also to split the CEE countries by giving better terms to those who agreed with China on other issues. Some people disagree with this point of view, saying that the goal has always been economic and that China's investments in the area have been small and full of failures. In 2019, China spent only €7.1 billion in the 11 EU countries that are part of the 17+1. This is only one-third of what China put into Germany. Chinese projects have been held up by things like delays, disagreements over money, and other problems.

People are much less interested in the 17+1 because of how China treats its people's rights, worries about Beijing's foreign policy, and the fact that some countries want to follow the United States' lead in international politics. The 2019 meeting in Croatia did not go well. China held a BRI meeting in the summer of 2020, but all members except Hungary, Greece, and Serbia didn't show up. In February 2021, a virtual summit was put together quickly, but it didn't go well because of a revolt led by Lithuania's new Atlanticist government and backed by Estonia and other countries. Even more:

- Estonia, Latvia, Lithuania, Bulgaria, Romania, and Slovenia rejected the summit invitation to send prime ministers or presidents;
- Attempts by China to insert political talking points into the communique prompted a boycott of the drafting process; and
- No announcement was made of the location or date of the next summit.
- Lithuania left the 17+1; Estonia has said it will reduce cooperation and has made no decision about future participation .

The event showed that China has some basic flaws in the way it does things, especially when it comes to dealing with small, faraway countries in a multilateral setting. It wouldn't work to treat them like European versions of Laos and Cambodia. From the start, it was a bad idea to think that anti-Western and mercantilist countries and pro-Atlanticist countries with strong anti-communist views and strong support for Tibet and other human rights issues would fit into the same framework. Planless talking points are not the same as a plan. Commentators in China say that the relationship with the CEE region has stalled because of ideological differences, pushback from the EU and the US (which has led to "distrustful" thinking in the US), stricter regulations, and the fact that the region's agricultural products are not competitive.

It's important to remember that China's approach is long-term, and that most 17+1 action happens outside of the high-profile annual summits and through bilateral relationships. For example, the annexe to the communique that came out after the Dubrovnik summit in 2019 names 71 related events and organisations, from meetings of central bankers to the "China-CEEC Veterinary Research Centre" that opened in December 2018 in Sarajevo. China thinks that these kinds of projects are important because they help build personal and bureaucratic relationships.

For now, the 17+1's main purpose is to give Euroskeptic leaders like Orban and Czech President Milos Zeman a chance to show their diplomatic independence by ignoring pressure from the US and other countries to stay away from the conference or participate less. Photos with Xi and other Chinese leaders are also good for politics at home because they counter the idea that the country is diplomatically isolated. But this doesn't help China's goals in the area very much.

The Performance Review

China and Russia's work in Central and Eastern Europe is not very impressive. But intentions and skills should be used to measure results. What do Moscow and Beijing want out of their relationship in Central and Eastern Europe? Is either side unhappy with how things have gone so far or afraid about how things will go in the future?

When it comes to this, less is more. Even though China and Russia don't work together much, it's more important that they don't fight with each other. What could have been a problem for their relationship has turned out to be anything but. Both sides seem happy with how things are going.

In Central Asia, where Beijing is following an ambitious, multifaceted, and well-funded agenda, the Kremlin can be sure that the Chinese have no plans or even the ability to replace Russian influence any time soon. In a strange way, China's small role in Central and Eastern Europe gives it room to work on some BRI-related projects. Since these things aren't seen as a threat to Russia's interests, Moscow isn't trying to stop them. Strategic safety leads to a lack of obstruction.

Way Ahead

The growing imbalance in the Sino-Russian relationship raises questions about how long it will last. Will Russian leaders accept that they will always be worse at strategy, or will they instead become more allergic and angry? Will the Chinese government overplay its hand and stop showing Moscow the respect that comes with being a big power? For a while, we won't know how to answer these questions. But it's already clear that how China and Russia deal in Central and

Eastern Europe won't have much of an effect on how their relationship grows as a whole. The big tests are in Northeast Asia, Central Asia, the Arctic, Antarctica, and the future of world order. If the way China and Russia engage in Central and Eastern Europe changes, it will be a side effect of a bigger structural shift.

It is hard to believe that Moscow would try to stop a conflict between China and the US in the Asia-Pacific by, for example, causing trouble in Ukraine, the Baltic states, and the Western Balkans. For one thing, acting as Beijing's agent in Central and Eastern Europe would put Russia's economic and security interests at risk without giving Russia any clear benefits. It would also go against Putin's main foreign policy goal over the past 20 years, which has been to make Russia an independent centre of regional and global power. Putin does not want Russia to be a "mere sidekick" to China. In the last two years, he has broadened Russia's relationships in the Asia-Pacific region, strengthened political and security ties with the ex-Soviet republics, flirted with mainstream European leaders like French President Emmanuel Macron, and worked harder to show that Russia is a good international citizen. In a fight between China and the US, his first goal will be to protect Russian interests. He may also be tempted to make Russia the "swing power" of the world, which would give it more influence with both China and the United States.

Even less likely is that China would get involved in a war in Europe. Not only does it not have the means to do so, but the Kremlin might also see such a move as an attempt to increase China's political power at Russia's cost. Beijing would probably not start a project so far from home that could upset Moscow, Washington, and Brussels at the same time.

Escalating Impact of Russia and China in the Western Balkans

This part talks about how Beijing and Moscow are becoming more powerful and influencing the Western Balkans (WB), especially in Serbia and Montenegro, and what this means for the European Union (EU). It uses both first-hand and second-hand sources and stories that are popular in Serbian and Montenegrin public conversation right now.

The "soft power" of a country comes from its culture, its political values, and its foreign policies. It can't survive without these three things. Talking about China's or Russia's "soft power" in the WB is impossible without also talking about their "hard power," like their military or economic power. Joseph Nye says that for a country to be successful, it needs both hard and soft power, or the ability to force people to do what you want and the ability to change people's long-term views and preferences. So, soft power is just one part of power, and it's not usually enough on its own.

That being said, the chapter mainly talks about the main economic, political, and cultural tools that Russia and China use to show that they can be good options to the EU.

Neopatrimonialism, state capture, and corruption are all problems that the WB has had a hard time getting rid of in order to join the EU. Regional political leaders are often corrupt, but they don't have to worry about being watched by China or Russia as much as they do about being watched by the EU.

Beijing and Moscow support very different models of development and government than the EU's idea of reforms, but they work better with the political elites in the area.

Nye says that evidence of soft power is not only the resources that are available, but also the fact that states that use soft power can change the behaviour of states that are being targeted by getting those states to support their own desires. When it comes to Serbia and Montenegro, business models and policies that were made possible by working together with Moscow and Beijing make their political and economic effects stronger. This part will talk about how Russia and China affect different areas before deciding if the EU is still an important outside actor in the WB.

Russia's Story of Influence

Over the last twenty years, Russia's political, cultural, and economic influence in the area has grown a lot. This paper is mostly about three main ways Moscow reaches its goals: 1) Business ventures, especially in Serbia's energy sector; 2) Traditions and culture; and 3) Regional media that are friendly to Russia or are owned by Russia.

Energy Sector

Russia can make progress in almost all Balkan countries thanks to their economic ties with Moscow. These ties cover business, energy, and tourism.

In 2017, about 2.7 billion cubic metres of gas were used in Serbia, making it the most important market for Gazprom in the WB. In the years since 2000, Lukoil and Gazprom have invested $20 billion in Serbia. It was agreed that Gazprom would pay 400 million euros to buy 51% of Naftna I nd ustrija Srbije (NIS) stock. Another underground gas storage station in Belgrade will be able to hold up to 750 million cubic metres of gas. This was agreed upon when President Vladimir Putin visited Belgrade in 2019.

Russia has spent about $1.4 billion so far to improve Serbia's gas infrastructure. This is so that Serbia can run the "Balkans Stream" gas pipeline project, which is a part of the Turkish Stream project that Serbia joined in

2019. The gas pipeline from the border with Bulgaria to Hungary, which is 403 kilometres long, was finished in January 2021.

Russia also has a lot of money invested in Montenegro. MONSTAT, the country's statistical agency, says that more than 30% of the more than 4,200 foreign-owned businesses that were working in Montenegro in 2015 were owned by Russians. The Russian Central Bank says that Russia's total investments in Montenegro in 2016 were more than $1.3 billion, which is 28% of all foreign investments in the country. Figure 4.1 shows that Russia is still putting a lot of money into Montenegro. In fact, they went up a lot in 2020, with RF coming back as the biggest investment in Montenegro with 118 million euros.

Figure 4.1: Russian investments in Montenegro 2010-2020; Source: Atlantic Council of Montenegro via Central Bank of Montenegro

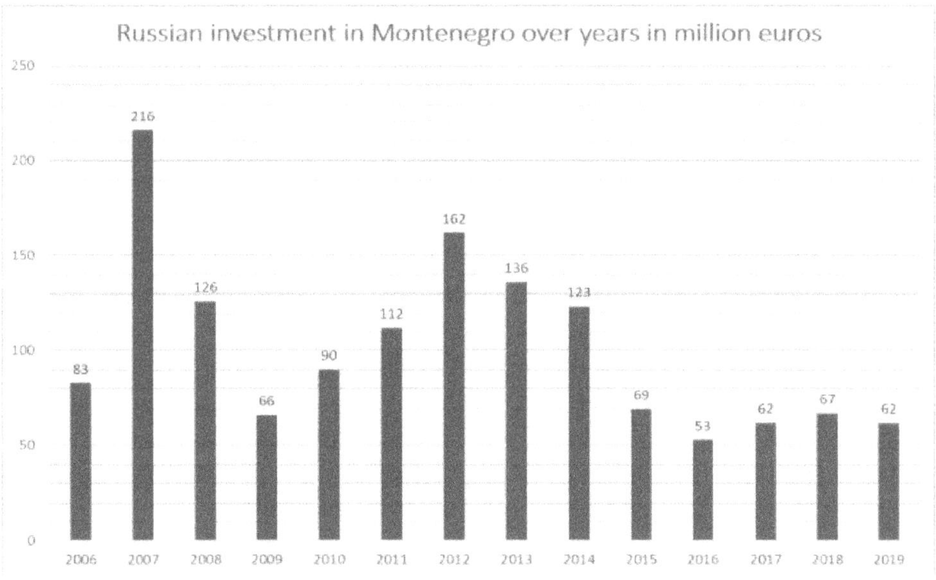

Russia has invested immensely in Montenegro's real estate, business, and tourism sectors. Although Montenegro is neither reliant on Russian energy investments nor connected to Russian gas pipeline networks, in September 2016, the Russian Gas company, Novatek, a partner with the Italian Eni, signed a 30-year concession for oil and gas contract with the Montenegrin Government.

The Power of Culture, Tradition, and Religion

To get along with Orthodox people is one of Russia's best traits in the Balkans. They think of Russia as the only power that can stand up to the West and protect Orthodox Christians in Eastern Europe. Russia and the Balkans are very connected in religious, cultural, and political levels. Russian media and public policy constantly talk about and sometimes exaggerate these ties. To "Russify" society, keep people interested in Russia, and promote what you could call "Orthodox conservativism" or "strategic conservativism" as a way to connect with European right-wing and nationalist groups, the Russian Federation manufactures stories.

Members of the ruling parties and, most importantly, the Serbian Orthodox Church (SOC), which is the Kremlin's biggest ally, assist it in both states. The Church has backed Russia's attempts to spread stories that are rude to Westerners. People have called the St. Sava Basilica in Belgrade "the new Hagia Sophia." It is the largest Orthodox church in the Balkans. Russians helped build it. Gazprom Neft gave EUR 4 million to ensure that the Basilica's interior was fixed up.

As a result, there are signs of friendship with Russia all over public spaces. For example, in 2014, Belgrade revealed a memorial to Nicholas II, the last Russian Tsar. Russian Patriarch Kirill blessed the monument. Montenegro's city, Podgorica, is where the "Moscow Bridge" is located. Moscow gave it to us as a gift in 2008. Popularised by local media and lawmakers, these kinds of symbolic acts are common. Their goal is to improve the "hundreds-years-long" friendship between the two countries.

Many Russian cultural sites are in the area, including the Centre of Slavic Culture in Belgrade, the Ruskiy Mir Centre in Niš, and the Russian Centre for Science and Culture in Belgrade (Rosstatnichestvo). Additionally, Serbia has a lot of dangerous groups that support Russia. These groups include the biker gang Serbian Night Wolves and the armed Balkans Cossack Army and Serbian Honour. Far-right Russian and Serbian groups also set up a camp in Serbia in 2018 where young people could learn how to be paramilitary.

Some Russian businessmen with ties to the ROC are actively pushing Russia's plan in the area. Konstantin Malofeev is the most famous of them. He started Russia's biggest Orthodox charity, which has a $40 million budget, and owns Tsargrad TV.

Media

The Centre for Euro-Atlantic Studies (CEAS) did research that showed 109 media outlets in Serbia that are backed by Moscow. By far, Sputnik Serbia is the most well-known Russian news source that works in the area. For instance, when the Serbian government was thinking about buying 1.8 million Pfizer vaccines from the US, Sputnik Serbia spread many stories saying that the American company was dishonest and "incomplete," while the Russian vaccine was better. These stories were heard all over Serbia and Montenegro.

China's Story of Influence

Chinese media and regional leaders often say that China's interactions with the WB are positive and don't cause problems. They also say that these interactions can help the economies of the surrounding areas grow.

China does not recognise Kosovo's independence. All WB countries have made bilateral agreements with China on the Belt and Road Initiative (BRI), except for Kosovo.

Figure 4.2: China-Western Balkans Trade; Source: UN COM Trade

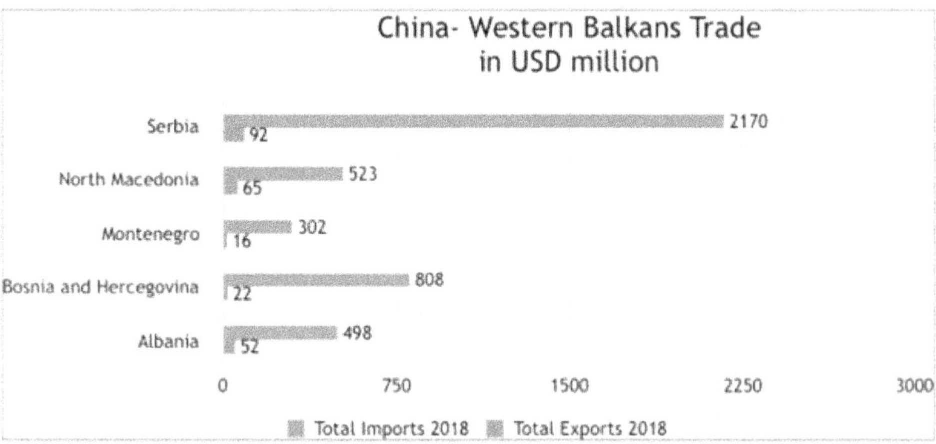

The trade between China and WB countries makes up only 4.3% of China's trade with CEI countries. On the other hand, the WB's trade with China ($4.5 billion in 2018) makes up only 5.5% of the region's total trade ($81 billion), with almost half of that being trade between China and Serbia (Figure 4.2). On the other hand, China gives loans to fund infrastructure development by the government, big industry projects, and nonrenewable energy sources (mostly coal-fired power plants). The Export-Import (EXIM) Bank and the Bank of China are two policy banks that do a lot of China's developmental loans. When Beijing gives these loans, it doesn't usually think about how well the countries will be able to pay them back, and for now, loan forgiveness isn't a choice.

Most investors stay away from Serbia and Montenegro because of their poor political and economic conditions. The BRI has helped China use the WB as a stepping stone to become less dependent on Western power economically, gain access to European markets, and balance its economy against the West.

China's Widening Reach

Serbia:

About 70% of the Chinese money that is invested in the WB is in Serbia. The Serbian National Bank said in a study that from 2010 to 2019, Beijing put more than $1.9 billion into Serbia (Figure 4.3). Furthermore, China has already loaned about $1.4 billion to Serbia, and the Serbian government hopes to borrow an extra $3.3 billion from China in 2021.

Figure 4.3: The Center for the Study of Democracy; policy brief 97, January 2021; China-Western Balkans FDI; Source: National Central Banks

Chinese Foreign Direct Investment Stocks (USD Million)

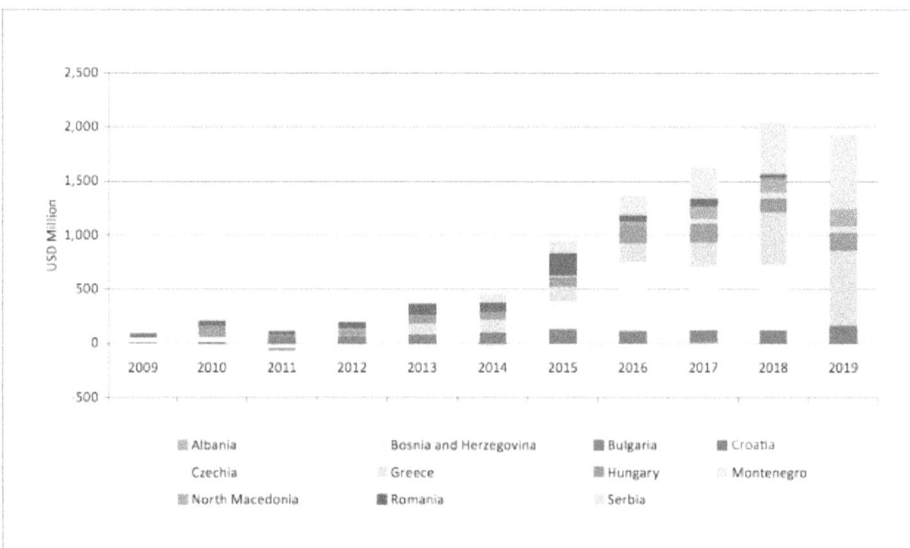

China also pays for regional highway projects to make it easier for Chinese goods to get from the port of Piraeus in Greece to markets in the EU. At the same time, Huawei has worked with the government of Serbia to make towns "safe" and "smart" in order to fight crime. In some of the same towns, Serbian and Chinese police have also been working together on regular basis. This has grown to include places that are important to China economically and strategically, as well as popular tourist spots. Recently, the Serbian government changed the story about joint police drills by saying that they were done to "counter-terrorism."

It's also important to note that Chinese companies have helped Serbian businesses and industries that were about to fail. The most well-known cases are when the Hesteel Group bought the closed Smederevo steel mill in 2016 and when Zijin Mining took over the mining and smelting company RTB Bor. Apart from building a tyre plant in Zrenjanin and an industrial park in Belgrade, Chinese companies have also worked on other projects.

Montenegro:

Japan's EXIM Bank gave Montenegro its first loan of $47.7 million in 2010 so that it could start rebuilding its trade fleet. Since then, EXIM Bank has given a $944 million loan to help build a highway from the port of Bar to the border with Serbia. China currently holds more than 25% of Montenegro's state debt, which was about $4.5 billion at the start of 2021. A study from the World Bank says that by the end of 2021, Montenegro's debt could reach 94.3 percent.

Based on figures from the Montenegrin Central Bank, China became the second most important investor in Montenegro in 2020, putting in over $71 million. With the sudden rise in Chinese FDI, there is a lot of serious discussion in the public sphere. China put ten times more money into it in 2020 than it did from 2010 to 2019.

Culture, Media and Medical Diplomacy

China uses Confucius Institutes, culture centres, the media, and now "medical diplomacy" to project its "soft power" in WB countries.

Seven Confucius Institutes can be found in the Balkans. Two are in Serbia and one is in Montenegro. China is currently constructing a culture centre in the area where its old embassy in Belgrade used to be. The strategic importance of the Belgrade site, where NATO bombed the wrong target in 1999, can't be ignored. It serves to remember people who are tired of NATO of one of its most famous mistakes.

Chinese companies work with Serbia's state-owned media to spread positive stories about China's domestic and foreign policies while leaving out negative views, especially those that talk about how China's actions might hurt the region.

Serbia and Montenegro went to China for medical help at the start of the COVID-19 pandemic, when the EU cut WB out of its vaccination programme. China's medical diplomacy began on January 17, 2021, when a million doses of the Sinopharm vaccine were sent to Serbia. Two weeks later, another half-million doses were sent. As the first pack of doses arrived in Belgrade, President Vucic of Serbia hailed China and kissed the Chinese flag.

The Collective Image of China and Russia

A poll done in November 2020 by the Belgrade Centre for Security Policy (BCSP) found that 75% of Serbians think China helped Serbia the most in the early stages of the pandemic. This may not come as a surprise. Ninety percent of Serbians polled recently think that China's impact in Serbia is good. This is thirty percent more than in 2017. With the support of 16% of the people, China is the second most popular country in Serbia.

Forty percent of Serbians think that Russia is their biggest ally, and seventy-two percent see Russia's impact as positive—a thirteen percent rise since 2017.

It is official that joining the EU is one of Serbia's top goals, but only 46% of citizens want to join, while 51% are against it.

Things are a little different in Montenegro. Four Western Balkan countries were surveyed in 2018 by USAID, the National Endowment for Democracy (NED), and the National Democratic Institute (NDI). The results showed that 45 percent of Montenegrins have a positive view of Russia, while 41 percent enjoy the same view of China and 40 percent enjoy the same view of the EU. It's interesting that a lot of people in Montenegro (47%) think that Russia's military is stronger than NATO's.

Authority of Persuasion

Along with Chinese and Russian investments and good public opinion, both Serbia and Montenegro have slowed down their reforms in six ways that are directly linked to their relationships with each other.

Corruption: In both Serbia and Montenegro, many projects involving Russia or China have been sources of controversy, including high-level corruption cases covered in secrecy and illegal schemes with partners from those two countries.

Financial Trap: Both states are now more dependent on Chinese loans, rendering them unable to negotiate better business deals with China in the future. Montenegro is in an especially difficult situation. Although Xinhua calls it the road to success, the highway project, sharply criticized by the International Monetary Fund, haunts Montenegro, which has recently asked the EC for assistance in paying off the loan.

Domestic Legislation: Chinese infrastructure projects are often exempt from national laws and do not meet EU standards in the field of public procurement, environmental standards, or competition. In Montenegro, the Chinese construction firms working on highways have been exempt from nearly all taxes and duties related to the importation of construction materials.

Environmental Impact: The region's generally low environmental and work standards have meant that China is placing itself in the position of doing business in countries where it is unlikely to receive the level of scrutiny for its practices as would otherwise be the case in the EU. In addition, Chinese undertakings in the region often result in increased industrial pollution.

Confidentiality: Most Chinese projects are veiled in secrecy and not available for public scrutiny. Montenegro's Central Bank declared any information about Chinese FDI confidential in 2018, 2019, and 2020. Presently, there are no official figures available about the volume and worth of the medical aid that China has provided to Serbia, as they are labeled 'state secrets.'

Diplomacy: Serbia has become Russia's and China's strongest ally in the Balkans, opening up a gateway for their further incursions into the WB. For example, even though, as an EU candidate country, Serbia has to abide by the EU's common foreign and security policy, with regards to Ukraine, Belgrade has opted to "remain neutral" and not follow Brussels' decision to impose sanctions on the Kremlin. Additionally, the Serbian government has given political support to Moscow several times by voting against UN resolutions concerning Russia's occupation of Crimea. In the face of EU concerns, Belgrade has also joined a group of 50 states that signed the so-called "second letter" backing Beijing's policy toward Xinjang's Uighur population. At the same time, Serbia needs Russia and China's support in its decades-long dispute over Kosovo's international status .

The case for Montenegro is more complicated. There have been some differences with Russia. For example, in 2014, Montenegro put sanctions on Russia for entering Crimea, and in 2016, there was a (alleged) coup attempt against the government that Russia backed. However, there seems to be a warming of relations. The pro-Russian Democratic Front, which is the largest alliance partner in the current Montenegrin government, has called for the lifting of sanctions more than once. The new Prime Minister Zdravko Krivokapic called the restrictions that were put in place "absurd." As for what's going on in Xinjiang, Podgorica has not taken sides.

EU as a Key Player

The EU has been the most important outside player in the WB since the 2003 summit between the EU and the WB in Thessaloniki. After that, the schedule gave Serbia and Montenegro the chance to become EU members and set up the rules for future cooperation between the two countries.

The EU is still the region's biggest investor, in addition to being a very important government partner. Between 2014 and 2018, EU member states put

12.7 billion euros into the WB. At the same time, the EU handles almost 70% of all trade in the region.

Figure 4.4: Trade between EU and the Western Balkans; Source: Eurostat

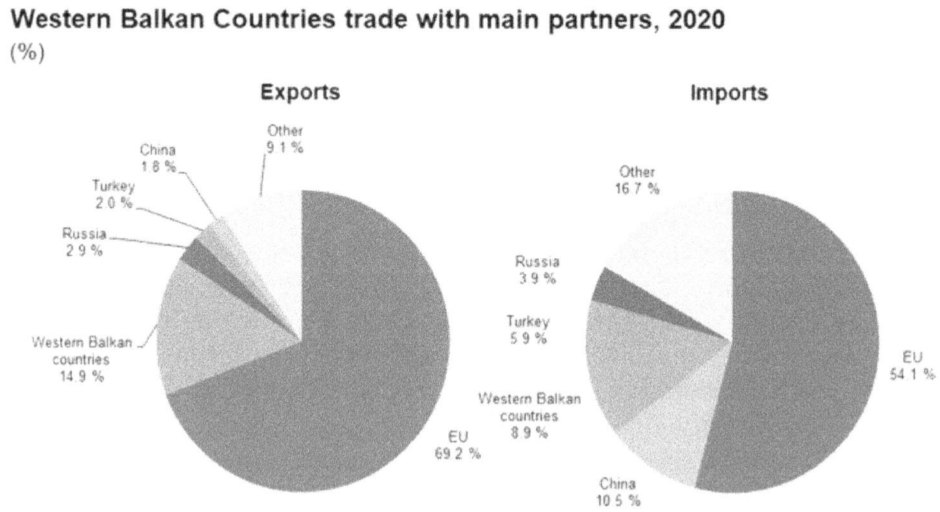

In 2019, 2 billion euros worth of FDI from the EU came into the WB. The EU is not only Montenegro's most important trade partner, but it is also the country that gives it the most money.

Also, the EU just passed a nine-billion-euro plan for investments and economic growth to help the WB's long-term economic rebound.

Prospects of joining the EU are still Brussels' most powerful soft power tool. In December 2011, Montenegro started talks to join the EU, and in June 2013, Serbia did the same. Then, in reaction to this incentive, these countries started the long and difficult process of becoming more democratic. As part of this, they had to change their laws to fit EU standards.

Now, though, it looks like the changes are going backwards, and the EU is worried. The EU has not let Serbia make any more progress towards membership for almost two years because changes have been slowed down. They say this is because of a lack of political will and the growing power of Beijing and Moscow. Along the same lines, 26 members of the European Parliament wrote to the European Council to voice concerns about the "impending environmental damage" caused by Chinese companies and China's "growing influence" in Serbia.

EU leaders, such as President Donald Tusk and Chancellor Angela Merkel of Germany, have often talked about how worried they are about Russia's growing power in the area.

Policy Takeaways

Factors contributing to the current decline of EU soft power include:

1. Brussels seems to lack an effective policy for countering Chinese or Russian transactionalism. Chinese investment offers are attractive precisely because they generally lack pre-conditions and circumvent the IPA (EU) legal framework.
2. The EU has neglected Europe's South-East corner as Brussels has been pursuing internal consolidation.
3. The prospect for EU membership has become a long shot. After the rough experience of the last waves of EU enlargement and current issues with some new members, old EU members have grown increasingly cautious and demanding. As Brussel experiences "enlargement fatigue," EU candidates from the WB experience "reform fatigue."
4. As corruption in the WB persists and rule of law and democratic standards continue to backslide, the abilities of China and Russia to flex their muscles in the region continue to grow.

The Way Forward

Many researchers in this book think that there is already some kind of alliance between Russia and China, or at least that a relationship based on alliance is starting to form. This opinion is backed up by research from all over the world. Different people have different ideas about how deep this connection is and how far each side is willing to go. But in general, the findings show that there is a lot of agreement.

From a European point of view, this piece answers the following questions: If Russia and China are making a military partnership, (1) what does that mean for Europe, and (2) what political and military conclusions will Europe have to make? The first question can be answered by looking at the European Union and Great Britain, but the second question has a problem: what does it mean for "Europe" to be a political actor? Is it the European Union, whose many national interests make it hard to have a shared foreign policy? Or is it the work of bigger and more important European countries like Germany, France, Italy, and Great Britain, even though Britain is no longer part of the EU? The author leans towards the second position and wants this contribution to be seen as a collection of ideas about how the major European states should react to a growing military alliance between China and Russia by working closely with EU institutions.

Historical Significance

When figuring out how important a military alliance between Russia and China would be from a political point of view, it helps to look at cases from the past that might be similar to the current situation. By talking about both what's the same and what's different, you might find a better way to understand what effects this existing or new union might have. There are three examples that come to mind: (1) the military alliance between the Soviet Union and the People's Republic of China in the late 1940s and early 1960s; (2) the Hitler-Stalin Pact from August 23, 1939; and (3) the German-Japanese-Italian Axis, which ran from 1936 to 1945. Why should we take these three cases into account? They were different in size and quality, but they all had one thing in common: they were military alliances between big military forces run by dictatorships that were aimed at the democracies of the West. Their main goal was to fight or even destroy the world of free societies by using cruel policies of subjugation, exploitation, and dominance.

The three groups did not stay together for long, though. The partnership between China and the Soviet Union lasted the longest, at more than 15 years. China no longer wanted to be the junior partner, so the deal fell apart. The Axis was made up of Germany, Japan, and Italy. It only lasted for 9 years before the Western forces and the Red Army beat them all. The Molotov-Ribbentrop Pact did not last for very long. During Operation Barbarossa, when Germany attacked Russia on June 22, 1941, it was moved out of the way.

All three cases have one feature in common: all of these alliances brought about major wars and, for the same reason, caused major policy changes on the side of major Western powers, in particular the United States:

- The Soviet-Chinese alliance led to the outbreak of the Korean War, which lasted from 1950 to 1953 and left four million dead . The Korean War led to fears in the West that an invasion similar to that initiated by the North Koreans and instigated by Stalin and Mao might also take place in Europe. Hence, it set off a debate among Western leaders, in particular in the US, about the difficulty of fighting two regional wars at a time on their own. Consequently, the North Atlantic Alliance gained in importance and even an effort towards German rearmament was initiated, since without a German military contribution to NATO's military posture in the centre of the Alliance's forward defence posture at that time, the defence of Europe was thought to be unrealistic.

- The Hitler-Stalin Pact led to both the German war of aggression against Poland and the Soviet wars of aggression against Estonia, Latvia, Lithuania and Finland, as well as to the annexation of the rest of Poland by the Red Army in October 1939. The Western response was the declaration of war against Germany by France and Britain and, later on, the issuing of the Atlantic Declaration as a signal for the need that something profound would have to change after the end of World War II. The United States' ultimate entry into the war against the Third Reich included a major effort by Washington to reset the international system both in Europe and globally after the eventual victory.
- The German-Japanese-Italian Axis paved the way for the Japanese aggression against the USA (first the attack on Pearl Harbor) and ended a long period of little interest in Pacific affairs by Washington. The alliance with Japan was of no use for the Third Reich, since Japan did not join Germany's war against the Soviet Union. On the contrary, Japan's attack against Pearl Harbor sped up the entry of the United States into the war against Germany in the European theatre. Again, as with the case of the war in Europe, the US remained the leading power in Asia- Pacific after World War II and started to reset the international framework in the region in conjunction with similar efforts in Europe.

In the end, there are three things we can learn from these cases from history: A Russian-Chinese union might not last too long, but it could lead to wars of a size we haven't seen since the Korean War or World War II, either directly or indirectly. This seems to be true since Russia is planning to invade Ukraine in February 2022. Another lesson is that it is up to the Western democracies to learn from the past and try to stop it from happening again by thinking ahead about what kinds of things might happen if Russia and China work together.

If you follow this line of reasoning, three important questions come up: (1) What can Western countries do to make sure that the alliance between Russia and China doesn't last as long as possible? (2) What kinds of war possibilities do we have to plan for if the Russian-Chinese Axis stays together? (3) What can Europe, the US, and other partners do together to stop the worst from happening?

Unity Between Russia and China Vulnerable

There are a lot of people who say that a union between Russia and China wouldn't last long because their goals would eventually be different. The biggest problem is that Russia seems to be a weaker partner than China. In almost every measure of power, China is much stronger than Russia, except when it comes to strategic nuclear arms. Russia has only 140 million people, while China has 1,4 billion. China is the second biggest economy in the world, after the US. In 2020, China had a gross national product (GNP) of 14.9 trillion US dollars (measured in dollars). Based on the value of the dollar, Russia's GNP in 2020 was $1.6 trillion, making it the 12th biggest economy. In terms of buying power parity, things would look a little different: China would have the biggest economy in the world, and Russia would be the fifth biggest economy, right behind Germany. China has many more conventional armed troops than Russia, and their quality is also getting better and better. China is becoming a leader in modern technologies and is seen as one of the most competitive industrial countries. Russia, on the other hand, is behind in most technologies (except defence technologies) and is seen as a power on the decline. Besides that, Russia has a lot of land in North Asia that China thinks belongs to them. China and Russia also have different ideas about how the economy in Central Asia should grow and how it should work with other countries. Lucas and Lo write in this book's part "Partnership Without Substance: Sino-Russian Relations in Central and Eastern Europe" that Russia and China don't seem to coordinate or work together much in Central and Eastern Europe.

In the past, both French President Emmanuel Macron and former German Chancellor Angela Merkel tried to persuade Russian President Vladimir Putin that it was in Russia's best interest to work together with Europe and not count on China. Some government leaders may have tried the same things. But so far, all of these attempts have been for nothing. Most experts in the academic world agree that the need for stability in Russia's government is so strong that there are no other choices. But things looked different when Dmitri Medvedev was in charge. Medvedev was very interested in working with the West to help Russia's economy and industry catch up with the rest of the world. Since 2012, when Putin became President of Russia again and a lot of Russians went out to protest against him, the tide has turned against him. Putin's strategy, both at home and abroad, is now focused on making sure his regime stays in power. A couple of expert studies have shown that Russia is run by a corrupt and kleptocratic power vertical whose top members have become very wealthy. Giving up power in politics would be a disaster for all of them. So, as resistance has grown at home in Russia, the government has made it harder for people to take part in politics. So, the Russian government has been going after and sometimes killing the leaders of the resistance. The Russian government is threatening anyone who tries to say something different. Russia has turned into a full-fledged dictatorship.

The Russian government thinks that any democratic resistance was started by democratic countries in the West, and that the domestic opposition has always been a tool of the West to make Russia unstable.1 This story is told everywhere in Russia's political class, and it is even part of the Russian military's official ideology. In this document, any resistance from within Russia is made to look like it was planned by the Western alliance as a way to make Russia unstable, like an invasion. So, Russia thinks it has the right to respond in kind and start its own actions that will make Western governments less stable.

Under these circumstances, it's hard to think that the current Russian elite would listen to the well-intentioned advice of Western leaders to break up with China. China is an even more authoritarian country than Russia, and it has many of the same characteristics that made great writers in the 1940s and 1950s talk about totalitarian rule. As long as the stability of the kleptocratic and autocratic regime is Russia's top concern, it is pointless to think that Russia will switch alliances. By being hostile to the West, Russia is making up for its lack of legitimacy at home. In a way, China is doing the same thing, since the Communist Party of China is also facing major problems at home. This keeps the two states together and makes it impossible for either of them to think about ending their partnership. This could change after Putin leaves office, but it could take a long time for that to happen. Instead of hoping that Russia can be persuaded to end its alliance with China, Europeans should look at the political and military risks that come with Russia's growing hostility towards the West and the risk that its alliance with China could lead it to risky military operations against Western states. This brings me to my next question.

War Scenarios

As was already said, a military partnership between Russia and China could make war more likely. But what kind of wars would we have to get ready for? There are many different kinds of war, from small, regional wars to big, intense wars between the most powerful industrial countries. There is reason to believe that there will be wars that start in a regional setting with hostile actions that don't go far enough to be violent, but which could turn violent after a short time, spread a lot, and turn into major wars with high-intensity fighting between powerful industrialised nations in different theatres in both the Euro-Atlantic and Indo-Pacific regions.

Academics are becoming more and more convinced that any big war could start with a regional war. As Brad Roberts has pointed out, both China's and Russia's armies have looked very closely at regional wars in order to learn how to win on the battlefield. Their goal would be to push Western powers back or to break up US-led alliances in their area. Regional wars, which are likely to happen on Russia's borders, are meant to be won by Russia, even if that means using nuclear weapons to stop the war from getting worse and help Russia reach its goals.

Regional wars are an important part of Russia's defence strategy. The Russian military knows that it could not win a long-lasting conventional fight with the West or a strategic confrontation with NATO and the US. But Russia's leaders think that a small-scale armed conflict could happen in Europe. This would give Russia a chance to weaken NATO's unity as an alliance, especially its willingness to protect itself. As part of Russia's "strategy of active defence," Russia's military theory says that regional wars are a key part of "pre-emptively neutralising threats." In contrast to Western military thinking, the Russian way of using military power in a conflict is not focused on avoiding or quickly ending the conflict and limiting the damage it causes. Instead, Moscow wants to win by taking advantage of the other side's weaknesses and stopping them from taking advantage of Russia's.

Regional fights, on the other hand, could be seen as the most extreme way for Russia to deal with its ongoing conflict with the West. The way Moscow tries to do this is called "hybrid warfare" in the West. Even when the West considers it to be at peace, Moscow's hostile actions include a wide range of military and non-military tools, such as disinformation campaigns, cyberattacks, and subversive actions, as well as meddling in national elections, turning energy supplies into weapons, and supporting extreme political movements. It also has military activities that are scary, like large-scale military exercises and building up the military in key areas, even with nuclear weapons, both in peacetime and during crises. Even though these actions don't involve direct military conflict, they are meant to make neighbours and enemies less stable, scare NATO and the EU, make it harder for NATO to make decisions, and limit its military choices. Even if a crisis turns into a military clash, the hybrid spectrum would still be used. For example, disinformation, propaganda, and malicious cyber activities would all be used as part of a larger military operation. If such a war happened, Russia's goal would be to gain a decisive military edge, fight a short war, and win strategically. In this situation, Russia's efforts also need to be seen in the framework of the last 20 years of systematic military reform and arming efforts.

Where could these kinds of wars happen? They could happen in places where Russia thinks it needs to regain control or where it sees a chance to completely change the strategic status quo in Europe by hurting NATO in a decisive way. This could happen if the economic situation in Russia gets worse and less people support the government. This would be even more likely if there were good strategic developments on a global scale, like the United States being militarily occupied in the Indo-Pacific region. Putin might be tempted to solidify his power with a decisive military action and the stirring up of nationalist feelings that comes with it. Russia's strategic and military policy is in line with this kind of situation.

At the moment, there are mainly two possible regional theatres: the first is the expansion of military operations in Ukraine with the goal of making it even less stable or even making it impossible for it to exist as an independent state; the second is a limited attack against one or more of the Baltic States and parts of Poland with the goal of making NATO look bad as a security provider. In both cases, Russia would try to use quick attacks to create military faits accomplis before the West, meaning the United States or NATO as a whole, could get involved militarily. In both cases, Russia's dual-capable intermediate-range missiles that could threaten or hit European cities and key military and civilian infrastructure would be a major factor in how well NATO would respond and defend itself as a whole.

The Russian invasion of Ukraine in February 2022, which was still going on as this piece was being written, shows how Russia is trying to start a war in the region. Moscow has tried to do two things: 1) topple the Ukrainian government and replace it with a puppet government; and 2) take over and finally annex large parts of Ukraine, especially the South and East. Even though the first goal couldn't be reached, Russia was able to take over most of the Donbass, which is in the south of Ukraine. Russia is still trying to take over Odessa, which is a port city in the south. The way the Russians fight in Ukraine is very typical. Russia used the army, the air force, and the navy to destroy Ukrainian military troops in all three ways. When it turned out that the Ukrainian defence was better than imagined, the Russian campaign turned into a brutal war against civilians and a war of total destruction against the Ukrainian infrastructure and industry. The mixed part, which includes cyber war, information war, etc., stayed small.

If Russia were to win, it would completely change the strategic situation in South-Eastern Europe and the Black Sea region, including Turkey, as well as the way military troops are set up in the area. Romania would face a clear military threat, and NATO would have to change the way it defends itself and tries to stop attacks. It would be important to set up a strong, permanent armed alliance presence along the whole eastern side of the country.

A similar move by the Russian government in the area around the Baltic Sea would be much riskier, but it couldn't be ruled out, especially after Russia's warning in December 2021. The Baltic States, Poland, Germany, and Denmark are all part of NATO, so the Washington Treaty's guarantee of collective protection would apply to them. Sweden and Finland are both members of NATO and have close ties to the organisation through things like joint drills and planning for operations. In Europe, especially in Germany and Poland, the US has strong ground, air, and naval troops. They also take part in regular exercises of land, air, and sea troops in the Baltic States and the area around the Baltic Sea.

If, on the other hand, Russia's leaders thought that the strategic situation as a whole would allow or even support a limited military attack, they could decide to move quickly with traditional armed forces into the Baltic States and parts of Poland. Moscow could try to destroy important targets for the deployment of NATO forces in Europe and across the Atlantic to help friends by using conventional strikes with a wide range. By threatening to use intermediate-range nuclear weapons with conventional or even nuclear warheads, European governments would be less likely to live up to their collective defence obligations and send troops to help their allies in the East, out of fear of a nuclear escalation. If Russian forces were able to take over the Baltic States or parts of them before NATO reinforcements could act decisively, Moscow could stop and force NATO to choose between a major war with unknowable chances of escalation or backing down and agreeing that, in the best case scenario, the Baltic States should leave NATO and become "neutral." There would be a lot of trouble for NATO and the security of Europe on the political level. It could be a sign that the partnership is over.

China, too, has plans for regional wars that would mainly take aim at the United States and its allies. For China, three different theatres of war seem to be the focus:

a. the occupation of the island of Taiwan (which was a colonial domain of the Chinese Empire for just 200 years, ending in 1895, but is claimed by Beijing as an integral part of China);
b. the South China Sea and the East China Sea, where Beijing wants to put huge maritime areas under its exclusive control; and
c. the possibility of a war on the Korean Peninsula.

In all three situations, China's war planners have to deal with the US or a country that is associated with the US. Due to the different geography of the Asia-Pacific region, most of China's war planning in the region is for maritime situations or mixed maritime, air, and land theatres. The goal of Russia's regional war planning is to quickly take over land to put the North Atlantic Alliance in a strategic bind. However, China's attempts to build up its military and other activities point to bigger goals. At their core are plans to block US forces from entering the whole area in a planned way by using a variety of weapons with different layers. Anti-access/area denial, or A2/AD, is the military word for this kind of plan. When you look at China's attempts to build up its military over the past 20 years, there is one thing that stands out: China wants to make the entire US military presence in East Asia, whether on land or at sea, vulnerable to a massive attack. It is what the Chinese call an ASCEL, which stands for active strategic assault on exterior lines. The A2/AD danger is mostly caused by China's deployment of reconnaissance-strike complexes to threaten US military bases and naval ships, especially carrier groups, in the area. China got these skills by putting money into modern satellite, anti-satellite, and weapon technology, as well as improving its submarine technology. In the meantime, China can attack US naval bases and ships with quite effective kinetic strikes from more than 2,000 km away from its coast. The Chinese People's Liberation Army (PLA) got these skills by spending a lot of money on modern technology.

In the not-too-distant future, the Chinese A2/AD powers could make it possible to deal a decisive blow to the US military presence in East Asia, or at least make the Chinese leadership think that this is a real possibility. Some people think that within the next ten years, the PLA might be able to do a lot of damage to all of the fixed sites that the US uses to support its military forces in the area. It might also be able to blind the main strategic intelligence and observation tools in the area and sink US naval ships, even aircraft carriers, up to 2000 km from the Chinese coast.

China's efforts to build up its military are so big that they will change the way the US plans for defence in a big way. Some people think this is similar to what Japan did in 1941 when it tried to push the US out of the Pacific. China's attempts to build up its military and its strategic goals are setting the stage for a major change in US defence policy and military strategy. The US government in Washington, DC, is preparing for the possibility of a big, high-intensity war in the West Pacific. This war could be started by Chinese leaders who want to show that they are in charge of that area. Also, it's not certain that the US and its allies in the area will be able to win this war quickly. So, the US has started to move its strategic attention to the Indo-Pacific. This change in the US's strategic direction will mean that the number and quality of US troops set aside for emergencies in Europe will drop by a large amount.

This leads to the most dangerous thing that could happen as a result of a Russian-Chinese military alliance: China could start a regional war in the West Pacific by striking and taking over Taiwan, and Russia could follow suit by taking over the Ukraine or the Baltic States. In this case, the US President will have to decide where to send US forces stationed in the continental US: either to help NATO prevent or, in the worst case, fight off a Russian attack, or to help US forces in the West Pacific who are in a tough fight against China. Most observers agree that protecting US positions and allies in East Asia or the West Pacific will be the top priority. This is because Washington sees China as the US's main strategic competitor, and China's regional and global ambitions are the biggest threat to the US and the rest of the Western democracies.

The most important fact is that the US is no longer willing to fight in two different wars at the same time. During the 1990s and the first decade of the 21st century, it was a good idea to be ready to fight two different wars at the same time. But because of the huge growth of China's military and technology, Russia's successful military reform and rearmament, and the US military's decline during the wars in Iraq and Afghanistan, the situation has changed in a major way. Both Russia and China are aware of this fact. If both governments agreed to start a "regional war" at the same time in their own backyards, it could mean the military defeat of the Western alliances in both theatres. This could lead to a new world order in which Russia controls large parts of continental Europe, China controls Asia, and the US controls only North America. This would be a world with an international "order" similar to what Carl Schmitt, a German jurist, political theorist, and member of the National-Socialist Party, drew up at the start of World War II. Schmitt's plans were mostly the same as Hitler's, but with Greater Germany instead of Russia.

The Significance of Europe

It is too soon to give a list of concrete policy choices for dealing with the risks and threats that the new strategic partnership between China and Russia poses. But it is important for the European governments, especially those in London, Paris, Berlin, and Brussels, to review their policies towards Russia and China in order to adapt to the new strategic situation in the area and the world. There are three important steps to do this.

Russian Military Threat

First of all, it's high time for European leaders to say out loud that Russia's military threat is a political fact and a reason to be worried that can't be ignored any longer. The German government is a good example of this. When Angela Merkel was chancellor, there was a big difference between what she agreed to at NATO Summit talks and what she said about Russia. Even though the NATO communiques didn't say anything about the military threat Russia poses to its allies, she never said anything at home that sounded like the words in the NATO papers she had also signed in Brussels. Former Chancellor Merkel did not have any plans to talk about or deal with military dangers. She never had a lot of respect for important institutions in the area of security and military policy. She used to have doubts about the BND, and she didn't know much about the Bundeswehr or Germany's defence policy in general. She was in office for

16 years, but she never gave a speech about Germany's security and defence policy. When she talked about these things, she always said things that could be taken in different ways. She didn't like or know how to think strategically, especially about whether military weapons were involved. "You can't solve political problems with military force," was one of her most well-known quotes.

For the same reason, her coalition's strategy towards Russia was, at best, ambivalent. Some have said that she was a "Putin whisperer," but that is not true. She knows Putin very well and has met him many times, especially when there was trouble in Ukraine in 2014. Putin told her lies over and over. Still, Merkel was sure that she could keep the peace by talking directly with Putin. She didn't seem to understand how to keep the peace through deterrence or protection. Many people from Central and Eastern European countries, especially the Baltic States, criticised her for this strategy of benign neglect. The Nord Stream 2 pipeline became a source of anger in Central and Eastern European countries as well as in Washington over Germany's mixed feelings about Russia and its poor defence policy. But when Russia started its aggressive war against Ukraine, everything changed in Germany. Even though the Social Democrats and the Greens were in charge of foreign and defence policy, they got over their pacifist ideas and decided to increase Germany's regular defence budget by more than 50 percent and spend an extra 100 billion euros to rebuild the German military after ignoring it for 20 years. Olaf Scholz, the German chancellor, has called it a "Zeitenwende," or a turning point in history. Also, the Nord Stream 2 pipeline project was scrapped, and the German government started a major plan to move away from Russia as a source of energy imports. In spite of earlier claims that they wouldn't add to the war, Germany has also sent weapons to the Ukraine.

But Germany was not the only country with an unrealistic attitude towards Russia. A similar attitude could be found in France, where President Emanuel Macron thought for many years that high-level diplomacy could help improve ties with Russia. His strategy was to try to figure out what the Russians were worried about and find a way out of the mess. But since Russia went to war with Ukraine, Paris is getting a more realistic view of the situation. In London, on the other hand, the Russian threat has always been seen with a bit more realism.

Since 2014, the NATO heads of state and government have chosen to slow down the efforts to arm their countries. This is because politicians like Merkel and Macron have signed off on different things in NATO documents and in their own countries' policies towards Russia. In particular, Germany is still a long way from meeting its obligations and commitments (see Rainer Meyer zum Felde's chapter in this book, "What a Military Alliance Between Russia and China Would Mean for NATO").

Worst Case Scenario

At least until recently, people in the German government thought that a Russian armed attack on the Baltic States and Poland was a very unlikely possibility. Moscow's defensive strategic worries and its desire to re-establish a buffer zone in its "near abroad" were thought to be behind its military's offensive stance. If the survival of the government was the most important thing, that would mean that the regime was not very willing to take risks. So, the worst could be avoided if the West kept a policy towards Russia that was based on calmness and talking. This way of thinking made sense most of the time. It was based on the (silent) assumption that, given their mutual interests and dependence on each other, this calculation could only be changed by a big event.

The Russian attack on Ukraine was a very important event. China could have made things worse if they had invaded Taiwan with their army at the same time. This would have put Russia in a situation where it would have had a real chance to change Europe's politics in a big way. By the way, the similarities with 1939 are striking. When the Molotov-Ribbentrop Pact was signed in August of that year, it gave Hitler the chance to follow through on his revisionist plans and attack Poland. It gave Stalin a chance to get back parts of the Russian Empire that had been lost, like Finland, the Baltic States, and the eastern parts of Poland. Taiwan is to China what Czechoslovakia and Poland were to Nazi Germany in the 1930s: the main target of a nationalistic and revisionist strategy based on military annexation. The Chinese did not attack Taiwan, which was a good thing. Given the many problems the Russian military has had with Ukraine's highly motivated defenders and the many problems inside Russia (failing logistics, lack of coordination and strategic leadership, loss of tanks and armoured fighting vehicles, poor performance of the Air Force, etc.), the Chinese military must have started to rethink their plans to invade Taiwan, since they might run into the same problems Russia did. This should give the Western world and Taiwanese people a little more room to breathe in the near future.

Reviewing Europe's Relationship with China

At the moment, the heads of state and government in the European Union all agree that China is both a partner and a foe in terms of how the world works. If rumours about China's military arming and huge buildup against the US and its allies in the West-Pacific are true, this formula will need to be carefully looked at. Especially, a change in overall strategy would be needed if a military alliance with Russia were to be made. In this case, China would be a military threat to both Europe and the United States. The threat would be more indirect, but such a union would definitely increase the risk of war in Europe and make it more likely that East Asia and Europe could both be involved in a war.

It seems like it would be much harder to change the way political leaders in Berlin or Paris think about China than it would be to admit that Russia has been a military threat since 2014. In the last ten years, the German government has been one of the strongest backers of China. Because of how well things went with China when she was handling the global financial disaster, Chancellor Merkel always had a good opinion of the country. During her time as chancellor, the German and Chinese economies have become very tied together. Today, the amount of trade between China and Germany is almost the same as the amount of trade between Germany and the United States and France. So, when she was chancellor, Merkel said many times that Germany did not want to get involved in a big power struggle between China and the US. Again, these comments show that she doesn't want to think about global strategy or strategic military competition. But China is building up a strong military force in the Indo-Pacific region against the US and its democratic allies. This has a huge effect on the security of Germany and the rest of Europe. Europe and Germany get most of their protection from the United States. If China is a military threat to the US, European nations can't be unaffected by this.

We hope that this pro-Chinese, no-questions-asked mindset will stop. The new alliance Government hasn't decided on anything yet, but that could change. In this way, it is up to other European powers to always question Germany's stance and push for a change in how Germany deals with China. In any case, there needs to be a conversation across the Atlantic about how to deal with China. In this way, the implementation of NATO's 2030 agenda, which was accepted by the Alliance's leaders at their Summit in Brussels in June 2021, and the development of NATO's Strategic Concept 2022 offer the chance to find a common, realistic position towards both Russia and China. This is a chance that should not be missed.

Conclusions

In conclusion, it is important for Europeans, especially those in Berlin, London, Paris, and Brussels, to re-learn how to think strategically and get a better idea of what really threatens the transatlantic community and the European Union, as well as how that threat could become real. Germany, which has been in a "end-of-history mode" for more than 20 years, needs to do this more than most. The EU External Action Service's strategic papers have helped people become more aware of strategic challenges and even threats. However, now that a Russian-Chinese alliance has formed or is forming, many of these assessments need to be looked at again. This alliance is a basic problem for Europe, and it could mean the difference between war and peace.

Chapter 5
International Relations Paradigms and The Future of a Military Partnership Between Russia and China

Relations between Russia and China were already very good before the conflict between Moscow and the West got worse. But since 2014, they have hit a whole new level. There have been more political talks, more military cooperation, and a lot of deals and plans for joint business projects. In June 2015, at the St. Petersburg International Economic Forum, President of the Russian Federation Vladimir Putin said, "As for the People's Republic of China, the level, nature, and confidence of our relations have probably reached a level that has never been seen before in their whole history."

As cooperation between Russia and China grows, the question of whether the strategic relationship between the two countries should be called an alliance has come up again. There are already some Russians who think that the relationship between the two countries is more like a union than an official alliance. They call it a "de facto alliance." To add to his voice, President Putin has spoken out on the matter, calling China a "natural ally" in October 2014. There were first articles in Russian and Chinese newspapers and magazines that called for the union to be made official by the law. Political scientist Yan Xuetong from China, for example, said that the US poses a threat to both countries, though in different areas. He said that Russia and China can't help each other and make their relationship stronger without a partnership. The Russian teacher of Asian studies, Y. Since Western countries are hurting Russia's interests, Tavrovsky wants a military-political union to be set up so that everyone can work together. He thought that a legally binding agreement would help both countries stand stronger on the world stage, build trust, stop China from claiming Russian territory, ensure Russia's fast growth with Chinese money, and stop the West from "internationalizing" Russia's natural resources.

The question of a Russia-China alliance makes sense, since alliances are usually made to fight threats and only then do they help reach specific goals.

The US is putting more and more pressure on Russia and China because it sees them as a threat to their own interests and the main strategy goal of creating a multicentric world order. Based on what A. China, Lukin, is a more dependable partner than Western countries because it doesn't try to force its own ideas on other people. And Moscow treats Beijing the same way.

Researchers who study Russia-China relations mostly look at how their political and economic ties have changed over time, how they work together on security issues, how they talk about important regional and global issues, and how they work together on military and technology issues. They also talk about the differences between the two countries, which are mostly about money, and show where their interests in Eurasia and Asia meet and differ. According to several experts who have looked at how Russia and China work together on security, their military ties are so strong that a military-political union is now just a formality.

This finding was strengthened even more when Vladimir Putin called the relationship between Russia and China "an allied relationship in the full sense of a multifaceted strategic partnership" in October 2019. He also said that Moscow was helping Beijing build a missile attack warning system that would "dramatically increase China's defence capability." The new stage of military cooperation between the two countries, which started in 2018-2019, is focused on strategic weapons, among other things. These facts are yet another reason to say that Russia and China are interacting at the highest level, which is typical of foreign groups. But at the same time, none of the agreements that the two countries have signed with each other require them to support each other in case of aggression. In June 2019, the Russian Federation and the People's Republic of China signed a joint statement on international relations entering a new era and global sustainable development. The statement says that the two countries are guided by three principles: they refuse to form allies, they don't fight, and they don't direct their actions toward third countries.

There aren't many detailed explanations in modern study for why Russia and China aren't in a hurry to make an alliance with legally binding obligations, even though they work together a lot. Most of the chapters that have come out have said that this is because both sides want to work together with the West. An alliance that is directly aimed at the United States would obviously make that impossible. So, if Moscow and Beijing agreed to bilateral legal guarantees, they would have less room to move. Some other reasons given for not wanting to form an alliance are that the two countries' economic models are different and their economic interactions don't work well together. This is because the people of Russia and China have different interests, bad memories of the past, and different ideas about how to understand the things they have both been through.

A number of studies look at how closely military cooperation between countries is like military-political alliances, but they don't actually answer the question of why countries don't make their agreements official. Kashin and Lukin say that there has been no political decision to form an alliance between the leaders of China and Russia. However, they don't rule out the chance of such a decision if the United States gets involved in a global armed conflict.

In general, the literature on how Russia and China are interacting right now doesn't have any broad theoretical bases, and it doesn't really talk about the modern theory of military-political partnerships. With this kind of theoretical support, it would be easier to understand why the parties haven't yet agreed to be allies with each other. This chapter's goal is to fill in this gap by looking at the main aspects of the strategic partnership between Russia and China. It does this by drawing on the theoretical work of Glenn Snyder and other writers. In this way, it will help figure out how stable the current model of relations between the two countries is and what is stopping them from forming a military-political alliance with legally binding responsibilities.

Before we look at the past of Russia-China relations and see how the theory of military-political alliances can be applied to it, let us first try to put military-political alliances as a way of working together into a bigger picture of other types of cooperative groups. This is what this part is for. We will also talk about the main ways that alliances are studied in the theory of international relations, what makes them unique, and why people might choose to work together in symmetrical or uneven ways.

The realist school of international studies is where a lot of the academic writing on alliance ideas can be found. Neorealism is based on the idea that the world is free of order and that each country's main goal is to protect itself. Balancing is one choice that states that are constantly threatened from outside can use. For internal balancing, you need to improve your own armed power. For external balancing, you need to form alliances to fight your enemies. Military-political alliances can form in hegemonic and bipolar systems, as well as in polycentric systems, where the main players use both conflict and balancing coalitions as ways to deal with each other.

As a state faces dangers, alliances help it figure out how to handle those threats and what kind of help it can expect from other countries. Stephen Walt says that an alliance is when two or more sovereign states work together in an official or informal way. This makes countries responsible to each other and gives each side some benefits. If the partnership ends or obligations aren't met, there are a lot of costs. When it comes to states that are a threat to them, states are more likely to try to balance their power than to join them. The amount of threat is affected by not only the combined power of a possible enemy, but also where it is located, how offensive its military might be, and what it wants to do.

One of the most important books on partnerships was written by Glenn Snyder. Snyder has a different view of alliances than Walt. He sees them as formal groups of countries that plan to use military force against countries that are not part of the alliance under terms set by the allies. Snyder says that the main goal of this method for cooperation is to combine efforts so that enemies' threats are less effective and people can feel safe. Alliances also have other benefits, such as making it less likely for enemies to attack friends, making sure that an ally doesn't become too friendly with an enemy, preventing an ally from attacking, and giving allies more power over their own politics. Even if it's not mentioned directly in the official alliance treaty, the fact that these countries are working together on collective defence means that they will support each other on a wide range of foreign policy issues as well. There are also costs that come with joining a partnership. The most important one is the risk of losing independence, which could mean having to fight an ally's side, getting involved in a conflict that it doesn't want to be a part of, or being part of a competitive alliance that limits future partners' options. So, for a partnership to be worth it, the possible benefits must be greater than the costs.

An anarchic international system is different from military-political associations because countries can't be made to keep their promises. This means that there is a chance that an ally will not do what it agreed to do. These risks get worse in a polycentric system; making linked relationships official lowers uncertainty but doesn't get rid of it completely. All partnerships have a dilemma: there is a chance that an ally will back out of the deal if there is a conflict, and there is also a chance that the country will be dragged into a conflict over ideas that it doesn't agree with.

When a country joins an alliance, it consciously limits its foreign policy choices in exchange for more safety. It might have to follow a path set by an ally or, on the other hand, give up on a strategy that would be best for its own country. Alliances can also form without written agreements, but in this case, a verbal agreement is needed and must be backed up by actions that show the country is living up to its promises. If not, the other parties may start to question the usefulness of the alliance. In order for an alliance to work well, states must agree on how their military and political leaders will work together in times of strife and how they will work together directly.

When a country decides to join an alliance, it is affected by both the international structure and the situational factors that affect the approach it chooses. These factors include the partners' interests, power, and level of dependence on each other. Similarities in interests are often needed for people to get along again, and when an alliance is made official, one side will often start to follow some of the other side's strategy goals, even if they didn't do so before. A big part of the choice to form an alliance is the balance of power. Interdependence can also show up in the area of security as well as the economy. This depends on how different their goals are, how likely it is that they will go to war, and how strong their military is compared to the enemy's. An alliance is either symmetrical, where countries of similar size have equal responsibilities, or asymmetrical, where the expectations of a stronger and weaker state are different. This is based on how much the states depend on each other. In the second case, this usually means that the bigger player is stronger than the smaller player. When a country buys new weapons or military technology, it becomes more likely to join an alliance. On the other hand, a fully independent military-industrial complex that can put new ideas into action lets the country keep its foreign policy independence.

Neoclassical realism adds something important to the meanings given above. Neoclassical realism goes beyond the idea that the structure of the international system is an independent variable and the strategy chosen by the state is a dependent variable. It also includes traits in the middle that show how domestic politics affect the situation. This factor can change how countries see threats from other countries and affect the approach they choose.

The idea of allies that this chapter is based on was created by Glenn Snyder. That one is based on the realist school of thought, but it also takes into account the factors thought of in the neoliberal and constructivist schools. It is the most complicated theory that tries to explain how military-political partnerships form and change over time. Snyder's way of thinking fits with the purpose of our study, which is to find out why Russia and China have never made their joint defence obligations official.

Along with a thorough review of the theoretical literature, what is also important for this study is how most people think about the modern nature of Russia-China ties and how they reflect the current stage of cooperation. The main idea in the study is that Russia and China's strategic partnership is not the same as a full-fledged allied relationship. Some researchers use the term "alignment" to describe this partnership. People form ideas about which states will back, oppose, or stay neutral in the future based on what they think will happen. But rapprochement can look like many things, including a formalized partnership, which is the most formalized form.

How a formalized alliance is put into action depends on how well the states understand each other's goals, options, and rules, as well as their duties within the alliance framework. Countries may expect help from a partner if they share an enemy, an ideology, or a group of people who are all the same race. They may also expect a partner to be able to improve security where they don't have the same skills. Joint actions, like military planning, exercises, diplomatic statements and agreements, and the formation of an alliance, can help a power feel more supported by another power. Forms of getting along can change depending on how power and interests are shifting.

Rapprochement comes in many forms, and different types can help states find more flexible ways to work together than formal agreements like a military-political alliance. A strategic partnership is an alternative to the latter. This is when two or more states work together in a planned way to come up with a better security solution than any one of them could provide on their own. When things are like this, rapprochement in foreign policy is more about achieving shared goals than protecting against a threat from a certain state. When comparing strategic partnerships to alliances, strategic partnerships have less strict rules about how to work together and lower costs for meeting obligations. This means that states can still have a lot of freedom to act.

At the same time, structured cooperation is what makes strategic partnerships unique. This can be seen in things like regular visits, relations between governments, joint military exercises, and so on. Often, they come with close cooperation in the military, the economy, and technology. China's partnerships are notable because they focus on working together in areas where everyone's interests and goals are the same, mostly in the economic sphere, and don't go into areas where people's goals and interests are at odds with each other. Partner relationships are less risky and more reasonable when people talk to each other on a regular basis. A study of China's partnerships in the real world shows that the country is motivated by practical concerns, mostly the strategic and economic importance of states, rather than ideological ones. Additionally, China wants to know how willing potential partners are to support its foreign policy strategy and help carry out China's strategic imperatives. China has built partnerships with dozens of countries since the early 1990s based on consultation, cooperation, and the search for mutual benefits. It has made full use of these partnerships to lower the level of conflict and greatly improve its own security. But the word "partnership" is neutral; it doesn't rule out problems and disagreements, or the fact that other countries may work with China and compete with it at the same time. These partnerships look, work, and talk about different things depending on the country.

The above-mentioned theoretical ideas helped shape the design of the empirical study, which described areas where Russia and China's interests overlap and the most important aspects of their political and military relationships. It then went on to explain why the two countries' growing friendship hasn't turned into formal obligations to protect each other. Therefore, in order to find out how important it is for states to form an alliance, the pros and cons of doing so will be weighed against each other, along with how the political and expert elites of both countries feel about the idea (this is called an analysis of the domestic political variable). Next, we will look at Glenn Snyder's list of variable interests, along with the balance of power and the level of interdependence between Russia and China, to figure out the most likely way for the two countries to work together.

There has been a deepening of relations between Russia and China, which can be described as a strategic partnership.7 The resumption of relations began with Mikhail Gorbachev's visit to China as president of the Soviet Union in 1989. During that visit, both countries signed an agreement not to fight, to settle disagreements through negotiations, and to work together in many areas. In a declaration from 1992, both sides agreed to see each other as friendly states and work toward good neighborliness, friendship, and cooperation that benefits both sides. In their 1996 joint declaration, they said they wanted to build "relations of equal and trusting partnership aimed at strategic interaction in the 21st century." They also made it clear that their cooperation was not meant to hurt other countries and did not mean they were making an alliance. Building a multipolar world order was a goal that both Russia and China set in 1997. In 1996 and 1997, the Shanghai and Moscow agreements were signed. These agreements strengthened military confidence-building measures and agreed to reduce the number of armed forces on the borders between China and four former Soviet republics.

The Treaty of Good-Neighborliness and Friendly Cooperation Between the People's Republic of China and the Russian Federation, signed in 2001, was the main document that set the stage for cooperation in many areas. In the Treaty, the relationship between the two countries is called a "strategic cooperative partnership of equality and trust." In 2001, Russia, China, and the Central Asian countries formed the Shanghai Cooperation Organization. A long negotiation process led to the signing of an agreement in 2004 on the border of the eastern part of the SCO. This helped settle the border dispute between the two countries. Russia and China said again in 2005 that the world needed a more fair order. Then, in 2010, they came up with a plan to build a "new security structure" in the Asia-Pacific region.

In 2014, relations between Russia and China reached a whole new level. After Moscow's relations with the West got worse, relations between the two countries got stronger. This led to a level of cooperation between the two that had never been seen before. In their Joint Statement on the Development of a Comprehensive Strategic Partnership, the People's Republic of China and the Russian Federation talked about these changes. They agreed to work together to connect the Eurasian Economic Union and the Silk Road Economic Belt as part of the Belt and Road Initiative in May 2015. In 2016, the leaders of Russia and China issued a joint statement on strengthening strategic stability. The statement talked about how important weapons other than nuclear ones are for keeping the world safe. Officially, relations between two countries are called a "comprehensive equal partnership and strategic interaction."

It has been over 30 years since Russia and China first started talking to each other, but official contacts between their representatives have become normal. Since 1996, the leaders of Russia and China have met every year, with each year being held in a different city in China. They also meet four to five times a year at international forums and conferences. Aside from that, the five intergovernmental commissions and the prime ministers of the two countries meet regularly. Contacts between departments and regions are also growing quickly. The leaders of Russia and China trust each other a lot, which has made it possible for their countries to work together more closely than ever before on foreign policy.

A strategic partnership between Russia and China is made up of a number of things. To begin, both Russia and China agree that a multicentric world order is a better way for the world to work. In an effort to make international relations more open and democratic, both countries want to be independent centers of power. Beijing and Moscow want to see an international order in which they and other non-Western countries are not below the US and its allies but are on the same level as them.

Second, both countries stress the importance of respecting sovereignty, territorial integrity, and other countries' internal affairs. This leads to a dislike of the US's unilateral actions and a desire to create an order that is focused on the US and doesn't let other countries reach their economic and potential goals. The growing relationship between Russia and China was a response to the bad changes in the world that came about when international law and the UN lost their importance. Russia and China both don't trust the US-built network of alliances and don't like how the US gets involved in other countries' affairs. The Trump administration's plan to keep Russia and China in check only brought the two countries closer together.

In a joint statement released in 2016, Russia and China said that the US and its allies were trying to save face by putting other countries' safety first and building up their armies so they could use force to reach their goals. They were also worried about the US putting up a missile defence system in Asia and Europe and about making space more military. People in the Asia-Pacific region think that Washington's actions make it impossible to build a single, open, transparent, and fair security architecture. Each country, Russia and China, is worried that the US is getting stronger near their borders. They want to make Asia a place where different groups can live together peacefully, which fits with their idea of a multifaceted world order. In June 2019, the leaders of Russia and China released a joint statement saying that their relations are still growing despite the unstable world order, growing competition, and the destruction of the arms control regime. They said that these relations act as a stabilizing factor in the international system.

Along with the shared views listed above, Russia and China work together because they both want to change the modern financial and economic system and the institutions that govern the world so that non-Western countries can play a bigger role. People believe that working together in groups like BRICS and the G20 is essential to reaching these goals. Russia and China agree that destroying the current system of agreements on arms control, disarmament, and non-proliferation is not acceptable. They also agree that there needs to be a multilateral treaty to stop weapons from being put into near-Earth orbit. The two countries are against protectionism, political blackmail by one country, monetary diktat in trade and economic relations, sanctions, trade wars, meddling in Venezuela's internal affairs, actions by one country against Iran, and international terrorism. They also want to end the conflict in Syria through political and diplomatic means and help build a nation in Afghanistan. Russia and China also don't like the way the US handles information space. They see the internet through the lens of national security.

China and Russia both want to find a solution to the problem on the Korean peninsula, which is another area where their goals are similar. In this way, they started a joint roadmap project to help North Korea and the rest of the world work out their differences. Russia and China both spoke out against the US THAAD system being put in South Korea at the same time. Since 2016, they have been working together on "Aerospace Security" exercises that focus on air and missile defence. The leaders of both Russia and China have worked hard to keep disagreements to a minimum throughout the whole history of their relationship.

Geostrategic factors determine how well Russian and Chinese interests match up with each other. China is mostly interested in East Asia, while Russia's foreign policy and efforts to integrate other countries are mostly focused on Eurasia. The two sides work together because they are both threatened by the same enemy in the areas that are most important to them. When it comes to Central Asia, Russia and China both want to keep things stable politically, make sure that secular regimes stay in power, and speed up economic growth so that the region stays stable. China also needs to work with Moscow to carry out its policy of reforms and openness and to make the world a better place for economic growth. In order to do this, Beijing had built ties with all of the world's major powers.

Russia and China could work together to create a cooperative order in the huge Eurasian space if they could successfully connect the EAEU and the Silk Road Economic Belt. They would be able to use each other's efforts to integrate, come up with common rules for the game, and help create indivisible security. Russia was able to act as an independent integration center and take advantage of China's desire to carry out bilateral and multilateral projects by promoting the idea of a Greater Eurasian Partnership. Beijing's initiative has a much better chance of succeeding in the region when it works with Moscow and its allies.

A lot of military-technical cooperation and military ties between the two countries show how strong the strategic partnership is. Russia and China's defence ministries made a deal in 1993 that allowed leaders from both countries' military departments to get in touch with each other. This included the chiefs of staff, the Security Council of the Russian Federation, and the State Council of the People's Republic of China. Every year, the Russian and Chinese militaries get together for 20 to 30 events, such as training sessions and joint exercises. The statements made after the two-way talks show growing concern about the threat from the United States, respect for each other's views on how the security situation is getting worse, awareness of the need to work together to solve problems, and so on. Russia and China don't talk about each other as a security threat in public or when they're talking to other countries.

China and Russia signed a Military-Technical Cooperation Agreement in 1992. This was the start of their large-scale interaction. As military contacts between the two countries have grown and tensions on the border have gone down since the agreements of 1996–1997, more advanced types of military equipment have been sent to China. Eventually, the sale of weapons gave way to the transfer of licenses and designs for Chinese orders. In the 1990s, military-technical cooperation grew. This helped China re-equip its armed forces and make huge progress with one or two generations of military equipment.

Around the middle of the 2000s, cooperation slowed down a bit because Russia's military-industrial complex was busy with orders from within the country, the country was busy expanding its list of export partners, and there was a growing chance that China would steal Russian technologies without a license. Between 2014 and 2015, China signed contracts worth more than $3 billion to buy 24 Su-35 fighters and at least six divisions of the S-400 long- and medium-range anti-aircraft system. This gave military-technical cooperation a new boost. China's growth in the military-industrial complex meant that Russia could give China the newest versions of its weapons, but Moscow ran the risk of having a smaller share of the Chinese market in the long run. According to the cost of the new supplies, China's possible enemies on its edges will be less likely to start fighting because of them. This will lower the risk that the US will use military action.

Since 2005, the Russia-China Peace Mission has held ground exercises together. In 2012, maritime interaction exercises were added to the schedule. Both have grown a lot over time, and so has the area they cover. Between 2015 and 2019, naval drills were held for the first time in the Mediterranean, South China, and Baltic seas. This kind of interaction plan has helped the groups be more consistent in areas like planning, intelligence, interoperability, communications, and logistics. It is through these drills that China has been able to work with one of the world's most experienced military powers, giving it training for combat missions in remote areas where Chinese ships don't usually go. The Russian and Chinese militaries have gained trust in each other through the joint exercises. They have also reaffirmed their friendly intentions toward each other and learned more about each other's fighting abilities.

2018 was the year that China and Mongolia took part in Vostok 2018, which was the biggest military drill in modern Russian history. Even though there were no agreements on collective defence, the presence of Chinese detachments made it possible for the two sides to work out technical issues of military cooperation. In this way, the conditions were set for an alliance to form, should that choice be made. Because of all of this, military experts say that the level of cooperation between the Russian and Chinese militaries is now higher than what is usually required for a military-political union to be formalized.

Long-range strategic planes from Russia and China went on their first ever joint patrol on July 23, 2019. The growing ways of working together are especially interesting because of the rising tensions between the US and China and between the US and Russia. A big part of Moscow's plan to show its power in the Asia-Pacific region is long-range strategic aviation. There are also plans to talk about the Military-Technical Cooperation Agreement again, which has been in place since 1993. The higher level of engagement we are seeing today should show up in the new version.

In October 2019, Vladimir Putin said that Russia was helping China build a missile warning system. This is more proof that relations between Russia and China have reached a whole new level. With this kind of system, it would be possible to launch a return attack before the enemy's nuclear weapon could reach the country. A single Russian-Chinese system with a single command was never going to happen, but the two countries can now share radar data in real time because they are working together. Because China has stations in the south and southeast and Russia has radars in the north, this kind of integration makes it harder to tell when a missile attack is coming.

As the conflict between Russia and China and the US and its allies gets worse, Moscow and Beijing may be able to work together militarily in more areas. A lot of experts say that these areas include hypersonic technologies, building nuclear submarines, strategic commandpost exercises, joint research and development in the field of military-technical cooperation, sharing information about US plans and actions, and more.

So, the warming of relations between Russia and China is based on facts and will last for a long time. It is because the two countries' strategic interests are close to each other. They can help each other in diplomatic, military, and economic ways when they are at odds with the United States thanks to the strategic partnership. Cooperation grew between the two countries in the 1990s and 2000s, and their priorities never changed. This built trust between the leaders of the two countries, with each knowing what the other was trying to do and how things would always go. In particular, it was expected that both sides would not send separatist forces into each other's countries or support policies that are hostile to third countries. Russia and China share a border, and the two countries work together very well, so it is not possible for either to be strategically surrounded. They are still each other's most important border partner, which is why they need to have stable, friendly relationships for their security and foreign policy. They could keep fewer armed troops on the border with the West and have more stable relations with the West if they had this kind of relationship.

According to standard language, the relationship between Russia and China is not an alliance because the two countries have not officially agreed to work together on defence and security. According to the Treaty of Good-Neighborliness and Friendly Cooperation Between the People's Republic of China and the Russian Federation, signed in 2001, they will not use or threaten to use force, will not aim strategic nuclear missiles at each other, will not join forces with anyone that would threaten the other party's sovereignty, security, or territorial integrity, and will talk and meet to get rid of threats. In other words, the document sets up obligations of non-aggression and mutual consultations that go beyond the guarantees that are usually part of these kinds of agreements. But it doesn't say that they have to defend each other if they are attacked with weapons, which is a key part of alliances.

We can't say for sure if Russia and China have obligations to each other that are the same as a defence pact based on information that is available to the public. The partner-ship between Russia and China is different from the military alliances the US has with several European and Asian countries because there are no formal agreements on joint actions and neither country is required to help the other in a conflict. This last point makes us wonder how stable mutual guarantees really are.

Because of the benefits and costs of an alliance for both Moscow and Beijing, this situation makes sense. It would not be in the best interests of either to sign one. From a practical point of view, an alliance would make it easier for both sides to stop the US. It would also make it less likely for the other side to warm up to the US, get rid of the threat of hostile actions, and give the US more control over its foreign policy actions. However, Russia and China must also think about the downsides of an alliance. These include the chance of getting sucked into a fight they don't want to be a part of, the fact that the US's network of alliances will get stronger because of the worsening security situation, and the fact that each country's foreign policy will be less independent because it will have to be coordinated with the other.

When Russia and China formed their strategic partnership, they made it clear that they were not working together to hurt other countries. At the time, this was because Western countries were not seen as a serious enemy that could not be worked with. Instead, both Moscow and Beijing wanted to get closer to the West in political, economic, and technological areas because it helped them grow. Coming together to fight against the United States would only be possible if there was a threat from the US that meant cutting all ties with the US and its allies.

There aren't any benefits to joining forces right now that are greater than the costs of keeping everyone safe. At the moment, neither country thinks that the US is a serious enough threat that they can't handle it on their own while keeping the same level of cooperation. Even though Russia's relationships with the US and NATO are getting worse, a direct military conflict is very unlikely thanks to its nuclear shield and advanced weapons, some of which have no counterparts anywhere else in the world. Russia is the only country in the world with the same level of global strategic potential as the US. It also has the ability to launch a nuclear retaliatory strike, which makes a conventional war much less likely. Russia's foreign policy is mostly about the area after the Soviet Union and its relationship with the EU. Even though the sanctions have hurt Russia's economic ties with Europe, they are still important for the country's growth. And technology makes it almost impossible to make more of them. In Asia, Russia also wants to broaden its foreign policy and economic ties by working together with India, Japan, South Korea, the Association of Southeast Asian Nations, and other nations.

Working together with the West is important for China because its growth depends on getting foreign investment, borrowing technologies, and selling finished goods. This is true even though China is in a trade war with the US and the US and EU both make it hard to share technologies. If China doesn't have to deal with energy exports, Russia is a much less appealing business partner. It can't get rid of its ties with the West.

Chinese investors want to put their money in other markets more. Due to the unique business climate in Siberia and the Russian Far East, as well as problems with the legal system and a lack of appropriate funding, cooperation across the border with Northeast China has not grown well, except for local trade. So far, it hasn't been able to help the economies of the two countries grow or bring them together more. It is hard to get Chinese investors to put money into the Russian Far East because the area isn't very developed yet. There isn't a big domestic market, there aren't enough workers, the transportation and production infrastructure isn't very good, costs are high, and the border crossings aren't very modern. Getting things back on track will take a long time.

China needs to build a more balanced economic model that includes both internal and export demand. This will take some time. In any case, these trends don't mean that the government should give up on its plans to do business abroad. The Made in China 2025 program also has a goal of catching up to the world's most advanced technological countries. However, it is hard to carry out because of many restrictions, and it can't be fully realized without working with the West, especially the US.

In its military planning, Beijing has set itself the goal of not only being defensive, but also increasing its chances of winning small, high-tech fights, with a focus on naval attacks. Even more than Moscow, it tries to keep possible enemies from getting to its edges. Russia and China are seen as strategic enemies by the Trump administration and the US policy that goes along with it. This has made Moscow and Beijing believe that the US's main goal in its relationship with them is to control them. Beijing is especially worried about the attacks that are meant to stop its technology progress.

Russia still wants to work with the US on arms control issues, and trade talks between Washington and Beijing led to the signing of an agreement on the first stage of a "trade deal" in January 2020. This shows that both Russia and China are willing to talk with the West. The United States is the most important country for China, both economically and strategically, when it comes to talks about the world and regional order. China wants to keep working with the US more than Russia does. It doesn't want to be seen as a power that wants to change the past. Beijing is still interested in changing the international order and the institutions that run it so that developing countries have a bigger role in them. Even though the Trump administration is acting unilaterally and ties between the US and China are at an all-time high, China is ready to work with other countries to keep the world order. The United States and China need to find a way to make their relationship more stable so that there is no more conflict in the world in the future. Experts from China keep saying that their work with Russia is not meant to hurt other countries.

Chinese researchers Feng Yujun and Shang Yu say it's hard to figure out what the benefits of a possible partnership with Moscow would be. Because of how complicated foreign relations are today, they may even turn out to be false. On the other hand, China would have to pay a very high price if its ties with the US got worse, and it would be hard to stop the situation from getting worse. Washington is not going to ease the pressure on either country. Even though the strategic relationship between Russia and China is growing, the US is still able to take action against Russia in Europe and China in Asia.

The model of conflict that would arise from a Russia-China alliance would not help solve world problems any more than it would hamper them. It would not make global and regional security better; in fact, it would make it worse. And there's no reason to think that such a union would help fix the problems between China and the US or between Russia and the US. Beijing thinks that the US would not ease its pressure on China even if they got closer to Moscow on the armed front.

Also, neither Moscow nor Beijing are trying to stop the other from making ties with Washington that are friendlier, let alone joining forces on this ground. The relationship between Russia and China is growing on a practical and non-ideological level, which is not true of either country's relationship with the West. Moscow sees Beijing as a more reliable partner than Washington, which it sees as an existential danger because of its tendency to get involved in liberal issues. In this way, it's hard to imagine a time when Russia would choose to build ties with the West over China. Due to the many problems between China and the US, the opposite scenario is also not likely to happen.

The idea that Russia or China would attack the other side is too crazy to be taken seriously. Even though both countries are planning for different possible futures in the world, their military preparations are mostly based on what might happen with the US, NATO, and the US's partners in Asia. Some people in Russia are still afraid that China will attack or try to take over more of their country, but experts are not sure. According to data from the Russian Public Opinion Research Center for October 2019, China is the country that Russia has the best ties with. Only 7% of Russians saw China as a threat. Many Russians (62% of those surveyed) think that China is a friendly country, while only 16% think that it is not. Also, 55% think that China's rise does not threaten Russia's interests, while only 26% think that it does. 20% of Russians think that it is more important to strengthen ties with the West, while 29% think that it is more important to strengthen ties with China, and 29% think that ties need to be When it comes to strategic possibilities, Russia still has a big advantage. Alarmist claims about the dangers of population growth are not backed up by evidence, which means there aren't any large-scale migration flows. Only about 330,000 Chinese people live in Russia, which is less than 3% of all the outsiders who live there.

So, both Russia and China think that their strengths are enough to protect themselves and fight a war on their own in the most likely situations. Because of this, the benefits of an alliance are not strong enough to make us want to look into the subject further. In fact, the countries would probably have to pay a lot of money because the conflict with the West would likely get worse and they wouldn't be able to work together on technology and economics if a union is made official. This is not possible: they can't join forces to stop other threats, like their partners getting closer to the US or Moscow or Beijing taking military action.

It's not possible to make military-political obligations in the area of collective defence official because there aren't any objective conditions and there are structural risks. These problems are on top of the political elites' views and some aspects of their own domestic politics. The leaders of both Russia and China don't want to form a partnership, either officially or in any other way. Most Russian observers think that the current ways of working together are enough to deal with the security problems, so they don't see the need for a full-fledged partnership. Chinese experts say that this kind of relationship between the two countries is the best choice because both the leaders and the people want it. People in these groups think that Moscow and Beijing will not be enemies or partners for a long time.

Moscow wants to be a great power, which shapes its strategic culture and makes it want to have its own foreign policy. In a message to the Federal

Assembly in February 2019, Vladimir Putin said that Russia had always been a separate country on the world stage and that this would continue to be the case. If it doesn't happen that way, it will either stop existing," which doesn't fit with the idea that formalizing a union would make people less independent.

Also, people in Russia are still talking about what kind of threat the West really is to Russia. In this case, the Russian expert S. According to Karaganov, the US and other Western countries should be clearly seen as Moscow's main strategic enemies. Sergey Lavrov, Russia's Minister of Foreign Affairs, told a press conference in January 2019 that the current bad mood in Russia's relations with the West is due to Washington's desire to control the world through force, economic pressure, and propaganda, and its refusal to "accept the reality of the emerging multipolar world." Lavrov said that Russia was still interested in getting back to normal relations with the US and the EU. Dynkin, a full member of the Russian Academy of Sciences, who stressed that Russia's move to get closer to China would make the country a junior partner or even a satellite of a growing power if an America-China world order comes into being. In this way, it would be good for Moscow to have more ties with Europe.

People in China don't like the memories of the times when they teamed up with Russia. This was one of the reasons given for China's refusal to sign official agreements on collective defence, which became a key part of its foreign policy. In this situation, China has no desire to join with other countries that are against the West in any way. Beijing wants to build relationships with Russia in different ways so that both countries can reach their growth goals and help each other more, which would make the international system more stable. China says that by strengthening their relationship, Moscow and Beijing will show the rest of the world how cooperation between major powers should work. They will show how to go from mistrusting each other to trusting each other, where countries try to avoid disagreements and work together on issues that are important to both of them. At the moment, neither Russia nor China wants to or is able to force their will on the other as part of an alliance, let alone lead one. In the same way, Chinese experts believe that the best way to move forward is to strengthen their relationships with Russia and India rather than joining forces with them to fight the West.

It's possible that a strategic confrontation with the US and its partners in the Indo-Pacific, a break in economic relations with Washington (which is not likely), or problems putting Beijing's own economic and technological strategy into action because of Western policies could push the city toward an alliance with Moscow. Chinese observers think that the US strategy of a Free and Open IndoPacific and the revival of the Quadrilateral Security Dialogue between the

US, Japan, Australia, and India is an attempt to contain China, stop the Belt and Road Initiative from happening, and make it harder for China to work with its neighbors.

The US's moves make it more dangerous for Beijing to be on the water in nearby areas and make things less stable in the South China Sea. Even though Washington has bad intentions, Chinese experts believe that the Indo-Pacific strategy will fail in the same way that the Obama administration's policy of strategic rebalancing to Asia did because Washington is inconsistent in how it treats its allies and partners and is ready to go to war with China. These goals will not be met, especially if China is smart enough to keep friendly relationships with countries it has always had ties with.

American economic tools are only one part of the American plan in the trade war with China, according to people in China who follow the conflict. This plan's goal is to slow down China's economic growth. The US is putting more pressure on China over security issues in the Indo-Pacific by working with allies and partners to escalate the arms race, weaken China's nuclear capabilities, and carry out high-profile military maneuvers. It has also given China ultimatums about its trade and industrial policy and taken sanctions and other anti-competitive actions against Chinese businesses.

The US is very interested in China's relationships with Taiwan, Tibet, Xinjiang, and Hong Kong, as well as human rights problems. All of these are very sensitive topics for the Chinese government. There are also limits on the amount of Chinese students who can come to the US and on contacts in the areas of science, technology, and humanitarian aid. It also runs a media operation to spread lies. Professionals from China say that what the US does threatens Russia's economic safety and causes problems for China in the food, energy, and banking sectors. In almost every area, including joint value chains and technology sharing, the US is trying to separate itself from China.

Meanwhile, China thinks that putting taxes on all of its exports would hurt its economy, but not so badly that it would be impossible to recover from. At the same time, US customers will also have to pay a lot. Beijing is not ready to give up its basic interests, such as security or authority, in this situation. Chinese experts think that these facts make Russia and China more politically and economically close. In any case, what the two countries want right now is to increase investments, work on joint projects, form scientific and innovative partnerships, and improve teamwork across borders. In other words, they want to strengthen the ties they already have.

The problem of trust between Russia and China needs its own section here. For Russia, the situation is complicated by the fact that China wants to develop

Russia's natural resources and Russia and China have different economic and population potentials. There are also different ideas about how to interpret some past events. Not trusting each other as much is slowly going away as the countries work together more. For example, people in the Russian Far East see China as a chance to grow rather than a danger. The way the two countries see each other is still affected by how they remember the time they settled their border disputes with the Soviet Union, especially in China. However, the leaders of both countries are trying to get along by focusing on things they have in common, like working together against a shared enemy in the Second World War.

Since 2014, many deals to work together on the economy have been signed, but many of them are still only on paper. There is a big difference between what the Russian side thought would happen and what actually happened when it comes to Chinese money coming into the country. Also, differences in culture and civilization, along with Russia's dislike of China's practicality, make the two countries less likely to trust each other in the future. Russia is worried about what Beijing really wants from the relationship, and China is unhappy with how unpredictable Russia's foreign policy is. It is often disappointing for China that many people in Russia still talk about the "Chinese threat" and that the country gets a lot of bad news in the Russian media.

Now, let's look at the three things that Glenn Snyder says determine the relationship between two groups and could affect the choice to form an alliance: interdependence, balance of interests, and balance of potentials. When a country negotiates with a partner, these factors affect how strong their stance is. They also affect the benefit-cost ratio of an alliance.

It is normal for the goals of great powers to sometimes overlap, sometimes differ, and sometimes be at odds with each other. A study of Russia and China's tastes shows that their goals are similar in many areas, including strategic ones. However, there are also some areas where their goals are different. Russia is mostly involved in conflicts in Europe and the area after the fall of the Soviet Union. China, on the other hand, is mostly involved in conflicts in East Asia. The countries can take a neutral stand on issues that affect one side's main interests but not the other side's. This is exactly what China did during the wars in Crimea and Ukraine in 2014 and Abkhazia and South Ossetia in 2008. Beijing's position is based on the fact that it doesn't want to put its relationship with the world's most powerful country at risk over things that don't affect its main goals. Also, because of the Taiwan problem and the separatist movements in China, supporting Russia's actions would set a bad example.

China is worried about many of Moscow's risky and uncertain moves. For a long time, China's more cautious stance, which rules out a direct conflict with the West, meant that it had to deal with lower political, economic, and military-strategic costs. China is also working hard to improve its economic ties with Central and Eastern European countries, as well as with Ukraine and other former Soviet republics. This is because these ties help the Belt and Road Initiative get done faster. The nuclear arms control regime is another possible area of disagreement. China does not think it is proper to be a part of this regime.

In the same way, Moscow doesn't want to help Beijing with its wars in the South China and East China seas. It also doesn't want to risk its relationships in Asia by staying out of China's problems with Vietnam, India, and Japan. Additionally, Russia does not support making man-made islands and putting armed bases on them. Instead, it supports using the 1982 United Nations Convention on the Law of the Sea to settle disputes peacefully. Moscow wants a legally binding code of behavior to be put in place quickly in the South China Sea and doesn't want other countries to get involved in disputes that are already going on. Except for the last point, Russia is more like Vietnam than China in terms of its stance. Beijing has said many times that Moscow is wrong for working with Hanoi to develop energy on the disputed shelf. Russia and China also have different ideas about how the government should be set up in East Asia. Beijing wants to become the continent's most powerful country, while Russia wants to strengthen its role as the region's main power. Even though China has spoken out against US actions and helped make a joint road map for the Korean problem, it rarely shows any desire to work together with Russia on issues in the region.

In the Eurasian area, Russia and China are also rivals. China wants to make the Belt and Road Initiative a place where people can work together in a way that suits China. It uses Chinese parts, services, labor, and tools, which helps China play a bigger role in value chains and achieve its economic and foreign policy goals. Focusing on two-way ties is important to Beijing. On the other hand, Russia wants international cooperation that doesn't slow down the process of integration in the EAEU. It wants gains to be shared more fairly, which would make the EAEU member states more competitive.

Because of this, it is still not clear what the real boundaries of the EAEU and Silk Road Economic Belt will be, or how the two countries will work together within the Greater Eurasia framework. China wants to create a free trade zone, but Russia and its partners don't want to go along with it because it would hurt their economies' ability to compete. China wants to open up economic ties and get rid of obstacles to the Belt and Road Initiative, which is why it doesn't like the EAEU's protectionist policy.

The two countries' business goals are often very different from one another. Russia wants to get away from the model of importing finished goods and getting energy from other countries. China, on the other hand, is happy with the way things are now. In this way, projects in areas other than resources are going along pretty slowly. This idea of a "community of common destiny for mankind" that Chinese President Xi Jinping uses to justify his foreign policy makes Moscow think hard: is it ready to back China's push for a leading role in Asia and the world as a whole?

We get a mixed picture when we look at the potentials of the two countries side by side, and Moscow is getting less and less of a boost. Russia's military-industrial complex is much more advanced than China's. Russia has big benefits over its strategic partner when it comes to air defence, some types of radar technology, building airplane engines, and building submarines. Chinese military equipment isn't even close to as advanced as Russian guns. However, Beijing has been quickly modernizing its military, which has helped it catch up to Russia and even beat it in some areas. The People's Liberation Army of China has been updated, military reforms began in 2015, and China has bought Russian weapons systems. These changes have given China more chances to take part in diverse military tasks.

In 2018, China's GDP was eight times bigger than Russia's in dollar terms and six times bigger in terms of purchasing power parity. This means that China had a bigger economic potential. China's economic growth may have slowed to 6–7% because of Russia's recession in 2014–2015. Russia's slow rebound has since made the difference in absolute economic performance even bigger. The size of a country's income also affects its ability to pay for its military. The Stockholm International Peace Research Institute says that China spent $250 billion on defence in 2018 while Russia only spent $61 billion. But this is the same as 3.9% of Russia's GDP and 1.9% of China's. China has been spending a lot more on its defence than Russia has for a long time now. Beijing's strategic potential isn't even close to that of Russia or the US, but if things keep going the way they are, it will only be a matter of time before it starts to build its own high-tech products. The question is: How much will the military-industrial complex be able to reinvent technology in important ways for modernizing the military? When will it happen?

Even though their economies are very different, Russia will probably still have the military and strategic tools to build relations with China on an equal basis in the 2020s. Also, it's still not clear whether Beijing will be able to deal with structural problems and actually hit a new level of technological development. But because the two countries' economic potentials are not equal, their total power is not equal neither. Since 2014, China has been paying more attention to this issue and telling Russia that it needs to meet China halfway in terms of its own interests, especially when it comes to economic issues.

The way that Russia and China rely on each other is also changing. As the imbalances in economic ties get worse, China is becoming less reliant on Russian equipment and parts. Beijing can fix problems with the uneven growth of different parts of the military-industrial complex and the slow production of some important parts by working together with Moscow on military-technical issues. It is only finished military equipment that is supplied on a large scale; no technologies or rights are transferred. Smaller deals for research and development are also being made.

As Chinese industry grows, Russia's role in it and its importance as a supplier are slowly decreasing. However, the most recent contracts are important because they help the People's Liberation Army of China fight better in the South China and East China seas and in Taiwan. China has now hit a point where it can improve and update its military hardware without Russia's help, though it will take some time. With that said, Beijing is likely to want to work with Moscow on military and technical issues in a number of areas over the next few years. The lack of intellectual property protection makes it hard for the two countries to move toward more complex forms of industrial and technological cooperation. For example, they can't work together on developing AI, laser weapons, robotics, and hypersonic technologies because they don't trust each other.

Even keeping up the level of military and technology cooperation that already exists doesn't make Russia and China want to form an alliance; things work out just fine for both countries as they are. While China is busy modernizing its military, Moscow is not likely to offer Beijing any security guarantees. This is true even if a war breaks out with the United States. It is literally impossible for China to count on Russia a lot when it comes to security.

There hasn't been a big change in the way businesses deal with each other, even though cooperation has grown and new industries have formed since the 2010s. There is a mismatch in the amount of trade going back and forth between the two countries. China buys two thirds of Russia's exports, which are natural resources. These are traded for produced goods and high-value goods. China has been Moscow's main trade partner since 2010. That year, it made up only 4% of Russia's trade, but by 2019, it made up 16.6%. In the same year, China's trade with other countries included only 4% with Russia.

Short-term changes in trade patterns are not likely to happen, and the problem of unequal economic ties between Russia and China will only get worse in the future. As of the end of 2018, the Ministry of Commerce of the

People's Republic of China said that China had made direct investments worth $11 billion in Russia. In contrast, Russia had only made investments worth $1.1 billion in China. China's investments are mostly in areas like energy, agriculture and forestry, construction, making building materials, trade, the textile and light industry, home products, and services. Speaking about China, Andrey Denisov, the Russian ambassador, said that as of the end of 2018, all of China's investments added up to about $30 billion. China has a hard time putting big amounts of money into the Russian economy in areas other than energy. Even though China has put money into new areas in the past few years, economic ties between the two countries haven't changed much.

The main way that Russia and China work together on technology is by sending Russian innovations to China to be used in their own products and for other uses. A lot of the time, Chinese companies work directly with Russian R&D. At the same time, Beijing hasn't been interested in Russian plans to form joint high-tech companies in areas where China is ahead of the curve and Russia is behind. That said, China still has some way to go to catch up with Western countries in terms of the level of technological development in most areas, and the quality of its hi-tech products, when the price increases are taken into account, is often below the required standard for Russian industry . When China does business with other countries, it mostly wants to sell finished goods made by its own tech companies. This gives China a higher place in the value chain.

As a result, economic ties between Russia and China are becoming more unequal, and political and economic cooperation is becoming less balanced. Further, there is a risk that Moscow could become dependent on Beijing both economically and technologically if the current trend towards the expansion of China's share in Russia's foreign activity persists in the long term, and if Russia opts to prioritize technological interaction with China .

There are good reasons why Russia and China haven't made their joint defence obligations official: the study of military-political alliances has made progress. Experts say that the two countries' chances of forming an alliance depend on how much they depend on each other and how much their interests overlap and differ. These variables are vital, both in terms of the prospects for a potential alliance, and in terms of how symmetrical such an alliance would be, what positions the parties would take within it, and how this configuration could change in the future.

Russia and China have had a close relationship since the 1990s. It hit a new level in the second half of the 2010s, when tensions with the US rose. A lot of global problems are important to both countries, but they are also different in some ways at the regional level. They have a lot of political agreement and have made trade and business ties stronger. In areas that are important for national security, both sides are willing to work together. This much is clear from the dialogue between the Russian and Chinese militaries, joint exercises of the armed forces, and the development of military-technical cooperation.

As a result, the bilateral strategic partnership is a very well organized model of getting along. Many experts see the strengthening of this partnership as a sign that Russia-China cooperation is moving towards what is traditionally seen as an alliance. Such developments are in many cases spun as desirable or expected. At the same time, both countries want to keep their options open in terms of possible interaction with third countries. Russia and China are highly dependent on cooperation with Western partners to achieve their development goals.

Our analysis revealed four groups of reasons that prevent Russia and China from forming a military-political alliance in the accepted understanding of the term. First, the advantages of this form of interaction are not attractive enough to the parties, who feel that they are able to ensure their own security and counter existing threats by themselves. Second, a Russia-China alliance would create significant risks of a further aggravation of the confrontation with the West, and a break in economic and technological cooperation with the most developed countries of the world. 'Third, the strategic culture of Moscow and Beijing encourages them to avoid actions that would limit their autonomy on the international stage, which is precisely what an alliance with another major power would do. Fourth, both Russia and China are concerned about being dragged into a conflict they would prefer to avoid.

For Russia, the risks of entering into an alliance with China are even more grave given the growing asymmetry of the economic potentials of the two countries and the growing imbalance of economic relations with China. The latter factor in particular increases the danger of Moscow becoming economically and technologically dependent on Beijing if its relations with the West do not improve. Russia's importance as a supplier of equipment and components for the Chinese market will in all likelihood start to fade. If the Russian economy fails to achieve sustainable growth and modernization, the alliance would likely tip in Beijing's favour (even if, to begin with, it would be balanced due to Russia's superior military potential). One of the biggest risks of forming an alliance with China is that Russia may be forced to support China in its confrontation with the United States in East Asia and be drawn into the conflict in the South China Sea. Cooperation with India and Vietnam would also likely suffer. Looking at potential worst-case scenarios, this could undermine Moscow's independence in Asia and call into questions the prospects for its turn to the East.

Unreserved support on the part of Russia for the Belt and Road Initiative without the establishment of the Greater Eurasian Partnership could lead to the erosion of the EAEU and its subordination to Chinese plans. Ultimately, this will contribute to the formation of an open hierarchical order in Asia and Eurasia, but one in which China will enjoy the leading position, and Moscow will be a significant but subordinate player.

These obstacles are unlikely to go anywhere soon, and will thus continue to block full-fledged treaty obligations in the sphere of collective defence in the future. Russia and China's current goals are best served if the existing formats of interaction are preserved. They leave the door open for further building cooperation without formal agreements. It seems likely that Russia and China will only move towards formal allied relations if the threat from the United States becomes so great that the elites of these countries have no choice but to significantly reduce the level of interaction with the West and conclude a military-political alliance. Despite the escalation of tensions in Moscow and Beijing's relations with Washington, such a scenario still seems unlikely. The key factors that may lead to a further deepening of the strategic partnership between Russia and China and a revision of the format of their relations, including the possible establishment of an alliance, are: a growth in strategic competition between China and the United States in the economic, technological and military-political spheres; the ongoing weakening of the interdependence between the world's biggest economies (decoupling); and the desire of the United States to limit China's cooperation with the West and its Asian allies while stoking the flames of the tensions in US- Russia relations.

Chapter 6
Russia and China Collaboration to Create a Counterweight to the United States

China and Russia both think that the way things are now in the world is unfair. They think that instead of the US being in charge, there should be a multipolar world order where countries like Russia and China have more say over how the world works and who benefits from it. But both China and Russia have ideas about how the international order should work and a lot of economic, military, and political power (though not all of it is equal) to change it. Today, these two countries are home to almost every major geostrategic danger, such as cyberattacks, nuclear weapons, military power, political power, and so on. Over the past ten years, China and Russia have often sided with each other to fight the West, especially the United States, and have stepped up their cooperation in both economic and armed areas.

This is more important than ever since the West put sanctions on Russia following the war in Ukraine in 2014 and since the US became more involved in Asia in search of partners to balance China.

This chapter will look at whether the relationship between China and Russia can grow into a partnership against the United States. To answer this question, we will first use the balance of power theory to explain the alliances that formed after the Cold War. The chapter will then look at the possibility of a partnership between China and Russia by looking at their place in the world (threat perception, challenges, and regional interests) and how they work together within their own countries (history and culture, mutual cooperation). Finally, the chapter will talk about how US strategy affects the relationship between China and Russia.

The chapter makes the case that Russia and China are "softly balancing" against the US, but there are too many differences between them to make a real armed alliance.

Balance of Power

The balance of power idea in realism tries to explain how power changes in global politics and why states try to get as much power as possible. It can also help explain how alliances are formed. Kenneth N. Waltz, who started the field of neorealism, says that states are unitary agents who will do whatever it takes to stay in power. You have to help yourself in the foreign system, and people who don't will fail. States try to get as much power as possible because of the system. States can increase their power both inside and outside their borders. For example, they can strengthen their military on the inside, and they can form alliances with other states to protect themselves from a stronger state (or perceived danger).

Liberalism was the main group that didn't like the balance of power idea because it didn't make sense in the world after the Cold War. Non-state actors are having a bigger impact on state policies, which makes states more ready to work together to fight them. As economies become more connected and the world economy grows, it becomes more expensive to compete harshly. To solve problems involving group action, foreign organizations have mostly been successful. The real-world example that liberals use most often is the fact that there has been no hard balance against the US's overwhelming power.

But the balance of power basically means cutting down on or matching the strengths of a bigger state. It shouldn't matter what kind of means are used in this case. TV Paul, a political scientist, takes the idea of balance of power in a new direction by describing three types of balancing: hard, soft, and unequal. Hard balancing is the standard realist argument for making military alliances, while soft balancing is more about building non-offensive coalitions, working together on the spot, and working together in international organizations. Asymmetric balance means protecting states from threats that come from outside of states.

It is important to think about balance of power in a broader way in a world where a country's power isn't just based on its armed strength, but also on its economy and the environment. There is still too much power difference between the USA and any possible rivals for anyone to publicly and aggressively challenge it. Also, the costs to the economy would be too high because of how much they depend on each other. In the fight against terrorism, which is now a fight between all major powers, the USA even works as a world police force. As a result, the idea of "soft balancing," which isn't just about "realistic" military balance, is better at understanding current world politics. It will also be used in this chapter to look at how China and Russia can work together.

Feasibility of a Sino-Russian Union

This Last chapter will look at China and Russia's place in the world and how their relationship has changed over time. The goal is to find out what the union between the two countries could be and how much it has grown.

Standing in the Global Arrangement

The idea of a common danger is one thing that drives countries to work together or form an alliance. This is because states tend to balance against an imagined threat. In the past ten years, ties between Russia and China have been shaped by both countries' views of the US as an outside threat. After the fall of the Soviet Union, both countries tried to keep each other in check by reducing uncertainty and suspicion. However, after the 2008 Georgia War and the US "pivot toward Asia," relations with the US and the West in general got worse, and China and Russia's foreign policies became more closely linked. What China and Russia think about the US's goals and whether they are dangerous is more important than what the US does.

Because both countries see a danger, there have been more high-level meetings and talks about a "comprehensive strategic partnership between both states." Since they are both permanent members of the UN Security Council, China and Russia have often taken the same stance on many security problems, most recently on Syria, and have vetoed resolutions proposed by the West. There have also been many problems that were important to both Russia and China that the other country did not speak out about. While China would have liked to keep good relations with Ukraine, which had become an important economic partner, it decided to side with Russia during its war with Ukraine in 2014. When it came to Ukraine, China didn't directly criticize Russia or join other Western countries in imposing sanctions against Russia. Instead, it used unclear language to call for a "peaceful solution." Even though this isn't an open backing, it shows that China values its relationship with Russia.

Russia and China both have to deal with problems in the international order, especially when it comes to the US. Inside their own countries, both China and Russia have a lot of different religious and racial minorities that question or could question the authority of the government. As a result, they are aware of how other states' political systems can affect their own, just as the US works to support freedom and democracy. People already strongly believe that the world's political and economic system is set up to benefit the US and the West as a whole, and that the US sees China and Russia as threats that need to be controlled.

Some political scientists, like G. Chang and R. Kaplan, say that China and Russia move when they are weak in the international system, which is why they are becoming more similar. China and Russia are both weak states, despite how they look from the outside. After Russia invaded Ukraine, the West put sanctions in place that hurt the already weak and oil-dependent Russian economy. In China, too, the economy is slowly getting worse. After the home and stock market bubbles burst in 2015, GDP growth dropped from double digits to an official 6.9%. People in both countries were afraid of domestic violence and governmental instability because of the economic problems. Russian and Chinese countries are also big and have a lot of different racial groups living in them. To make up for it, China and Russia, especially, went to nationalism to distract their unhappy people, which made them more hostile toward the West. China was smarter about what it did in East China and the South China Sea, while Russia was very direct in Ukraine. But it will take some time to see if China's political problems will make it more active in the world.

At the international level, China and Russia formed the Shanghai Cooperation Organization in 1996 to work together with their weaker neighbors to deal with them. The main areas of cooperation are fighting terrorism, extremism, and secession in the region. However, China and Russia have also taken part in a number of military drills in recent years as part of the SCO. As of now, the SCO is not a defensive alliance, but it is moving toward becoming a regional security ally. Russia works with other countries in the area on defence through the Collective Security Treaty Organization, but China is not a part of this group. Not only does it show that Russia doesn't want China to get in the way of its security in the region, but it also shows that Russia knows it needs to include China. That's why there are two organizations that do almost the same thing.

On the other hand, Russia's interests in the region might be at odds with China's, even though there are already rules in place. Turkey, Malaysia, and Indonesia are just a few of the Southeast Asian countries that buy weapons from Russia because they are afraid of China's rise. Russia is also friendly with Mongolia and other Central Asian countries that used to be part of the Soviet Union. These countries are also worried about China's growing power. Russia has been trying not to depend too much on the Chinese market, which has made it easier for them to work with other countries in the area. So far, it hasn't made things worse between them and China, but if these countries start to fight China, it will. The struggle for power in the region also goes the other way. Russia is worried that China's "silk road," which aims to connect trade and investment in Central Asia, will weaken Russia's position as a power in Eurasia. Russia and China are more of rivals than partners when it comes to their relationships with other countries in the area. However, they have tried to work together through regional frameworks because they know how valuable each other is. This makes it less likely that there will be a formal agreement, but it doesn't rule out soft balancing.

Even though Russia and China both see a threat, face problems in the international order, and care about the environment in the region, aren't the West and the USA too important for Russia and China to work together against them? The imbalance of power and the need to count on each other may make it too expensive. It's not openly hostile toward the US like it was during the Cold War. China and Russia may need the US more than they need each other in the long run. Even though China and Russia have worked together more on the economy in recent years, the European and American markets are still better for them than the Chinese and Russian markets. This is mirrored in their cooperation with each other.

Domestic Dynamics within the China-Russia Connection

Russia and China have had a rough recent past, marked by mistrust between them. During the Cold War, they both believed in Soviet ideas, but their goals were different. Stalin died in 1953, and Nikita Khrushchev took over as leader of the Soviet Union. He began to move away from Stalinism, which led to the split. China supported more traditional Soviet ideas over the Soviet Union's plan for a new kind of world socialism. China thought that Moscow had too much power when the Soviet Union was in power. The worst part of this was when China and the Soviet Union fought with weapons over the border in 1969. The people in charge of both countries are still aware of this troubled past.

Russians and Chinese people are also not very close when it comes to culture. In the past, most of Russia was more connected to Europe, especially after the 18th century, when Europe was seen as the center of the world. The only part of Russia that doesn't have a cultural divide with China is the Far East, which probably has stronger cultural ties with China than Moscow. This is also clear from the fact that official government-level cooperation is decades ahead of culture exchange, tourism, and general contact between people.

But if the states didn't trust each other and didn't really share any cultural or ideology beliefs, then why did they decide to put aside their differences and work together after the Soviet Union fell apart? One thing is that they share a long land line that is over 4,000 kilometers long. In addition, they often needed to work together with the other state. However, this need is still met with some doubt and care.

When Russia and China worked together in the 1990s, it was mostly to keep the border between them calm so that both countries could focus on their own problems and economic growth. It wasn't really possible to work together more deeply yet; they mostly just sold arms and worked with other countries in the area.

This has changed over the past ten years. The countries are now closer together, both politically and economically, because they see a shared threat.

The economies of Russia and China work well together. China's economy is based on industry, and Russia has a lot of natural resources that China doesn't have. The oil and gas market is getting extra attention, but teamwork isn't getting too tight because this part of business in Russia is very politicized and because Russia still benefits more from Western markets. That's not all—China is also wary of Russia's market and doesn't want to rely too much on one source. Even so, Russia and China signed a 400 billion dollar deal in 2014 to buy Russian gas over the next thirty years. This is the newest and most important energy deal between the two countries. It builds on other oil trade deals that they have already made. Russia might want to trade more with the West because it makes more money, but it may have to trade more with China because it needs to invest in gas and oil areas that are farther away, like those in Siberia, which is close to China. Russia has the upper hand when it comes to getting energy from Russia, but China can still choose its own energy sources.

In the same way that Russia is a market for Chinese items, the Western market is a much more important one for China. Not just in the energy sector, Russia would like to see more spending in high-tech fields. Russia and China have a history of working together on arms deals, but things are going in the wrong direction now: Russia isn't able or willing to trust China enough to give it high-tech weapons. Furthermore, China is beginning to sell guns and might turn into a rival in the area. The economies of the two countries are still not fully integrated, and their unity is based on self-interest, in part because they compete with each other and don't trust each other.

Russia and China are becoming more similar in their foreign policies, economies, and even armies. However, they are becoming less similar in terms of their power in the world order. China has a bigger economy than Russia does, and its military power is rising. This makes Russia a less important player in these relationships. The rise of China makes Russia suspicious and wary of another country. The sparsely populated Far East of Russia is a good example of this. This area shares cultural ties with China. Russia is worried that as China grows, Chinese people will move to the Far East and take economic control of the area's huge natural resources that aren't being used yet. Even though this hasn't happened yet, it shows one way in which Russia is worried about China's growth.

China still needs Russia domestically, even though it is growing. China is already having a hard time getting partners in the area, especially since the US is putting a lot of effort into doing the same. But China would rather have Russia as a "safe rear" than as a "strategic encirclement" if it sides with the US. The other country is a "strategic cushion" for both China and Russia against the West. Within this trio, both Russia and China would rather work together than be left out if one side sides more with the USA.

US Factor

In this triangle of power, both the US and China have had different policies toward each other over time. This part will talk about the latest US strategy toward China and Russia in order to figure out what role the US plays in the relationship between the states.

Obama, as president, set the tone for how the US deals with China and Russia these days. The world economy was in bad shape when he was elected, and the US had failed in Iraq and Afghanistan. As a result, he was more ready to be friendly with China and Russia in order to make friends in politics and business. This was made in the form of a "G-2 proposal" for China and a "reset policy" for Russia. Russia and China have different levels of power toward the US, as shown by their different responses to these ideas and changes in ties since then.

Between 1972, when President Nixon normalized diplomatic ties between the US and China, and the fall of the Soviet Union, the US and China were "allies of convenience." After that, they turned into strategic rivals who tried to find a balance between working together and competing. In 2009, Barack Obama asked China to join the "G-2," which would be a form of global leadership. China turned him down because it felt strong after getting out of the economic crises mostly unscathed. China didn't feel like it had to follow the rules set by the US-led international order, and over the next few years, China became more aggressive.

China, on the other hand, took a different path. From 2009 to 2010, there was a "reconciliation" between China and the USA. The US changed their stance on missile defence and gave up on their plans to put up a missile defence system in Poland. Russia and the US held nuclear arms control talks and set up a dozen working groups to talk about things like energy and civil society. The "reset policy" did not work out in the end, though, because both states were not ready to change how they saw and dealt with each other.

This shows that Russia and China are not on the same level of power. Beijing feels more powerful toward Washington than Moscow does. First, because the economies of the US and China are linked; and second, the Middle Kingdom sees itself as the only country that could truly challenge US dominance in the future. The United States has changed its policy to be more open to China's rise to power, so it can play a part in the international scene. This is to make sure that China's growth doesn't make the international system less stable. The USA are ready to let China change some parts of the global order that they think are wrong. Such as helping to make worldwide rules and laws about cyber security, for example.

China is stronger in terms of material things, but Russia is very strong when it comes to politics, as we saw in Georgia and Ukraine. No longer is it the "Soviet Union" that threatens the US, but it is still against the West and can make risks that directly hurt US interests. At least for the US, it's important because it has a huge nuclear stockpile. China is a bigger and stronger country, but the USA still needs to pay attention to this one.

Even though China and Russia had different policies toward the US at this time, their cooperation did not decrease; in fact, it grew. In this case, China and Russia are working together to do more than just fight the US. In the many areas of shared interest we've talked about so far, they stand on their own. But it's also true that ties between China and Russia got even better after 2012, when the US started to shift its focus to Asia and gave up on its "reset policy" toward Russia. This was because both countries saw a common threat. China-Russia ties are complicated and can't be boiled down to the US, but the US's policy toward Russia and China has a big impact on how closely these two countries work together.

Conclusion

Russia and China should work together and form a relationship for many reasons. They both see threats the same way, face problems in the international system, have similar government systems at home, and see each other as a partner for both economic and political reasons. As a result, they work together more in real life, including in the military, and their foreign policies are more similar. But it would be very strange for neighbors with such a long border to not work together at all. In fact, this could be seen as a way to keep the USA in check. Russia and China work together because they want to, but they don't trust each other and have a lot of doubts about each other's goals in the area. Russia is the first country in history to be a junior partner to China. This is especially true for Russia. Russia and China both want the other side to move closer to the US so they don't get left out. Russia especially doesn't want to become a second-tier power while the US and China set the strategic direction of the world.

All of this means that China and Russia probably won't be able to form a formal, trustworthy military partnership. They don't make an alliance, but they do work together strategically in economic, political, and military areas. This is called "soft balancing." They work together in a flexible enough way that they don't have to cut ties with the West, which they need for both economic and political reasons. It's scary to think that China and Russia might join forces, which keeps the West and the USA on their toes.

Even though there is soft balance, that doesn't mean it won't hurt the USA. The US's policy in the region affects how close China and Russia become as a partner, but it's not the only thing that affects their relationship. China and Russia could even work together on a military level, which would be very bad for the West. This could happen in East Asia, where China and the US have many disagreements, or it could happen in the Middle East, where China and Russia agree on what to do about Iran and Syria, and China is becoming more aggressive because it needs natural resources.

So, US policy should continue to strike a balance between working with China and competing with it. It shouldn't make China and Russia angry for no reason, but it should also make it clear what the limits are that can't be crossed. The US would like China and Russia to stay involved in world politics and work to change the idea that the US wants to keep China and Russia in check. A formal alliance between China and Russia could happen in the future, but a lot will rest on how the US handles its foreign policy and how well it can avoid making it seem like China and Russia need an alliance.

Index

L

M

N

O

P

R

S

www.ingramcontent.com/pod-product-compliance
Ingram Content Group UK Ltd.
Pitfield, Milton Keynes, MK11 3LW, UK
UKHW021321020826
14184UKWH00003B/18